ZAGATSURVEY®

2001

BOSTON
RESTAURANTS

Editor: Sinting Lai

Local Editor: Nichole Bernier Ahern

Local Coordinator: Maryanne Muller

Published and distributed by
ZAGAT SURVEY, LLC
4 Columbus Circle
New York, New York 10019
Tel: 212 977 6000
E-mail: boston@zagat.com
Web site: www.zagat.com

Acknowledgments

We gratefully acknowledge the assistance of the following people and organizations:

Tom Ahern; Annie B. Copps; Jon Davis and Evelyn Rubak; Julie Fox; Perry Garfinkel; Chris Haynes; Bill Kirtz; Lisa, Alex and Langley Pierpont; Sarah Wilcox and Todd Adelman; *The Martha's Vineyard Times*; The Charlotte Inn; Bunch of Grapes Bookstore, Martha's Vineyard; and *The Cape Cod Times*. A special thanks to Jen Murphy and Sarah Reddington, and to all the Boston-area chefs who returned calls promptly and endured exhaustive questions.

This guide would not have been possible without the exacting work of our staff:

Phil Cardone, Erica Curtis, Laura du Pont, Jeff Freier, Sarah Kagan, Natalie Lebert, Mike Liao, Dave Makulec, Jefferson Martin, Andrew O'Neill, Bernard Onken, Robert Seixas, Zamira Skalkottas and LaShana Smith.

Contents

About This Survey

This *2001 Survey* is an update reflecting significant developments since our last *Boston Restaurant Survey* was published. We have included more than 50 key places that were not in the previous book, as well as made changes throughout to indicate new addresses, branches and phone numbers, plus decor, chef changes and other new developments.

As a whole, this *Survey* covers more than 830 restaurants in the Boston area, including Cape Cod, Martha's Vineyard and Nantucket, with input from more than 3,650 people. We sincerely thank each participant. This book is really "theirs." By surveying large numbers of regular restaurant-goers, we have achieved a uniquely reliable guide.

To help guide our readers to Boston's best meals and best buys, we have prepared a number of lists. See, for example, Boston's Most Popular Restaurants (page 11), Top Ratings (pages 12–17) and Best Buys (page 18). On the assumption that most people want a "quick fix" on the places at which they are considering eating, we have provided handy indexes.

We are particularly grateful to our editor, Nichole Bernier Ahern, a restaurant writer and contributing editor for *Boston* magazine and *Condé Nast Traveler*, and to our co-ordinator, Maryanne Muller, a freelance caterer and cooking instructor in Boston.

We invite you to be a reviewer in our next *Survey*. To do so, simply send a stamped, self-addressed, business-size envelope to ZAGAT SURVEY, 4 Columbus Circle, New York, NY 10019, or e-mail us at boston@zagat.com, so that we will be able to contact you. Each participant will receive a free copy of the next *Boston Survey* when it is published.

Your comments, suggestions and even criticisms of this *Survey* are also solicited. There is always room for improvement with your help.

New York, New York
October 2, 2000

Nina + Tim
Nina and Tim Zagat

What's New

Diners, take your seats – the new millennium is in full swing, and the options for eating in the Boston area are more appetizing than ever.

Call it the year of the spin-off. Buoyed by a booming economy and popular demand, established chefs and restaurateurs branched out. Frank McClelland, chef-owner of L'Espalier, opened his more casual Provençal eatery Sel de la Terre by the waterfront. Impresario Todd English, never one to rest on his Figs (or Olives), debuted his KingFish Hall, which brings seafood to a double-decked Faneuil Hall setting. And Jasper White, Boston's big kahuna of crustaceans, went slumming this year with his no-frills Jasper White's Summer Shack in Cambridge.

Other area standouts saw an opportunity to spruce up. In the Back Bay, the bastion of beef Grill 23 & Bar is doubling its space. And Les Zygomates, a hip Leather District bistro and wine bar, added a cafe and private dining room. In some cases the makeover has been more radical. The Theater District's Mercury Bar became the Soviet-chic Pravda 116, and the South End Grill morphed into the Southwestern newcomer Masa. Finally, La Bettola has been revamped into a midpriced Mediterranean, South End Galleria.

Some chose to retire from the scene altogether, including the traditionally French Du Barry on Newbury Street; Le Midi, Moncef Medeb's corporate hangout in the Financial District; Somerville's refined Union Square Bistro; and the Brighton Cal-Italian, Uva.

But at the same time, certain neighborhoods have proven fertile ground for clusters of newcomers. In the Theater District, Fleming's Prime Steakhouse & Wine Bar brings surf 'n' turf to the Wang Center environs, while elsewhere on Stuart Street, Flashes is out to steal the show with funky New American fare. Adjacent to the Theater District, the South End claims its own boomlet. The Dish is a new nook on Shawmut Avenue, and a few blocks away, Garden of Eden opened in an airy space for casual dining and gourmet-to-go. Nearby, java junkies get their fix at Rave, a sleekly retro cafe serving three meals a day.

Down the Cape, fresh finds like Cafe Tsunami on Martha's Vineyard and Nantucket's 56 Union compensate for the departure of faves Red Cat and Moona Grille.

And here's another morsel of good news: the average price of a meal remains a reasonable $24.96. So eat up, Boston.

Boston, MA
October 2, 2000

Nichole Bernier Ahern

Dining Tips

Over our 20-plus years of surveying restaurant-goers, we've heard from hundreds of thousands of people about their dining-out experiences. Most of their reports are positive – proof of the ever-growing skill and dedication of the nation's chefs and restaurateurs. But inevitably, we also hear about problems.

Obviously, there are certain basics that everyone has the right to expect when dining out: 1. Courteous, hospitable, informative service; 2. Clean, sanitary facilities; 3. Fresh, healthful food; 4. Timely honoring of reservations; and 5. Smoke-free seating.

Sadly, if these conditions aren't met, many diners simply swallow their disappointment, assuming there's nothing they can do. However, the truth is that diners have far more power than they may realize. Every restaurateur worth his or her salt wants to satisfy customers, since happy clients equal a successful business. Rather than the adversaries they sometimes seem to be, diners and restaurateurs are natural allies – both want the same outcome, and each can help the other achieve it. Toward that end, here are a few simple but sometimes forgotten tips that every restaurant-goer should bear in mind:

1. Speak up: If dissatisfied by any aspect of your experience – from the handling of your reservation to the food, service or physical environment – tell the manager. Most problems are easy to resolve at the time they occur – but not if management doesn't know about them until afterward. The opposite is also true: if you're pleased, speak up.

2. Spell out your needs ahead of time: If you have specific dietary requests, wish to bring your own wine, want a smoke-free (or smoking) environment, or have any other special needs, you can avoid disappointment by calling ahead to make sure the restaurant can satisfy you.

3. Do your part: A restaurant's ability to honor reservations, for example, is largely dependent on diners honoring reservations and showing up on time. Make it a point to cancel reservations you're unable to use and be sure to notify the restaurant if you'll be late. The restaurant, in turn, should do its best to seat parties promptly, and, if there are delays, should keep diners informed (a free drink doesn't hurt either).

4. Vote with your dollars: Most people tip 15 to 19%, and often 20% or more at high-end restaurants. Obviously, you have the right not to tip at all if unhappy with the service; but in that case, many simply leave 10% to get the message across. If you like the restaurant, it's worth accompanying the low tip with a word to the management. Of course, the ultimate way to vote with your dollars is not to come back.

5. Put it in writing: Like it or not, all restaurants make mistakes. The best ones distinguish themselves by how well they acknowledge and handle mistakes. If you've expressed your complaints to the restaurant management but haven't gotten a satisfactory response, write to your local restaurant critic, with a copy to the restaurant, detailing the problem. That really gets the restaurateur's attention. Naturally, we also hope you'll express your feelings, pro and con, by voting on zagat.com.

Key to Ratings/Symbols

This sample entry identifies the various types of information contained in your Zagat Survey.

(1) Restaurant Name, Address & Phone Number

(2) Hours & Credit Cards

(3) ZAGAT Surveyor Ratings

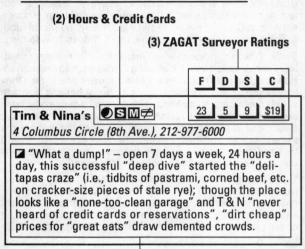

F	D	S	C
23	5	9	$19

Tim & Nina's ◐ⓈⓂ⌿

4 Columbus Circle (8th Ave.), 212-977-6000

◪ "What a dump!" – open 7 days a week, 24 hours a day, this successful "deep dive" started the "deli-tapas craze" (i.e., tidbits of pastrami, corned beef, etc. on cracker-size pieces of stale rye); though the place looks like a "none-too-clean garage" and T & N "never heard of credit cards or reservations", "dirt cheap" prices for "great eats" draw demented crowds.

(4) Surveyors' Commentary

The names of restaurants with the highest overall ratings, greatest popularity and importance are printed in **CAPITAL LETTERS**. Address and phone numbers are printed in *italics*.

(2) Hours & Credit Cards

After each restaurant name you will find the following courtesy information:

◐ .... *serving after 11 PM, Monday–Thursday*

Ⓢ .... *open on Sunday*

Ⓜ .... *open on Monday*

⌿ .... *no credit cards accepted*

(3) ZAGAT Surveyor Ratings

Food, **Decor** and **Service** are each rated on a scale of **0** to **30**:

F	D	S	C

F .... *Food*
D .... *Decor*
S .... *Service*
C .... *Cost*

23	5	9	$19

0 - 9	*poor to fair*
10 - 15	*fair to good*
16 - 19	*good to very good*
20 - 25	*very good to excellent*
26 - 30	*extraordinary to perfection*

▽ 23	5	9	$19

▽ .... *Low number of votes/less reliable*

The **Cost (C)** column reflects surveyors' estimated price of a dinner with one drink and tip. Lunch usually costs 25% less.

A restaurant listed without ratings is either an important **newcomer** or a popular **write-in**. The estimated cost, with one drink and tip, is indicated by the following symbols.

–	–	–	VE

I	*$15 and below*
M	*$16 to $30*
E	*$31 to $50*
VE	*$51 or more*

(4) Surveyors' Commentary

Surveyors' comments are summarized, with literal comments shown in quotation marks. The following symbols indicate whether responses were mixed or uniform.

◪ .... *mixed*
◼ .... *uniform*

Boston's Most Popular

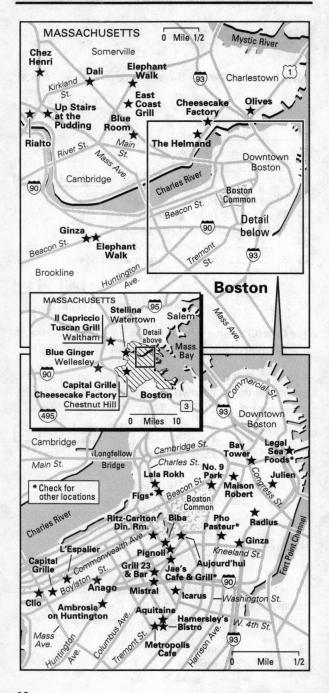

MASSACHUSETTS

0 Mile 1/2

Mystic River

Somerville

Charlestown

Chez Henri

Dali

Elephant Walk

East Coast Grill

Cheesecake Factory

Olives

Kirkland St.

Up Stairs at the Pudding

Blue Room

The Helmand

Rialto

River St.

Main St.

Mass Ave.

Cambridge

Charles River

Beacon St.

Downtown Boston

Boston Common

Detail below

Ginza

Elephant Walk

Brookline

Beacon St.

Huntington Ave.

Tremont St.

Boston

MASSACHUSETTS

Il Capriccio Tuscan Grill Waltham

Stellina Watertown

Salem

Blue Ginger Wellesley

Detail above

Mass. Bay

Capital Grille Cheesecake Factory Chestnut Hill

Boston

0 Miles 10

Cambridge

Commercial St.

Downtown Boston

Longfellow Bridge

Cambridge St.

Charles St.

Bay Tower

Legal Sea Foods*

Main St.

Lala Rokh

No. 9 Park

Julien

* Check for other locations

Figs*

Beacon St.

Boston Common

Maison Robert

Charles River

Ritz-Carlton Din. Rm.

Biba

Pho Pasteur*

Radius

L'Espalier

Pignoli

Ginza

Capital Grille

Grill 23 & Bar

Jae's Cafe & Grill*

Aujourd'hui

Kneeland St.

Clio

Boylston St.

Anago

Mistral

Icarus

Washington St.

Ambrosia on Huntington

Aquitaine

Hamersley's Bistro

W. 4th St.

Mass Ave.

Huntington Ave.

Columbus Ave.

Tremont St.

Metropolis Cafe

Harrison Ave.

0 Mile 1/2

10

www.zagat.com

Boston's Most Popular

Each of our reviewers has been asked to name his or her five favorite restaurants. The 40 spots most frequently named, in order of their popularity, are:

1. Aujourd'hui
2. Olives
3. Hamersley's Bistro
4. Elephant Walk
5. Rialto
6. Blue Ginger
7. L'Espalier
8. Clio
9. Legal Sea Foods
10. Biba
11. Dali
12. Ambrosia on Huntington
13. Mistral
14. Blue Room
15. Icarus
16. East Coast Grill
17. Anago
18. Capital Grille
19. Up Stairs at the Pudding
20. Jae's Cafe & Grill
21. Helmand, The
22. Radius
23. Il Capriccio
24. No. 9 Park
25. Maison Robert
26. Tuscan Grill
27. Figs
28. Ginza
29. Cheesecake Factory
30. Grill 23 & Bar
31. Ritz-Carlton Din. Rm.
32. Chez Henri
33. Pignoli
34. Pho Pasteur
35. Metropolis Cafe
36. Bay Tower
37. Julien
38. Lala Rokh
39. Aquitaine
40. Stellina

It's obvious that many of the restaurants on the above list are among the most expensive, but Bostonians also love a bargain. Were popularity calibrated to price, we suspect that a number of other restaurants would join the above ranks. Thus, we have listed 80 Best Buys on page 18.

Top Ratings*

Top 40 Food Ranking

28 L'Espalier	No. 9 Park
Aujourd'hui	Grill 23 & Bar
27 Olives	Mistral
Hamersley's Bistro	Sakurabana
26 Caffe Bella	Mamma Maria
Julien	Helmand, The
Il Capriccio	Biba
Radius	Morton's of Chicago
Saporito's	Galleria Umberto
Rialto	Seasons**
Lumière	Bristol Lounge
Sage	Tosca
Icarus	Ritz-Carlton Din. Rm.
Blue Ginger	Oak Room
Clio	Tuscan Grill
25 Silks	Pignoli
Maurizio's	**24** Blue Room
Ginza	Capital Grille
Terramia	Ambrosia on Huntington
La Campania	Brown Sugar Cafe

Top Spots by Cuisine

American (New)
28 Aujourd'hui
27 Hamersley's Bistro
26 Sage
Icarus
24 R Place

Barbecue
24 East Coast Grill
23 Uncle Pete's Hickory Ribs
22 Blue Ribbon BBQ
Jake's Boss BBQ
Redbones

American (Regional/Trad.)
25 Grill 23 & Bar
24 Rowes Wharf
23 Harvest
Scandia
22 Henrietta's Table

Chinese
23 East Ocean City
Lotus Blossom
New Shanghai
22 Chau Chow City
Grand Chau Chow

Asian/Fusion
26 Blue Ginger
24 Ambrosia on Huntington
23 Elephant Walk
JP Seafood Cafe
21 Bernard's

Chowder
21 Legal Sea Foods
Turner Fisheries
20 Locke-Ober Cafe
19 Jimmy's Harborside
15 Joe's American B&G

* Excluding restaurants with low voting.
** Tied with the restaurant listed directly above it.

Continental

- *24* White Rainbow
- *20* Locke-Ober Cafe
- *19* Andover Inn
- *18* Cafe Escadrille
- Hartwell House

Eclectic/International

- *26* Blue Ginger
- Biba
- *24* Blue Room
- Ambrosia on Huntington
- Metropolis Cafe

French (Bistro)

- *27* Hamersley's Bistro
- *26* Lumière
- *23* Chez Henri
- Truc
- Aquitaine

French (Classic)

- *25* Mistral
- Ritz-Carlton Din. Rm.
- *24* Maison Robert
- Le Bocage
- *22* Cafe Fleuri

French (New)

- *28* L'Espalier
- *26* Julien
- Radius
- Clio
- *25* No. 9 Park

Hamburger

- *21* Tim's Tavern
- *20* Mr. & Mrs. Bartley's
- *19* Audubon Circle
- *16* Sunset Grill & Tap
- *14* Charley's Saloon

Indian

- *24* Tanjore
- *22* Rangoli
- India Quality
- Kashmir
- *21* Kebab-N-Kurry

Irish Pub

- *21* Matt Murphy's
- *15* Grafton St.
- *14* Burren, The
- Green Dragon Tavern
- Doyle's Cafe

Italian (North)

- *26* Il Capriccio
- Saporito's
- *25* Mamma Maria
- Tosca
- Tuscan Grill

Italian (North & South)

- *25* Maurizio's
- Terramia
- La Campania
- Pignoli
- *24* Pomodoro

Italian (South)

- *25* Galleria Umberto
- *24* Trattoria A Scalinatella
- *23* Giacomo's
- *22* Antico Forno
- Pagliuca's

Japanese

- *25* Ginza
- Sakurabana
- *23* Fugakyu
- *22* Tatsukichi
- Jae's Cafe & Grill

Jewish

- *18* S&S Rest. & Deli
- Rubin's
- *17* Milk Street Cafe
- Zaftigs
- *16* B&D Deli

Mediterranean

- *27* Olives
- *26* Rialto
- Caffe Bella
- *25* Maurizio's
- *22* Casablanca

Mexican/Tex-Mex

- *21* Olé, Mexican Grille
- Casa Romero
- *20* Anna's Taqueria
- Sol Azteca
- La Paloma

Middle Eastern

- *23* Lala Rokh
- Sultan's Kitchen
- *22* Kareem's
- *18* Cafe Jaffa
- Karoun

Top Food

Pizza
25 Galleria Umberto
23 Café Louis
22 Santarpio's
21 Pizzeria Regina
   Figs

Seafood (American)
25 Grill 23 & Bar
24 East Coast Grill
22 Daily Catch
21 Legal Sea Foods
   Turner Fisheries

Seafood (Ethnic)
23 Giacomo's
   East Ocean City
   JP Seafood Cafe
22 Grand Chau Chow
21 Ocean Wealth

Spanish/Portuguese
24 Dali
23 Atasca
   Tapeo
22 Rauxa
   Tasca

Steakhouse
25 Grill 23 & Bar
   Morton's of Chicago
   Oak Room
24 Capital Grille
21 Abe & Louie's

Thai/Malaysian
24 Brown Sugar Cafe
22 House of Siam
   Rod Dee
   Penang
   King & I

Vietnamese/Cambodian
25 Viet Hong
23 Elephant Walk
22 Carambola
21 Pho Pasteur
21 Saigon

Top Spots by Special Feature

Breakfast (casual)*
22 Sound Bites
20 Charlie's Sandwich
19 Geoffrey's
18 Johnny's Luncheonette
17 Zaftigs

Brunch
24 Blue Room
   Metropolis Cafe
   Rowes Wharf
23 Harvest
19 Geoffrey's Cafe & Bar

Dessert
26 Radius
24 Ambrosia on Huntington
   Anago
22 Rauxa
   Finale

Dim Sum
22 Chau Chow City
21 Bernard's
   China Pearl
20 Golden Palace
16 Dynasty

Diner
20 Charlie's Sandwich
18 S&S Rest. & Deli
   Mike's City Diner
   Johnny's Luncheonette
15 Rosebud Diner

Family
23 Red Clay**
21 Figs
18 Johnny's Luncheonette
17 Full Moon
16 Iguana Cantina

---

* Other than hotels.
** Low votes.

Hotel Dining
- **28** Aujourd'hui
- **26** Julien
- **25** Seasons
    Bristol Lounge
    Ritz-Carlton Din. Rm.

Landmark
- **24** Library Grill
    Maison Robert
- **20** Locke-Ober Cafe
- **16** Union Oyster House
- **15** Warren Tavern

Lunch (Power)
- **28** Aujourd'hui
- **26** Radius
    Julien
- **25** No. 9 Park
- **20** Locke-Ober Cafe

Lunch Spot
- **23** Café Louis
    Harvest
    Claremont Café
- **19** Sonsie
    29 Newbury

Newcomers/Unrated
- Bomboa
- Butterfish
- Jasper White's
- KingFish Hall
- Sel de la Terre

People-Watching
- **26** Radius
- **25** No. 9 Park
    Mistral
- **19** Sonsie
- **16** Armani Cafe

Pre-Theater
- **24** Galleria Italiana
- **22** Finale
- **21** Montien
- **19** P.F. Chang's
- **–** Pravda 116

Worth a Trip
- **28** Topper's
    Nantucket
- **27** L'Etoile
    Martha's Vineyard
- **26** Chillingsworth
    Cape Cod
- **25** Silks
    Tyngsboro
- **–** Back Eddy
    Westport

Yearlings/Rated
- **26** Radius
    Lumière
- **23** Fugakyu
    Harvest
    Red Clay*

Yearlings/Unrated
- Back Eddy
- Cassis
- Federalist, The
- Restaurant Bricco
- Torch

---

* Low votes.

Top 40 Decor Ranking

28	Aujourd'hui		Maison Robert
27	L'Espalier		Biba
	Julien		Dali
	Bristol Lounge		Icarus
	Ritz-Carlton Din. Rm.		Ritz-Carlton Cafe
	Oak Room		Copley's
	Rowes Wharf		Wayside Inn
26	Bay Tower		Hamersley's Bistro
	Clio		Up Stairs at the Pudding
25	Spinnaker Italia		Pignoli
	Top of the Hub	23	Anago
	Silks		Pillar House
	Seasons		Tosca
	Fugakyu		Capital Grille
	Rialto		Barker Tavern
	Hungry i		Veronique
	Mistral		Mamma Maria
	Radius		Helmand, The
24	Ambrosia on Huntington		Laurel
	Lumière		Grill 23 & Bar

Outdoor

Armani Cafe	Hamersley's Bistro
Barking Crab	Henrietta's Table
Casa Romero	Maison Robert
Daddy-O's	Stephanie's on Newbury
Davio's (Cambridge)	Up Stairs at the Pudding
Garden of Eden	Water Club

Romantic

Cafe Budapest	Hungry i
Casa Romero	Julien
Chanterelle	L'Espalier
Clio	Maison Robert
Dali	Trattoria A Scalinatella
Euno	Truc

Room

Aquitaine	No. 9 Park
Cranebrook Rest. & Tea Rm.	Parker's
Grill 23 & Bar	Red Clay
Harvest	75 Chestnut
Lala Rokh	Sophia's
Library Grill	Tapeo
Locke-Ober Cafe	Vault

View

Anthony's Pier 4	Ritz-Carlton Din. Rm.
Aujourd'hui	Rowes Wharf
Bay Tower	Spinnaker Italia
Biba	Tavern on the Water
Davio's/Cambridge	Top of the Hub
Jimmy's Harborside	Water Club

Top 40 Service Ranking

28 Aujourd'hui
27 Ritz-Carlton Din. Rm.
   L'Espalier
26 Julien
25 Bristol Lounge
   Oak Room
   Silks
   Radius
   Ritz-Carlton Cafe
   Lumière
24 Seasons
   Hamersley's Bistro
   Rowes Wharf
   Maison Robert
   Icarus
   Clio
   Rialto
   Grill 23 & Bar
23 Salts
   Morton's of Chicago

Il Capriccio
Ambrosia on Huntington
Lala Rokh
Saporito's
Capital Grille
Up Stairs at the Pudding
Sage
Le Bocage
Atasca
Mamma Maria
Blue Ginger
Saraceno
No. 9 Park
Mistral
Locke-Ober Cafe
Pillar House
22 Anago
   Olives
   Cafe Budapest
   Tosca

Best Buys

40 Top Bangs for the Buck

This list reflects the best dining values in our *Survey*. It is produced by dividing the cost of a meal into the combined ratings for food, decor and service.

1. Anna's Taqueria
2. Baja Betty's Burritos
3. 1369 Coffee House
4. Galleria Umberto
5. Charlie's Sandwich
6. Sound Bites
7. Caffe Vittoria
8. Hi-Rise Bread Co.
9. Wrap
10. Mr. & Mrs. Bartley's
11. Blue Ribbon BBQ
12. Boca Grande
13. Baker's Best
14. Purple Cactus
15. Rosebud Diner
16. Country Life Vegetarian
17. Sultan's Kitchen
18. Tim's Tavern
19. Saigon
20. Mike's City Diner
21. House of Tibet
22. Other Side Cosmic Cafe
23. Zaatar's Oven
24. Johnny's Luncheonette
25. Rod Dee
26. Buddha's Delight
27. Taqueria Mexico
28. Demo's
29. Blossoms Cafe
30. Jake's Boss BBQ
31. Brown Sugar Cafe
32. Pizzeria Regina
33. Audubon Circle
34. Finale
35. Cafe Jaffa
36. Santarpio's
37. Sichuan Garden
38. Cornwall's
39. Centre Street Café
40. Milk Street Cafe

Additional Good Values

(A bit more expensive, but worth every penny)

Addis Red Sea
Amarin of Thailand
Atasca
B&D Deli
Bangkok Cuisine
Bluestone Bistro
Bombay Bistro
Burren
Cafe Barada
Cafe of India
Chau Chow City
Delux Cafe
Doyle's Cafe
Erawan of Siam
Gardner Museum Cafe
Goemon Noodle
Green Dragon Tavern
House of Siam
Indian Cafe
Indian Club

India Pavilion
India Quality
Le Gamin
Matt Murphy's Pub
Miracle of Science B&G
Neighborhood Rest.
Olé, Mexican Grille
Pho Pasteur
Rangoli
Rudy's Cafe
S&S Rest. & Deli
Siam Cuisine
6 Burner Urban Diner
Skewers
Tacos El Charro
Tandoor House
Tanjore
Uncle Pete's Hickory Ribs
Vicki Lee Boyajian
Zaftigs

Alphabetical Directory of Restaurants

Boston

| F | D | S | C |

Abbondanza Ristorante Ⓜ ▽ | 18 | 11 | 17 | $18 |
195 Main St. (Broadway), Everett, 617-387-8422
☑ Find "good, basic Italian" at this "neighborhood-style"
place in Everett that caters to families and the "blue-rinse
crowd"; regulars say the "food is fresh and tasty" and
there's "lots" of it, but some wish the menu offered more
choices for "non–pasta lovers"; despite a "take-out
atmosphere", it's "comfortable and homey" enough.

Abe & Louie's Ⓢ Ⓜ | 21 | 22 | 22 | $46 |
739 Boylston St. (bet. Exeter & Fairfield Sts.), 617-536-6300
☑ The business crowd gains another "deal-clinching spot"
in this "masculine", "good-looking" steakhouse in the Back
Bay; "don't go unless you're hungry", because the "too-
large" portions of "solid" prime meat seem to provide
"enough food for a week"; detractors, though, grouse that it
"comes up mediocre for the price" and say "it's trying too
hard to be a Boston institution."

Addis Red Sea Ⓢ Ⓜ | 20 | 19 | 17 | $19 |
544 Tremont St. (bet. Clarendon & E. Berkeley Sts.), 617-426-8727
■ Traditional Ethiopian cuisine fits right in to the "culturally
diverse neighborhood" of the South End, and at this "fun
alternative" enthusiasts enjoy "yummy, unusual fare served
on spongy bread in pleasant surroundings"; the "exotic"
food (with "lots of vegetarian options") is offered the
authentic way – sans utensils – making for a "sensory
experience" that's especially "fun with a group."

Ajanta Ⓢ ▽ | 21 | 16 | 21 | $16 |
*145 First St. (bet. Bent & Binney Sts.), Cambridge,
617-491-0075*
■ At this Indian restaurant with "all the right stuff" in
Kendall Square, the "great lunch buffet" is a "good deal"
and it's presented in a "nice atmosphere"; while the room
is nothing to look at, the "owners are lovely" and the
"friendly" staff is "outstanding", leading admirers to urge
"try it – you'll like it."

Akbar India Ⓢ Ⓜ | 16 | 13 | 16 | $17 |
*1248-1250 Cambridge St. (Prospect St.), Cambridge,
617-497-6548*
☑ "True, it may be one of Cambridge's 250 Indian places",
but this offbeat Inman Square "standby" is "dependable"
for "hearty fare", particularly the "delicious" lunch buffet;
while critics yawn "run-of-the-mill", many laud it as a
"bargain" "ethnic experience."

Al Dente ⓈⓂ   ▽ 17 | 10 | 15 | $21
109 Salem St. (Parmenter St.), 617-523-0990

◨ "Substantial servings" of "good, basic pastas" make this "comfortable" North End Italian a standby for some locals, who also recommend the bruschetta as "a must"; critics, however, find it "slightly boring" and "too crowded" and say the service needs major improvement.

Alloro Ⓢ   21 | 14 | 19 | $27
351 Hanover St. (bet. Fleet & Prince Sts.), 617-523-9268

◨ This "romantic", "cozy North Ender" earns points as a "great date place" for those who favor a "postage stamp–sized room" (there are only 26 seats) and "minimalist decor"; as the kitchen sends out "huge portions" of "simple", "savory" (if a bit "oily") Italian dishes prepared with "Mediterranean influences", loyalists are surprised that it's "often not crowded", given this overcrowded end of town.

Amarin of Thailand ⓈⓂ   20 | 18 | 19 | $20
287 Centre St. (Galen St.), Newton, 617-527-5255
27 Grove St. (Spring St.), Wellesley, 781-239-1350

◨ Suburbanites say it's "good to have these Thais nearby" for their "nice variety of dishes" with "clean, clear tastes", "interesting decor" and a staff that's "accommodating of substitutions"; but despite an "upscale" ambiance, some feel "the prices are too high for ordinary" fare.

AMBROSIA ON HUNTINGTON ⓈⓂ   24 | 24 | 23 | $50
116 Huntington Ave. (bet. Dartmouth & Newton Sts.), 617-247-2400

◨ This "flashy" Back Bay spot "hits the mark" with "great eye appeal" and a "chic, sophisticated ambiance"; equally noteworthy is its "inventive" Franco-Asian cuisine that some call a "tasty but precious" example of "fusion intrusion" – the "ingredients sometimes seem strangely combined" and the desserts look like "architectural projects"; still, the service is "attentive" (if "pretentious") and the "sexy bar" attracts a "glitzy" clientele; P.S. don't forget to "bring your platinum card."

Amelia's ⓈⓂ   14 | 14 | 14 | $19
Marina Bay, 305 Victory Rd., North Quincy, 617-471-1453

◨ "The best thing" about this Marina Bay Italian-American is its "lovely view of the Boston skyline"; otherwise, the interior is as "unimpressive" as the pastas, but even so, "dining outside" on the roofed patio is pleasant.

Amrheins ⓈⓂ   14 | 12 | 16 | $18
80 W. Broadway (A St.), South Boston, 617-268-6189

◨ At this "old-fashioned" South Boston bar that doubles as a "neighborhood political institution", the "middle-class boys-club atmosphere" is spiced by "waitresses who call you hon" and bring you dishes of "basic" New England fare; it may be "plain cooking, but it's well done."

ANAGO 🔲 Ⓜ   24 | 23 | 22 | $49

Lenox Hotel, 65 Exeter St. (Boylston St.), 617-266-6222

☑ Since moving recently from Cambridge to the "trendy" Lenox Hotel in the Back Bay, this little red room has become quite the "happening scene" with a "young, professional crowd", which "feels quite regal" dining on "innovative" American cuisine in the "high-ceilinged" space; dissenters, however, find it "overrated", "overpriced" and "snooty" and wonder "what all the fuss is about."

Anchovies ●🔲Ⓜ   16 | 14 | 16 | $17

433 Columbus Ave. (bet. Braddock Park & Holyoke St.), 617-266-5088

■ For an "anything-goes atmosphere", an "electric crowd" flocks to this "dark" and "smoky" publike mecca known for its "funky decor" and "huge portions" of "great, basic Italian"; insiders say "this is the best of what the South End can offer – good food at great prices in a totally hip" haunt.

Andale! Taqueria Mexican   ▽ 19 | 7 | 13 | $11
Grill 🔲Ⓜ

513B Medford St. (Broadway), Somerville, 617-625-5454

■ Surveyors in Somerville report this "great, quick" Mexican is "worth the money" for "authentic", "flavorful" eats; some swear the burritos are among "Boston's best", so despite "slow service", it's a "favorite."

Andover Inn 🔲Ⓜ   19 | 22 | 20 | $39

Phillips Academy, 10 Chapel Ave. (Rte. 28), Andover, 978-475-5903

☑ "Preppy elegance" distinguishes this "formal, starched" room at Phillips Academy, which offers a "charming New England experience"; the Continental-American menu may be "a bit boring", but the "famous" Sunday night Indonesian rijsttafel is "a wonderful treat."

Angelo & Son's Seafood 🔲Ⓜ   ▽ 19 | 14 | 18 | $25

297-299 Chelsea St. (bet. Day Sq. & Putnam St.), East Boston, 617-567-2500

■ For decades, this "homey" East Boston Southern Italian fish house has been dishing up "excellent" "Sicilian-style" seafood, notably "always good shellfish"; despite "simple" decor, it charms with a "delightful and intimate" atmosphere.

Angelo's Ⓜ   20 | 14 | 17 | $35

575 Boylston St. (bet. Clarendon & Dartmouth Sts.), 617-536-4045
237 Main St. (William St.), Stoneham, 781-279-9035

☑ Fans praise the "quaint" Stoneham flagship as a "miracle" on this stretch of "food-forsaken" Main Street, providing "well-prepared" Italian food to the hungry in "low-key" – or is that "uninviting"? – surroundings (and "the BYO policy is a plus"); meanwhile, the Copley branch offers "fun alfresco dining" and "a nice view of Trinity Church", but most sense that both are "overpriced."

Anna's Taqueria ⓈⓂ⊟　　　20 | 9 | 17 | $8
446 Harvard St. (Thorndike St.), Brookline, 617-277-7111
1412 Beacon St. (Summit Ave.), Brookline, 617-739-7300
822 Somerville Ave. (White St.), Cambridge, 617-661-8500
■ Mexican aficionados swear that the "best burrito in Boston" can be found in Brookline at these taquerias where the "cheap fill-up" is "always fresh because the lines are always long"; most locals prefer takeout to sidestep the "cafeteria setting"; N.B. there's a new and unrated branch in Cambridge.

Anthony's Pier 4 ⓈⓂ　　　14 | 15 | 15 | $34
140 Northern Ave. (Pier 4), 617-423-6363
◪ While this harborside "landmark" seems to have "been around since the Mayflower", nostalgists "still love going here" for "classic" New England–style seafood; even if it's both "passé" and a "tourist trap", detractors concede it may be "worth it for the view."

Antico Forno ⓈⓂ　　　22 | 16 | 20 | $25
93 Salem St. (bet. Cross & Parmenter Sts.), 617-723-6733
■ "Step into this cozy" (or is that "cramped"?) North End trattoria, complete with an "authentic beehive"-shaped brick oven, and enjoy "large portions" of Neapolitan favorites, such as "terrific thin-crust pizzas" and "excellent pastas"; the staff is "friendly" and "knowledgeable", but now that it's "been discovered", prepare for the "crowds."

Antonio's Ⓜ　　　▽ 20 | 13 | 19 | $21
288 Cambridge St. (opp. Mass General), 617-367-3310
■ For nearly "perfect Italian without the hassle of traveling through the Big Dig to the North End", those in the know in Beacon Hill head to Cambridge Street for "unpretentious, straightforward cooking"; the "waiters are real characters" and there's "a nice neighborhood feel" to the room, making it a "consistently good" pick near Mass General.

Apollo Grill ●ⓈⓂ　　　▽ 19 | 15 | 15 | $23
84-86 Harrison Ave. (Kneeland St.), 617-423-3888
◪ A "popular post-club hangout" in Chinatown, this "pleasant" Japanese-Korean "after-hours retreat" feeds the hungry with "large portions of sushi and sashimi" that some say is "delicious", though others advise "stick to the barbecue"; the service is likewise "inconsistent", but nobody's complaining much at 4 AM.

Appetito ⓈⓂ　　　19 | 17 | 18 | $28
1 Appleton St. (Tremont St.), 617-338-6777
761 Beacon St. (Langley Rd.), Newton, 617-244-9881
◪ "Convenient and comfortable", these Italian "staples" "always have long waits", with locals lining up for some of the "best bread in Boston" and "full-flavored" pastas, as well as for the "rockin' Sunday brunch scene"; regulars at the "lively" South End venue adore its "stylish" patio.

Aquitaine [S][M] | 23 | 22 | 20 | $42

569 Tremont St. (Clarendon St.), 617-424-8577

Bringing "France to the South End", this "beautiful" "find" appeals with "quintessential French bistro fare" prepared with "flair" (notably "great steak frites"), accompanied by an "excellent wine list"; while critics grumble that it's "overrated", "pretentious" and staffed by an unusually "loud" bunch, devotees insist it's "warm and welcoming, and we could stay all night", then come back for brunch.

Arirang House [S][M] | ▽ 12 | 7 | 13 | $14

162 Mass Ave. (Belvedere St.), 617-536-1277

While the Korean "buffet isn't a culinary masterpiece", it does the job when you're looking for a "half-decent place near Symphony Hall"; the quality of the "homestyle" dishes is "variable" – some praise the "tasty" *kalbi* (barbecued short ribs), but others cry "tired, sad food"; in any case, it's "cheap."

Armani Cafe [S][M] | 17 | 18 | 14 | $34

214 Newbury St. (bet. Exeter & Fairfield Sts.), 617-437-0909

"Against all odds, the food is quite good" at this "très" "fashionable" Newbury Street "hangout for the Euro crowd" tucked inside the Armani boutique; while "watching the beautiful people shop" (you better "dress the part"), nibble on "trendy", "overpriced" Italian fare; expect "attitude" aplenty and "smoky" surroundings, but it's a "great outdoor lunch spot in the summer" "for the wanna-be rich and famous."

Armida's | ▽ 20 | 13 | 17 | $23

135 Richmond St. (Hanover St.), 617-523-9545

Set in a "nice location" near the Paul Revere House, this North End Italian turns out "uneven" fare: the kitchen can achieve moments of "greatness", as in what partisans claim is "the best ravioli ever", but it can also be "underwhelming."

Artu [S][M] | 19 | 13 | 16 | $22

6 Prince St. (bet. Hanover St. & North Sq.), 617-742-4336
89 Charles St. (bet. Mt. Vernon & Pinckney Sts.), 617-227-9023

Enjoy "more than just pasta" at these Italian nooks in the North End and on Beacon Hill, which also feature "amazing" antipasti, "great sandwiches" and "alluring specials"; even if the decor resembles a "cafeteria" more than a trattoria, "who cares" when "yummy" food is this "affordable"?

Aspasia | – | – | – | E

377 Walden St. (Concord Ave.), Cambridge, 617-864-4745

An ever-evolving menu showcases New American fare at this Cambridge rookie, a cozy dinner-only charmer done in muted tones and exposed brick; the weekday prix fixe menu supplements rotating specialties like pea flan and beef Wellington, and the handsome walnut bar is a magnet for elbow-benders.

Assaggio ●Ⓢ🅜   21   20   19 $28
29 Prince St. (Hanover St.), 617-227-7380
■ Little Italy denizens call this "find" more than "a cut above the standard", with "decent, if not memorable, Italian" food (but the "risotto is fabulous"); though the "teeny" tables are squeezed "too close together", "friendly", "attentive" service helps make this a "favorite" among admirers, who whisper "let's keep it a secret."

Atara Bistro & Wine Bar 🅜   –   –   –   M
1418 Commonwealth Ave. (Kelton & Warren Sts.), Brighton, 617-566-5670
Creative cuisine and a casual ambiance characterize chef Larry Kessler's new Brighton bistro in the former location of Uva; the menu offers Mediterranean specialties, and an adjacent bar and cafe provide a soothing refuge for relaxed regulars; N.B. dinner only.

Atasca Ⓢ   23   20   23 $24
279 Broadway (bet. Columbia & Prospect Sts.), Cambridge, 617-354-4355
■ Alas, this "delightful" family-run Cambridge "treasure" is "no longer undiscovered", so Iberian loyalists must now "reluctantly share" their find with novices; rated by many as the "best" of its genre in a very ethnic neighborhood, this "real thing" shines with "authentic" Portuguese "home cooking", "imaginative decor" and "sincere" service.

Atlantic Fish Company Ⓢ🅜   16   14   16 $27
761 Boylston St. (Fairfield St.), 617-267-4000
◪ Relocated post-*Survey* a few doors down from its former site (thus outdating the decor score), this Back Bay fish house continues to prepare "all the basics just right"; the menu may be "nothing special, but it's reliable" and fairly priced, making it a "good old standby" for many locals.

Atlantic 101 Ⓢ🅜   18   21   18 $34
Mercantile Wharf, 101 Atlantic Ave. (bet. Commercial & Richmond Sts.), 617-723-5101
◪ Relatively new, this seafood house overlooking the harbor has already gone through a "change of chefs"; some say the kitchen turns out "tasty" fish and praise the "friendly" staff that's "steadily improving", but more carp that it "misses the boat" with a "mediocre" yet "overpriced" menu.

Atlas Bar & Grill Ⓢ🅜   13   16   12 $18
145 Ipswich St. (Landsdowne St.), 617-437-0300
■ "Fun and games abound" at this "lively" "sports bar with a dance club–wanna-be personality" housed in Jillian's entertainment emporium; a "loud, younger crowd" "likes" that there are "TVs at every table", though the "over-30" set wonders "whatever happened to conversation?"; "oh yeah, they serve food too", but it's "blah" American pub grub.

Audubon Circle [S][M] | 19 | 19 | 16 | $17 |

838 Beacon St. (Arundel St.), 617-421-1910

■ Proximity to Fenway Park makes this "casually hip" New American a "best bet" for a pre– or "post–ball game" stop among a "young, professional crowd"; the "Frank Lloyd Wright–inspired decor" is a smart backdrop for a "variety of tasty treats", and though it's a "high-decibel experience", satisfied regulars say with "great burgers, great potstickers and good-looking people, who needs much more?"

AUJOURD'HUI [S][M] | 28 | 28 | 28 | $64 |

Four Seasons Hotel, 200 Boylston St. (bet. Arlington & S. Charles Sts.), 617-351-2071

■ "Heaven's main dining room", according to disciples, is in the "luxurious" Four Seasons Hotel where pampered diners are virtually guaranteed "an elegant", "world-class" evening; in a "magnificent" space with "regal decor" and a stellar view of the Public Garden, an "impeccable" staff proffers "glorious" New American cuisine layered with French and Asian accents; Boston's Most Popular Restaurant, it also ranks as the No. 1 restaurant overall in the city, with the top combined scores for Food (No. 2), Decor (No. 1) and Service (No. 1).

Aura [S][M] | 23 | 19 | 22 | $44 |

Seaport Hotel, 1 Seaport Ln. (bet. Congress St. & Northern Ave.), 617-385-4300

◪ Once past the shock – "imagine a waterfront restaurant with no windows!" – diners settle in a "beautiful room" and enjoy New American fare that admirers say is "superb", notably a "spectacular raw bar, exceptional sushi" and a "fabulous brunch"; dissenters, however, are "not impressed" with the "dull" menu, having "expected more from the hype", but do commend the "attentive" staff.

Back Eddy, The [S][M] | – | – | – | E |

1 Bridge Rd. (Rte. 88), Westport, 508-636-6500

On an appropriately aquatic site, this spacious riverside fish house in Westport (courtesy of Chris Schlesinger, chef-owner of the East Coast Grill & Raw Bar) buzzes with action; the kitchen specializes in grilled seafood with a twist and bases its menu on other local ingredients, such as produce, cheeses and wines; plus, the docks outside are a casually nifty setting for the tempting raw bar.

Baja Betty's Burritos [S][M]💳̸ | 18 | 11 | 17 | $9 |

3 Harvard Sq. (bet. Harvard & Washington Sts.), Brookline, 617-277-8900

◪ For "a quick and creative Cal-Mex fix" that's "tasty" and "healthy", aficionados make tracks for this Brookline "hole-in-the-wall" to devour "huge" burritos ("with a variety of sauces to heat them up") and other "great, cheap eats", washed down by "fresh lemonade"; P.S. beware that the "joint" has only 15 seats.

Baja Mexican Cantina [S][M] 14 | 13 | 14 | $20
111 Dartmouth St. (Columbus Ave.), 617-262-7575
◪ At the crossroads of the South End and the Back Bay, this "funky" Mexican attracts an "after-work crowd" that drops in for "tart margaritas" and "great chips and salsa", then stays for "sizzling fajitas"; it's "nothing fancy", but many find it a "reliable", "convenient" cantina with a "fun atmosphere" enhanced by "personable servers."

Baker's Best Cafe [S][M] 22 | 12 | 16 | $14
27 Lincoln St. (Walnut St.), Newton Highlands, 617-332-4588
■ A boon to Newton Highlands, this "imaginative" American cafe and "appetizing" take-out spot offers "fantastic sandwiches", "fresh salads" and prepared foods prized by "harried moms" and hosts scrambling for "last-minute holiday fill-ins"; while bargain-seekers complain about its "price chutzpah", admirers appreciate it as the "best suburban brunch spot", where "everything looks great and tastes even better."

B & D Deli [S][M] 16 | 9 | 13 | $13
1653 Beacon St. (Washington St.), Brookline, 617-232-3727
◪ Some mavens swear that "Jewish soul food better than mom's" can be found at this "next best thing" to a NYC deli, a "solid, old-time" Brookline "favorite" famous for a latke sandwich that's "a heart-stopping delight" and a plate of lox and scrambled eggs that must be a gift "from the gods"; even if there's "too long a wait" and the room needs "updating", loyalists demand "where else can you get a tongue omelet?"

Bangkok Basil [S][M] 16 | 13 | 17 | $17
1374 Beacon St. (Centre St.), Brookline, 617-739-1236
◪ They're "not afraid to make the food spicy" at this "low-key" Coolidge Corner Thai that turns out pretty "tasty" "standards", including "delicious vegetarian" dishes; detractors, however, are "disappointed" in "uninspired" fare and reserve extra knocks for the "clueless service."

Bangkok Bistro [S][M] 18 | 12 | 16 | $17
1952 Beacon St. (Chestnut Hill Ave.), Brighton, 617-739-7270
◪ Follow the "college crowd" to this Brighton "find" for "straightforward" fare, especially "excellent pad Thai", delivered by a "friendly", "quick" staff; despite "tacky" decor ("pink-and-green everything") and "difficult parking", it's among the "best values in town."

Bangkok Blue [S][M] 19 | 14 | 16 | $20
651 Boylston St. (opp. Boston Public Library), 617-266-1010
■ "One dish stands out – shrimp with crispy basil" – at this Copley Square spot that's "a cut above the rest of the Boston Thai scene", featuring "reliable, if typical", fare "with a few original touches"; it's "small, so there may be a wait", but it's "worth it" for "fresh tastes" at "reasonable prices."

Bangkok Cuisine S M
21 | 14 | 18 | $19

177A Mass Ave. (bet. Boylston St. & Huntington Ave.),
617-262-5377

■ "One of the original Thai restaurants in Boston", this "old favorite" "convenient" to the Berklee School of Music is "still consistently good after all these years"; the menu includes "detailed descriptions to take the mystery out of Asian dining", making this a "safe choice"; if only the somewhat "cold atmosphere" were as "hot" as the food.

Bangkok House S M
18 | 13 | 16 | $18

50 JFK St. (Mt. Auburn St.), Cambridge, 617-547-6666

◪ An "extensive selection" of "flavorful", "appropriately spiced" dishes differentiates this basement-level Harvard Square Thai from others of its ilk; critics gripe "they can't even make a decent pad Thai", and few are soothed by the "tired" decor, but many feel it's a "good value."

BARCODE ◑ S M
− | − | − | M

(fka Division Sixteen)
955 Boylston St. (bet. Hereford St. & Mass Ave.), 617-421-1818

Behind its supermarket scanner−striped logo, this Back Bay newcomer cultivates a colonial look with bamboo, mahogany and palm trees, lending exotic flavor to the Asian fusion fare of chef George Leu; dishes such as sugarcane-skewered beef and ginger-brined pork chops spice up the menu, and a bar with ceiling fans occupies the entrance.

Barker Tavern, The S
22 | 23 | 22 | $34

21 Barker Rd. (bet. Hatherly & Jericho Rds.), Scituate,
781-545-6533

■ Sample a "taste of olde New England" at this "beautiful" 1634 house in Scituate with a "colonial" "tavern" setting and "gracious" service; the "tried-and-true" American menu "isn't too creative", but when the kitchen's "areas of excellence" include the "best swordfish anywhere", who needs "innovative" cuisine?

Barking Crab, The S M
15 | 14 | 13 | $20

88 Sleeper St. (Northern Ave.), 617-426-2722

◪ "Boston's equivalent of a clam shack", this "ultracasual" "hut" "on the waterfront" may be a "summer tourist attraction", but it's the "best place in town to get down and dirty" with a plate of clams, crab or lobster; even if some find the food "marginal", most say it's a "fun, unique experience."

Bar 10 ◑ S M
− | − | − | M

Westin Hotel, 10 Huntington Ave. (Dartmouth & Stuart Sts.),
617-424-7446

The new lounge at the Westin in Copley Square is part watering hole, part Mediterranean eatery, and thoroughly sleek and modern; dishes like margherita flatbread pizza and tuna niçoise are capably delivered to diners nestled in candlelit banquettes.

Bawarchi [S][M] ▽ 17 | 12 | 13 | $16
636 Beacon St. (Commonwealth Ave.), 617-424-1499
◪ While it's certainly "not the best Indian restaurant", this "sweet, family-owned" spot in Kenmore Square is "decent", and many "take advantage of the average but inexpensive lunch buffet"; critics, however, point out that "you get what you pay for" – "mediocre quality at bargain prices" – and warn the room is "as dark as a dungeon."

BAY TOWER, THE [M] 20 | 26 | 22 | $50
Faneuil Hall Mktpl., 60 State St. (Congress St.), 617-723-1666
◪ "Swanky" and "romantic", this "formal" Financial District New American is justly renowned for the "breathtaking" vista from its 33rd-floor perch, reason enough why it's "wonderful for special occasions"; while "nothing else here can come close" to that "intoxicating view", the "splendid" fare is "catching up" to the "outstanding service"; indeed, this "true treat" is "a splurge", but "great dancing" is available gratis.

B.B. Wolf [S][M] 13 | 12 | 15 | $18
109 Brookline Ave. (Yawkey Way), Brookline, 617-247-2227
◪ A somewhat "upscale imitation of a downscale BBQ joint", this American "delight for carnivores" in the "shadow of Fenway Park" is known for its "Fred Flintstone–sized servings of ribs" paired with a "fantastic beer selection" (48 choices); critics gripe "tasteless", but fans say the "backyard" setting (complete with a picket fence) and "whimsical staff" always "put them in a good mood."

Bella's [S][M] 21 | 16 | 18 | $31
933 Hingham St. (Rte. 3), Rockland, 781-871-5789
◪ For "consistently good Italian", notably "delicious veal dishes" and the "best eggplant parmigiana around", Rockland locals head to this "basic" standby; supporters say it's "top quality for the 'burbs or anywhere", but dissenters find it "run-of-the-mill" and detect "attitude"; still, as there's usually a "long wait", most must feel it's more than "ok, even if nothing exceptional."

Bernard's [S][M] 21 | 15 | 18 | $23
Mall at Chestnut Hill, 199 Boylston St. (Hammond Pond Pkwy.), Chestnut Hill, 617-969-3388
■ "Don't let the mall location scare you", because this "gourmet" Asian in Chestnut Hill is "not your basic egg roll and spareribs" joint; taking the "neighborhood Chinese concept to a whole different level", the kitchen turns out "adventurous", "addictive" specials that are an "awesome" "alternative to the usual"; it's all served by "happy people" in an "understated" room at "moderate prices"; boosters swear "you can't do better" while shopping.

Bertucci's ⓢⓜ
15 | 12 | 14 | $16

Faneuil Hall Mktpl., 22 Merchants Row (State St.),
617-227-7889
90 Main St., Andover, 978-470-3939 ●
412 Franklin St. (Five Corners), Braintree, 781-849-3066
4 Pearl St. (bet. Brookline Ave. & Rte. 9), Brookline, 617-731-2300
21 Brattle St. (Harvard Sq.), Cambridge, 617-864-4748 ●
14 E. Littleton Rd. (Rte. 110), Chelmsford, 978-250-8800 ●
1405 Providence Hwy. (Sumner St.), Norwood, 781-762-4155
197 Elm St. (Davis Sq.), Somerville, 617-776-9241
475 Winter St. (Rte. 128), Waltham, 781-684-0650
17 Commerce Way (New Boston St.), Woburn, 781-933-1440
▨ "Yummy" "yuppie pizzas" with "fresh", "inventive"
toppings draw in the hordes to this "absolutely reliable"
Italian chain of "family eateries"; despite the "sterile"
"Pizzas-R-Us" setting and "iffy" service, regulars say it's
"a favorite for an inexpensive, satisfying meal."

Betty's Wok & Noodle Diner ⓢⓜ
– | – | – | M

250 Huntington Ave. (Mass Ave.), 617-424-1950
Take a wok on the wild side at this Symphony-area Asian
noshery where a '50s-diner feel and red quilted booths
define the campy throwback sensibility; picking your own
noodle, vegetable and sauce combos makes for a creative
customized bite at an affordable price.

BIBA ⓢⓜ
25 | 24 | 22 | $52

272 Boylston St. (bet. Arlington & S. Charles Sts.), 617-426-7878
▨ Among the city's premier "power dining spots", this "oh-
so-chic" Back Bay New American boasts a "fantastic view
of the Public Garden" from the "fabulous" Adam Tihany–
designed room and "inspired", "innovative" dishes from
chefs Lydia Shire and Susan Regis that are admittedly
"sometimes weird"; but even if the "menu is too avant-
garde, this is still one of Boston's best tables"; P.S. the
"buzzing" bar is a "good place to eat and people-watch."

Billy Tse ●ⓢⓜ
20 | 13 | 17 | $22

240 Commercial St. (Atlantic Ave.), 617-227-9990
441 Revere St. (Pierce St.), Revere, 781-286-2882
■ "Thumbs up, Billy!" for giving Boston twin "oases" of
"inventive" Pan-Asian fare, featuring "Chinese with a twist"
and "wonderful sushi", as well as "out-of-the-ordinary" Thai
and Vietnamese dishes; both the North End and Revere
branches are "lively" and the staff is "accommodating"
and "informed", so you'll leave "smiling."

Bishop's ⓢⓜ
20 | 12 | 19 | $28

99 Hampshire St. (Lowell St.), Lawrence, 978-683-7143
▨ "It's worth the trip" to Lawrence for "excellent" Middle
Eastern savories such as "heavenly hummus" and the "best
charbroiled lamb chops"; a handful of detractors say this
"nondescript place" is "tired", but most count on it as a
"consistent" "standby" with "good value."

Bison County BBQ 🆂Ⓜ   17 | 12 | 15 | $18
275 Moody St. (Crescent St.), Waltham, 781-642-9720
◪ "Memphis it ain't", but this BBQ "meat fix" "isn't bad for
Waltham", dishing up "tender", "tasty" bison, "great ribs"
and "awesome" sweet-potato fries; critics cite "surprisingly
mild" (read "bland") vittles and a "moderately competent"
staff, but at least "you'll never go home hungry."

Bistro 5   – | – | – | M
5 Playstead Rd. (High St.), Medford, 781-395-7464
A whimsical clown theme shares center ring with Northern
Italian fare at this newly reopened Medford bistro; baby
octopus salad and lamb with gnocchi are mainstays, livened
up by an interior done in bright harlequin colors, with
menus hanging on the walls to double as decor; N.B. BYO.

Bisuteki 🆂Ⓜ   17 | 15 | 18 | $26
Howard Johnson Hotel, 777 Memorial Dr. (Pleasant St.),
Cambridge, 617-492-7777
Howard Johnson Hotel, 407 Squire Rd. (Rte. 60 W.),
Revere, 781-284-7200
◪ At these Japanese "circus acts" in Cambridge and
Revere it's always "show time", with "entertaining chefs"
and their "flying knives" in the center ring preparing "tasty"
steak and other morsels at your "communal" table; the
unamused complain about "chop, chop, chop, boring" food,
but defenders insist this "gimmick" "still works."

Black Goose Ⓜ   15 | 14 | 14 | $24
21 Beacon St. (Bowdoin St.), 617-720-4500
◪ Expect to "hobnob with the law" at this "power-lunch"
Italian near the State House on Beacon Hill while dining on
housemade pastas; despite food that "sometimes lays an
egg", it remains "popular with politicians and lobbyists",
proving that its "convenient location" "keeps it going."

Black Rose, The 🆂Ⓜ   13 | 14 | 14 | $17
Faneuil Hall Mktpl., 160 State St. (Commercial St.),
617-742-2286
◪ "Forget the world – drink, sing" and be merry at this
"spirited Irish pub" in Faneuil Hall, "one of the best beer
houses in Boston"; the "menu isn't very extensive", which
is a plus, because the "typical" grub is "unexciting"; "the
big draw here is the live music" featured nightly.

Blackstone on the Square ●🆂Ⓜ   – | – | – | M
1525 Washington St. (W. Brookline St.), 617-247-4455
Overlooking Blackstone Park, this Contemporary American
in the South End appeals to a hip, largely gay clientele with
its active bar scene and modern, industrial setting that's
juxtaposed with such Gothic touches as stained glass and
church-pew booths; the seasonal menu features appetizers
like a paper bag filled with fried Maine clams, herb-grilled
prime rib and broiled Cape bluefish.

Blossoms Cafe Ⓜ | 17 | 12 | 13 | $13 |
99 High St. (Congress St.), 617-423-1911
◪ As a "creative alternative" for a weekday breakfast or lunch in the Financial District, try this "hidden jewel" that presents "offbeat salads" and "delicious" sandwiches for a "quick" bite, along with "more substantial meals" from a California-style menu; though some write it off as a "nothing-special corporate cafeteria", more appreciate it as a "blooming good" option.

Blue Cat Cafe ●ⓈⓂ | 16 | 18 | 17 | $24 |
94 Mass Ave. (Newbury Ave.), 617-247-9922
◪ "Cool" jazz plays all night long at this "trendy" Back Bay American hangout that's "dark, funky" and perhaps "too sexy" for its own good; a "hip" crowd gathers at the "easygoing bar", sips "excellent martinis" and admires the "old-fashioned working telephones" on each table; the "limited menu" is mostly "lackluster", but food really isn't the point here.

Blue Diner ●ⓈⓂ | 13 | 13 | 12 | $16 |
150 Kneeland St. (South St.), 617-695-0087
◪ Downtown's "late-night nosh central" "isn't like it used to be" at its previous location, but it's still a "reliable", all-American "joint" with a "real diner" flavor, and it continues to feed the "post-clubbing" set and a "bizarre cast of characters" with "hearty breakfasts anytime"; critics, though, sigh it's "lost its charm" and gripe about "truck-stop food at airport prices."

BLUE GINGER Ⓜ | 26 | 22 | 23 | $41 |
583 Washington St. (Rte. 16), Wellesley,
781-283-5790
■ "Good luck getting reservations" at "brilliant chef" Ming Tsai's "casually elegant" "gem" in Wellesley, "but if you do, you're in for a treat" because his "exciting East-meets-West fusion" cuisine is "uniquely" "exquisite", infused with an "outstanding blend of flavors" (don't miss his "awesome" signature sake-marinated Chilean sea bass); despite some negative marks for the "hard-edged decor", most "welcome" it as a "first-class" "oasis in the Western suburbs."

Blue Ribbon BBQ ⓈⓂ | 22 | 12 | 17 | $13 |
908 Mass Ave. (Highland Ave.), Arlington, 781-648-7427
1375 Washington St. (Elm St.), Newton, 617-332-2583
■ Someone thankfully "sent the BBQ gods" to Newton and Arlington to educate the Yanks about "authentic Southern cooking"; the kitchen at this pair of "roadhouses" turns out "monster portions" of "mouthwatering" ribs and pulled pork that's "knock-your-socks-off spicy"; there's "scarce seating", so it's "mainly for takeout."

BLUE ROOM, THE 🄢🄜   24 | 20 | 22 | $36
1 Kendall Sq. (bet. Broadway & Portland St.), Cambridge,
617-494-9034

◪ In Kendall Square, this "upbeat", "always satisfying"
experience seems to "get even better every year"; chef
Steve Johnson's "fabulous" Eclectic menu (with "Asian
touches") is "innovative and flavorful, based on unexpected
combinations that work", and it's matched with a "killer
wine list"; the "attractive, relaxed" surroundings make
this an "all-around great hangout", and "you'll leave as
happy" as Julia Child (this "jewel" is one of her favorites).

Bluestone Bistro 🄢🄜   18 | 13 | 15 | $16
1799 Commonwealth Ave. (Chiswick Rd.), Brighton,
617-254-8309

◪ "They should patent" the "terrific" pizzas with "great
crusts" and "eclectic toppings" at this "local favorite" of
the Brighton "college crowd"; the "funky, casual" room is
a bit "cramped", and service swings between "friendly"
and "dazed and confused", but it's "always crowded" for
a "delicious" reason.

Boathouse Grille 🄢🄜   17 | 18 | 18 | $31
(fka Scullers Grille)
Doubletree Guest Suites, 400 Soldiers Field Rd. (River St.),
Allston, 617-783-0090

◪ Some sing the praises of the "surprisingly good food"
at this recently renamed New American in the Doubletree
Guest Suites in Allston, but many more find it hits a sour
note with only "ok food" and "mediocre service"; the
common refrain: "there's no reason to eat here unless
you're seeing a show" at the jazz club next door; N.B. a
revised menu may outdate the score for Food.

Bob the Chef ◖🄢   19 | 16 | 18 | $20
604 Columbus Ave. (Mass Ave.), 617-536-6204

■ This Soul Food "landmark" in the South End is a "feel-
good kind of place" to chow down on "tasty" "home
cookin'" "done right" – "falling-off-the-bone" ribs, "gold-
standard fried chicken" and sweet-potato pie that's "a
must"; it's all served by a staff that "makes you feel like
a regular"; P.S. "great jazz brunch on Sundays."

Boca Grande 🄢🄜   15 | 7 | 11 | $9
149 First St. (Bent St.), Cambridge, 617-354-5550
1728 Mass Ave. (Linnaean St.), Cambridge, 617-354-7400
1295 Beacon St. (bet. Harvard & Pleasant Sts.), Brookline,
617-739-3900

◪ "Speedy Gonzalez meets the Frugal Gourmet" at this pair
of "really inexpensive" Mexican joints that cater to
Cambridge students and the "high-tech" set with "killer
burritos"; detractors cite "bland" grub and "sterile decor",
but many depend on it for a "simple", "filling" fix; N.B.
there's a new and unrated branch in Brookline.

Bombay Bistro S M   21 | 15 | 19 | $19
1353 Beacon St. (bet. Harvard & Winchester Sts.), Brookline, 617-734-2879

◪ "A wonderful neighborhood treasure", this "soothing" Coolidge Corner Indian – "one of the best in Boston" – delivers "awesome, spicy" dishes with "clear flavors"; even if the menu is "predictable", the food is "solid" and served by a "gracious" staff in "pleasant" surroundings.

Bombay Cafe S M   18 | 15 | 17 | $18
175 Mass Ave. (bet. Boylston St. & Huntington Ave.), 617-247-0555

◪ This "small", colonial-style Indian eatery near Symphony Hall is "reliable, if not extraordinary"; the menu is "pretty standard", as is the "decent lunch buffet", but the wine list is surprisingly "nice" and tabs are "affordable."

Bombay Club S M   20 | 17 | 16 | $22
Harvard Sq., 57 JFK St. (Winthrop St.), Cambridge, 617-661-8100

◪ "Wraparound windows overlooking Harvard Square" vie with the "amazing selection" of "fresh" dishes at this "upscale" Cambridge Indian; the "yummy buffet with a four-star condiment array" wins kudos, but "disinterested" service leads some surveyors to conclude "too pricey."

Bomboa ◕ S M   – | – | – | E
35 Stanhope St. (bet. Berkeley & Clarendon Sts.), 617-236-6363

A fusion of French and Brazilian marks the explosive debut of chef Michael Reidt's latest venue in the former location of Zinc, straddling the Back Bay and South End; culinary highlights include cachaça-marinated tuna and a Brazilian pot-au-feu, and the zinc bar shares the stage with zebra-striped banquettes and a saltwater aquarium.

Boodle's ◕ S M   17 | 16 | 18 | $32
Back Bay Hilton Hotel, 40 Dalton St. (Belvedere St.), 617-266-3537

◼ Specializing in mesquite-grilled dishes, this "pleasant" American in the Back Bay Hilton makes a "convenient" starting place on "symphony nights"; most find it "perfectly satisfactory, though nothing more", with a "no-surprise" menu, "comfortable seating" and "unpretentious" service.

Border Cafe ◕ S M   16 | 15 | 15 | $17
32 Church St. (Palmer St.), Cambridge, 617-864-6100
817 Broadway/Rte. 1 (bet. Lynn-Fells Pkwy. & Main St.), Saugus, 781-233-5308

◪ "Big margaritas" draw the "college crowd" to this "perennial Harvard Square favorite", as do the "huge portions" of Tex-Mex staples like fajitas and popcorn shrimp; the "rowdy atmosphere" makes it particularly "fun for groups", though dissenters dismiss it as "faux Mexican" for the "fake-ID bunch"; N.B. there's also a branch in Saugus.

Boston Beer Garden [S] [M] — 14 | 14 | 14 | $17

734 E. Broadway (L St.), South Boston, 617-269-0990

◪ For "good, cheap eats" in a beer-basted "sticky floor" setting, the "twentysomething" crowd heads to this "loud" South Boston suds emporium known for its "large-screen TVs" and "'70s disco" music; but those over 30 sniff it's "just a bar with about as much charm as the Fleet Center."

Boston Beer Works 🌙 [S] [M] — 15 | 14 | 14 | $17

61 Brookline Ave. (Fenway Park), 617-536-2337

◪ "Great cask-conditioned beers" poured in a "fun and funky setting" near Fenway make this American brewpub "dive" popular before or after a ball game, even though fans admit "acoustically it's a nightmare" and tabs are "a little pricey"; N.B. a new menu outdates the above food score.

Boston Sail Loft [S] [M] — 15 | 15 | 16 | $21

80 Atlantic Ave. (Commercial St. & Lewis Wharf), 617-227-7280
1 Memorial Dr. (bet. Kendall Sq. & Main St.), Cambridge, 617-225-2222

◪ Regulars at these "picturesque" waterfront Americans advise stick to the "superb chowder" and "best fish 'n' chips"; even if the rest of the "basic seafood" is only "mediocre, the riverside tables are an excellent antidote to a sticky summer night", and the staff is "friendly and upbeat."

Brandy Pete's [M] — 12 | 11 | 13 | $19

267 Franklin St. (Batterymarch St.), 617-439-4165

◪ While most veterans agree that this Financial District "watering hole" was "a better place years ago" before "the move from Broad Street", it's still "a great place for burgers" and a good "after-work dive"; but the discerning yawn "tired" and bet there's "not one healthy item on the menu."

Brasserie Jo 🌙 [S] [M] — 20 | 21 | 19 | $35

Colonnade Hotel, 120 Huntington Ave. (W. Newton St.), 617-425-3240

◪ "Bravo for late-night" rejoice Francophiles who flock to this Symphony-area brasserie that features "typically Parisian" dishes, particularly "awesome" escargots served "the traditional way"; but detractors say it's "a great concept halfheartedly done", though a post-*Survey* chef change might be remedying the situation.

Brew Moon 🌙 [S] [M] — 16 | 17 | 16 | $21

115 Stuart St. (bet. S. Charles & Tremont Sts.), 617-742-2739
South Shore Plaza, 250 Granite St. (South Shore Plaza Rd.), Braintree, 781-356-2739
50 Church St. (bet. Brattle St. & Mass Ave.), Cambridge, 617-499-2739

◪ The "interesting" microbrews at this "trendy" trio of brewpubs is the main draw for most quaffers, much more so than "pretentiously priced" grub; many like the "cool, modern design", but others snarl "surreal factory decor."

BRISTOL LOUNGE, THE ●🅂🄼   25 | 27 | 25 | $39
Four Seasons Hotel, 200 Boylston St. (bet. Arlington &
S. Charles Sts.), 617-351-2053
■ "Affordable luxury" awaits at this glass-walled lounge on
the first floor of the Four Seasons Hotel with "wonderful
views of the Public Garden"; diners dressed in "jeans or a
tux" are welcome in one of Boston's "nicest places to
meet" for brunch, lunch, afternoon tea or dinner; many
admirers feel the "exquisite" New American cuisine is
nearly "as good as the food upstairs" at the more formal
Aujourd'hui, but at far less precious prices – think of this
as the "Four Seasons on a budget."

Brown Sugar Cafe 🅂🄼   24 | 14 | 20 | $18
129 Jersey St. (Boylston St.), 617-266-2928
1033 Commonwealth Ave. (Babcock St.), 617-787-4242
■ For "superb Thai", MFA wanderers find their way to this
"small", "hidden" "storefront" "gem" in the Fenway that
entices with "dreamy" dishes and "homey" decor made
"romantic" at night with candlelight; what's more, the
"cheerful" staff seems to "remember" all the "diverse"
patrons drawn here in spite of "impossible parking"; N.B.
there's a new and unrated branch near Brighton.

B-Side Lounge ●🅂🄼   21 | 19 | 19 | $21
92 Hampshire St. (Windsor St.), Cambridge, 617-354-0766
■ This "cool, retro spot" fast won raves from the "beautiful"
people of Kendall Square, who like the "adventurous"
American food and "groovy" decor ("like a 1958 lounge");
the downside, however, of being so "trendy" and "already
too well-known" is that the "sassy service" and the long
"waits" are unlikely to soon abate.

Buddha's Delight 🅂🄼   18 | 10 | 16 | $13
3 Beach St. (Washington St.), 617-451-2395
404 Harvard St. (bet. Beacon St. & Commonwealth Ave.),
Brookline, 617-739-8830
◪ "Chinese for strict vegetarians" is the mission of this
pair of inexpensive Asians in Chinatown and Brookline;
the "creative" kitchen so cleverly employs "mock meat"
that carnivores probably won't miss it; despite a rather
sober atmosphere and "slow" service, the open-minded
appreciate its "novel approach."

Bugaboo Creek Steak House 🅂🄼   12 | 15 | 14 | $19
551 Mahar Hwy. (Pearl St.), Braintree, 781-848-0002
345 Cochituate Rd. (bet. Rtes. 9 & 30), Framingham, 508-370-9001
North Shore Mall, Rte. 114, Peabody, 978-538-0100
Arsenal Mall, 617 Arsenal St. (Elm St.), Watertown, 617-924-9000
◪ Dining with "Crocodile Dundee and the family" is how
some surveyors think of this "Disney-esque" meat house
"theme" chain with "corny" decor and "mediocre" steaks
and burgers; "kids love" the "talking moose", "dancing trees
and flapping fish", but the shtick fast "grows annoying."

Bukhara ⓢⓜ   ▽ 20 | 17 | 15 | $20
701 Centre St. (Burroughs St.), Jamaica Plain, 617-522-2195
✉ "Finally, Indian comes to Jamaica Plain" cheer supporters
of this "welcome addition" to the neighborhood that
"beautifully presents delicious", "well-spiced" South Indian
specialties; even if the "friendly" service is a bit "slow",
appreciative palates just hope it'll "improve with time."

Bull & Finch Pub ◗ⓈⓂ   12 | 15 | 14 | $20
84 Beacon St. (bet. Arlington & Charles Sts.), 617-227-9605
■ Even if nobody really "knows your name" here, that
doesn't stop "busloads" of "out-of-towners" from flocking
to this Beacon Hill pub that inspired the TV show *Cheers*,
though the American eats are "nothing special"; local wags
can't help but sing this is "where everybody knows . . . it's
a tourist trap", so go "buy your aunt a shirt and leave."

Burren, The ⓈⓂ   14 | 18 | 14 | $15
247 Elm St. (Davis Sq.), Somerville, 617-776-6896
■ Pub crawlers get their Irish up at this "endearingly dark
and smoky" Somerville bar, which "pours the best pint of
Guinness around" and features "traditional sessions" of
live music nightly; this is "everything an Irish pub should
be", "ok" "comfort food" included.

Buteco ⓈⓂ   20 | 12 | 18 | $19
130 Jersey St. (Park Dr.), 617-247-9508
■ "Food is all" at this tiny, "no-decor" Fenway "storefront",
which "sticks with Brazilian basics and gets it right"; most
of the dishes are "boy-oh-boy" "fabulous", but you "must
try the manioc with carrot sauce", plantain chips and "tasty"
collard greens ("surprisingly", there's a "great choice for
vegetarians"); it's "plain", but "cheap" and "friendly."

Butterfish American Bistro Ⓢ   – | – | – | E
*5 Craigie Circle (bet. Brattle St. & Concord Ave.), Cambridge,
617-497-5511*
The crisp blue-toned interior and fresh Contemporary
American cuisine more than compensate for any parking
hassles at this newcomer west of Harvard Square, on the
site vacated by Cafe Celador; the kitchen keeps things
interesting with an oft-modified menu.

Cactus Club ⓈⓂ   15 | 15 | 14 | $21
939 Boylston St. (Hereford St.), 617-236-0200
✉ A "fun, lively atmosphere" is the reason a "young crowd"
joins the "after-work" fiesta at this Back Bay Tex-Mex that's
as much a "pickup joint" as a restaurant; nachos with salsa
are the "best" of the "generic" picks, but the "big drinks
make the food taste better."

Cafe Barada M
18 | 12 | 16 | $16
201 Mass Ave. (Lake St.), Arlington, 781-646-9650
■ "Classic Middle Eastern food" offered in a "relaxing environment" adds up to "the tastiest little deal in Arlington"; "locals love" to begin with the "outstanding" hummus, follow with a "tantalizing" lamb entree and end with "superb" baklava; even though the "grumpy" "servers never smile" and the decor is "totally bland", it's "worth it" for these "delicious, cheap eats."

Cafe Brazil S M
19 | 11 | 19 | $19
421 Cambridge St. (Harvard Ave.), Allston, 617-789-5980
■ Rio comes to Allston at this "funky little place" with "good staples like rice and beans" and "fabulous" fish dishes; top it off with a "hearty coffee" while listening to live music, and the "slummy" ambiance soon morphs into an "inviting" one.

Cafe Budapest S M
22 | 21 | 22 | $46
Copley Square Hotel, 90 Exeter St. (bet. Boylston St. & Huntington Ave.), 617-266-1979
☑ "Long live the cherry soup" hail regulars of this Hungarian "time warp" in the Back Bay, a "sentimental favorite" for its "cozy and romantic" "old-world charm"; even if you can "feel your arteries clogging", "calories be damned" when the menu features "heartily" "wonderful" goulash, paprika chicken and "sour cream in everything."

Cafe China S
19 | 14 | 18 | $21
1245 Cambridge St. (Prospect St.), Cambridge, 617-868-4300
☑ "Unique" Chinese with European touches makes this "small", "crowded" Inman Square "find" a "creative alternative to Chinatown"; enthusiasts laud the "imaginative flourishes", but purists feel "Chinese dishes would be better left alone, not gussied up like here"; nevertheless, many say this "different" spot is "worth a visit."

Cafe de Paris S M ⇦
12 | 10 | 10 | $13
19 Arlington St. (bet. Boylston & Newbury Sts.), 617-247-7121
☑ "Convenient to the Public Garden", this "shopping pit stop" is a "popular" place to "grab a bite" in a "cafeteria setup"; there's a "good sandwich selection" and "great desserts", but critics quip that given these "outrageous prices" it should be dubbed "Cafe de Rip-Off" and rant "I've been in sushi bars more Parisian than this."

Cafe Escadrille M
18 | 17 | 18 | $33
26 Cambridge St. (Rte. 128, exit 33A), Burlington, 781-273-1916
☑ This Burlington Continental is a "conservative choice" for a "business lunch", providing a "great selection" (some complain there's "toooo much to choose from") of "well-prepared", if "predictable", fare (a "Caesar salad for the table is mandatory"); detractors, though, find it "over-everything – done, sauced, priced."

Cafe Fleuri S M   22 | 21 | 22 | $38
Le Meridien Hotel, 250 Franklin St. (Pearl St.), 617-451-1900
◪ Remodeled not long ago, this "gardenlike" French cafe in Le Meridien Hotel is a "premier" destination for "power" breakfasts, lunches and dinners; while some grumble about "small" portions and a "stuffy" atmosphere, everyone raves about the "dreamy" Saturday chocolate buffet (September–May) and Sunday brunch – "boy, do they know how to put out a spread."

Cafe Jaffa S M   18 | 10 | 15 | $14
48 Gloucester St. (bet. Boylston & Newbury Sts.), 617-536-0230
■ "Fast and affordable Middle Eastern food" is the draw at this "true bargain" in the Back Bay, which offers "high-quality" "basics" including "great falafel" and "yummy" kebabs; even if you're "served with a frown", you're still served "large portions" of "hearty" "ethnic specialties."

Café Louis M   23 | 19 | 21 | $44
Louis, 234 Berkeley St. (Newbury St.), 617-266-4680
◪ Fashionistas urge don't "spend all your money" while shopping at the Back Bay's Louis, because its "innovative and stylish" cafe boasts a "terrific" Northern Italian menu that spotlights "excellent" pizzas and "dynamite pastas"; the room is "frightfully loud", the ambiance is a bit "cold" and the prices are, well, "pricey", but "you'd never believe you could get food this good at a clothing store."

Cafe Marliave M   15 | 14 | 17 | $24
10 Bosworth St. (bet. Tremont & Washington Sts.), 617-423-6340
◪ Downtown Crossing business execs "step back in time" and get their "lasagna fix" at this "tried-and-true" Italian landmark known for its "solid" lineup of "the classics with red sauce"; though the dishes "aren't exactly inspired", the "cozy little booths" enhance a "homey" atmosphere that's as "old and charming" as the staff.

Cafe of India S M   20 | 18 | 17 | $19
52A Brattle St. (Hilliard St.), Cambridge, 617-661-0683
◪ One of "the best Indians in Cambridge", this "casual", "reasonably priced" entry delivers "generally good" "standards", notably a "flavorful" lunch buffet and a "neat *lassi* yogurt drink"; a few think the "room lacks warmth", but most find it "pleasing" enough.

Cafe Pamplona ● S M ⊅   – | – | – | I
12 Bow St. (Mass Ave.), Cambridge, 617-547-2763
It's been going strong for 43 years, and the locals are still bullish on this Cambridge cafe, one of Boston's most distinguished java outlets; it offers light bites and a cuppa from late morning till 1 AM, along with pastries and chocolates to satisfy the sweetest tooth.

Cafe St. Petersburg 🇸
19 | 18 | 19 | $27

236 Washington St. (Harvard St.), Brookline, 617-277-7100
■ Those longing for Leningrad can find "a taste of old-world Russia" at this "lively neighborhood spot" in Brookline that features "authentically" "heavy" but "delicious" dishes; "shots of housemade cranberry vodka" and live classical and gypsy music add to the "delightful" "ethnic" ambiance.

Cafe Suisse 🇸🅜
▽ 20 | 17 | 20 | $33

Swissôtel Boston, 1 Ave. de Lafayette (bet. Chauncey & Washington Sts.), 617-451-2600
☑ "Try the Swiss specialties" at this Downtown Crossing hotel cafe that offers a "very Euro" breakfast and a "quiet" environment that makes it "a good place for a business lunch"; those who are "not impressed" can't help but notice that it doesn't seem to get "a lot of customers."

Cafe Sushi 🇸
19 | 10 | 15 | $21

1105 Mass Ave. (Putnam Ave.), Cambridge, 617-492-0434
☑ Count on "perky sushi" at this "nothing-fancy", "family-owned" Cambridge Japanese, which also offers "great sake options" and "interesting teas"; even though the "brightly lit" room is "nondescript", the atmosphere is "relaxed" and "comfortable."

Cafe Three Hundred 🅜
▽ 22 | 15 | 15 | $14

300 Summer St. (D St.), 617-426-0695
■ A "great alternative to the office cafeterias" Downtown, this "funky" lunch-only cafe lures workers away from their desks with "interesting choices" of "creative and delicious" American fare; "though the menu is limited, it never fails to please"; N.B. open weekdays only.

CAFFE BELLA 🅜
26 | 19 | 22 | $34

19 Warren St. (bet. Main St. & Rte. 139), Randolph, 781-961-7729
■ Set in a strip mall in Randolph, this "unbelievable" Mediterranean gem is the "South Shore's culinary trophy"; revel in the "divine" creations of "genius" chef-owner Patrick Barnes Jr. – "perfectly prepared" dishes with "wonderful flavors" – accompanied by an "incredible wine list"; it's "too loud" and "crowded", with "squishy seating" and "ridiculous waits", but even so, devotees "could dine here nightly"; "don't miss this one."

Caffe Luna 🇸🅜
19 | 14 | 17 | $24

Old Chestnut Hill Shopping Ctr., 11 Boylston St. (Hammond St.), Chestnut Hill, 617-734-8400
■ "Fine" for a "weekday quickie" "before the movies" or as "a break from shopping", this "simple" Chestnut Hill "storefront" satisfies with a "reliable" Northern Italian menu; regulars "recommend all the salads", the "scrumptious pizzas" and the "great focaccia sandwiches."

Caffe Paradiso ◗ⓈⓂ   16 | 13 | 13 | $14

255 Hanover St. (bet. Cross & Richmond Sts.), 617-742-1768
1 Eliot Sq. (Winthrop St.), Cambridge, 617-868-3240

■ "Rich desserts" are why the "after-dinner" crowd ends their evenings out at this "popular" duo of Italian cafes in the North End and Harvard Square; early birds like it "best as an afternoon place for tasty treats", but most everyone agrees this is a "perfect" "place to gain weight in Boston."

Caffe Vittoria ◗ⓈⓂ⇴   19 | 19 | 15 | $13

294 Hanover St. (Prince St.), 617-227-7606

■ Making the "best cappuccino and cannoli in Boston", this "colorful" "institution" in a "retro" setting "couldn't be more Italian"; it's "a must for dessert after dinner in the North End", and the "mix of locals and visitors makes for great people-watching" too; admirers "could stay here for hours sipping and eating."

California Pizza Kitchen ⓈⓂ   14 | 12 | 14 | $17

Prudential Ctr., 800 Boylston St. (Ring Rd.), 617-247-0888
Natick Mall, 1245 Worcester Rd. (Speen St.), Natick, 508-651-1506
137 Stuart St. (bet. Charles & Tremont Sts.), 617-720-0999

◩ When "unavoidable hunger strikes", these "good" casual eateries provide quick relief with "fresh" "gourmet" pies offered with "unusual toppings"; critics, however, mutter about the "bright", "cafeterialike" setting, but at least there's "something for everyone"; N.B. the Stuart Street branch is new and unrated.

Cambridge Brewing Co. ⓈⓂ   12 | 12 | 13 | $17

1 Kendall Sq. (Broadway & Hampshire St.), Cambridge, 617-494-1994

◩ "Beer heaven" in Kendall Square, this "sparse" brewpub is a "noisy" MIT hangout that pours "extremely tasty" suds (including "great pumpkin ale" in the fall); there's a "limited" choice of "blah" grub, but quaffers advise "forget the food, ignore the setting", "sit at the bar" and hoist a glass.

Cambridge Common ◗ⓈⓂ   13 | 12 | 15 | $15

1667 Mass Ave. (Wendell St.), Cambridge, 617-547-1228

◩ Harvard Square locals gather for "cheap pints" at this "comfortable" "neighborhood joint" that serves "typical" American "bar food" like "big burgers" and "the best sweet-potato fries", all priced for a "student's budget."

Cantina Italiana ⓈⓂ   21 | 15 | 20 | $26

346 Hanover St. (Fleet St.), 617-723-4577

■ Since 1931 this "North End classic" has been preparing "generous portions" of "basic Southern Italian at its best (terrific red sauce)"; there's "nothing creative on the menu", and the "pleasantly tacky" "decor could be freshened up", but the "wonderful" staff "treats diners so well" that it's long been a "favorite stop" for many.

CAPITAL GRILLE 🅢🅜 | 24 | 23 | 23 | $48 |
359 Newbury St. (bet. Hereford St. & Mass Ave.), 617-262-8900
250 Boylston St. (Moody St.), Chestnut Hill, 617-928-1400
■ "Bring your wallet and heart monitor" to this "clubby" pair of "NYC-style" chophouses in the Back Bay and on Chestnut Hill, where "impressive", "juicy" steaks prepared "any way you want" and "great martinis" constitute "power meals" for the "expense-account crowd"; it may be "a bit too manly and brash", but it's "well worth it" for what many "consider to be the top steakhouse in Boston"; P.S. don't overlook the "superb wine selection."

Caprice Restaurant & Lounge 🅢🅜 | – | – | – | E |
Tremont Hotel, 275 Tremont St. (Stuart St.), 617-292-0080
The Theater District's Tremont Hotel has a new French-Med dining room and lounge, serving morning to night in a site convenient to the Wang and other area playhouses; capricious rumba enthusiasts will find a Cuban band on hand Sunday nights.

Captain's Wharf 🅜 | 16 | 10 | 15 | $19 |
356 Harvard Ave. (Coolidge Corner), Brookline, 617-566-5590
☑ "Everything is fried" except the salad at this "low-end" seafood "shack" in Brookline frequented by "lots of senior citizens"; purists dismiss this "tried-and-tired" "institution's" "dull", "greasy" food, but the "elderly crowd" say the "fish is always fine and reasonably priced, and there's plenty to eat."

Carambola 🅢🅜 | 22 | 17 | 19 | $24 |
663 Main St. (Moody St.), Waltham, 781-899-2244
■ "Jaded palates" are promised an "adventurous" boost at this "intriguing" Cambodian "find" (cousin to Elephant Walk) in Waltham, where chef Nadsa de Monteiro creates "exciting, fascinating" dishes; novices are advised to ask the "helpful" staff for guidance because the menu can be "confusing", but the already smitten vow that "every bite sparkles", making a meal here "a pure delight."

Carla's 🅢🅜 | 19 | 19 | 19 | $30 |
171 Nahatan St. (Central St.), Norwood, 781-769-9000
☑ Set in an "interesting old firehouse" in Norwood, this "solid" Northern Italian is "a pleasant suburban restaurant" with a "pretty good" menu and a "friendly" staff that makes diners "always feel welcome"; detractors, however, say it's "not all that hot" – "dull food and atmosphere."

Carlo's Cucina Italiana 🅢🅜 | 24 | 11 | 20 | $21 |
131 Brighton Ave. (Harvard Ave.), Allston, 617-254-9759
■ "*Bellissimo*" rave admirers of this "gem" in Allston that offers "outstanding" "Italian home cooking" ("wonderful pastas") at "inexpensive" prices; the "big portions" are delivered by a "thoughtful" staff in a "tiny" room, but the food – "prepared with love" and so "authentic" it "belongs in the North End" – definitely makes it "worth the squeeze."

Casablanca [S][M] 22 | 20 | 18 | $29

40 Brattle St. (Harvard Sq.), Cambridge, 617-876-0999

◪ The mural on the wall will "make you think you're in Morocco" if you haven't already been transported by the "exotic ambiance" at this Harvard Square "favorite", an "oasis" for "top-notch" Mediterranean; chef Ana Sortun's "flashes of brilliance" leave fans wanting to "play it again."

Casa Mexico [S][M] 19 | 17 | 19 | $23

75 Winthrop St. (JFK St.), Cambridge, 617-491-4552

■ Harvard Square's best-hidden Mexican, this "basement" "gem" is "worth the search" for "authentic", "homestyle" "standouts" served in a "cozy and quaint" (or "dark and cramped") room by a "friendly" staff; it's "underappreciated" "after all these years", but that suits aficionados just fine.

Casa Portugal [S][M] 19 | 15 | 19 | $21

1200 Cambridge St. (bet. Prospect & Tremont Sts.), Cambridge, 617-491-8880

◪ At this "homey" "little piece of Portugal in Cambridge", the "comfort food" is the "real" thing and so are the "warm" people who provide "lots of nice touches"; those in the know recommend "anything with seafood" but concede that other dishes can be on the "heavy" side.

Casa Romero [S][M] 21 | 22 | 20 | $29

30 Gloucester St. (bet. Commonwealth Ave. & Newbury St.), 617-536-4341

■ The "romantic patio" at this "upscale" Mexican in the Back Bay makes it a "great date spot", providing a "subterranean escape" off a secreted alley, and the interior is equally "charming", with "beautiful", "colorful tiles"; the "delightful" staff, overseen by a "genial host", serves a "limited menu (but it's good across the board)", as well as the "best margaritas"; "take someone special here."

Cassis – | – | – | M

16 Post Office Ave. (Main St.), Andover, 978-474-8788

The "charming owners", a husband-and-wife team, have fast cultivated a loyal following at their little jewel box in Andover by presenting "generous portions" of "wonderful" French bistro fare (with a focus on classic dishes from Dijon and Provence) in an intimate room with a "romantic" feel.

Centre Street Café [S][M] 21 | 13 | 18 | $17

669A Centre St. (bet. Burroughs & Myrtle Sts.), Jamaica Plain, 617-524-9217

■ Relocated a couple of years ago, this "downscale" Eclectic hangout in Jamaica Plain remains beloved for its "funky, organic menu" of "earthy but not alienating food" (with an emphasis on "vegetarian-with-flavor" dishes); little matter that seating is "cramped" and service "spotty", because weekend brunch is such an "institution" that "every neighborhood" should be so lucky.

Changsho [S] [M] | 19 | 19 | 18 | $20

1712 Mass Ave. (bet. Linnaean & Martin Sts.), Cambridge, 617-547-6565

◪ "The most appealing Chinese dining room" can be found at this "classy yet casual" "oasis" outside Porter Square, a "lovely" backdrop for "light, innovative dishes" served by an "attentive" staff; dissenters, however, cite merely "adequate food" and wonder "could Chinese be any less Chinese?"

Chanterelle French Country Bistro [S] [M] | 20 | 20 | 20 | $36

226 Newbury St. (bet. Exeter & Fairfield Sts.), 617-262-8988

◪ "Romantics" duck into this "intimate", "subdued" Back Bay French bistro "for a civilized evening out", dining on "authentic country" classics delivered by an "excellent" staff; some find it "pretentious", but it's "like being in France."

Charley's Saloon [S] [M] | 14 | 14 | 15 | $20

284 Newbury St. (Gloucester St.), 617-266-3000 ◐

Mall at Chestnut Hill, 100 Boylston St. (bet. Hammond Pond Pkwy. & Langley Rd.), Chestnut Hill, 617-964-1200

◪ "Consistency is the key" to these "decent burger-and-beer places" on Newbury Street and Chestnut Hill that function as "great meeting places"; there's "no fancy-schmancy stuff" here, just "basic food" from an American menu that has "lots of choices"; critics sniff "generic pseudo-pubs", but "in a pinch, it's food."

Charlie's Sandwich Shoppe [M] ≠ | 20 | 13 | 17 | $11

429 Columbus Ave. (bet. Dartmouth & Newton Sts.), 617-536-7669

■ "An institution" that's "been around forever", this "old-fashioned" South End "greasy spoon" with "great local color" draws in the hordes with its "fantastic breakfasts" – "heaping plates" of "legendary turkey hash", "amazing omelets" and the "best pancakes in town"; you'll either love or hate the "cheek-by-jowl" "community tables", but this American "classic is not to be missed"; N.B. no dinner.

Chart House [S] [M] | 18 | 19 | 19 | $32

60 Long Wharf (Atlantic Ave.), 617-227-1576

◪ In a "wonderful setting on the Harbor" with a "beautiful view", this "dependable" chain American adheres to its proven "formula" – "simple" seafood and steak "done well"; "though it's not very exciting", many find it "pleasurable"; N.B. a $2 million renovation has spruced up its locale in the historic Gardiner Building, outdating the score for decor.

Chau Chow City ◐ [S] [M] | 22 | 11 | 16 | $18

83 Essex St. (Oxford St.), 617-338-8158

■ For "gourmet Chinese in a low-rent setting", head to this "winning" late-night Chinatown "dive" to enjoy "flavorful", "real-deal" "Hong Kong–style seafood" and dim sum; the somewhat "dingy" atmosphere is actually "pleasurably seedy" and service is "quick and attentive."

CHEESECAKE FACTORY ●⬤ⓈⓂ | 18 | 16 | 16 | $21 |
Cambridgeside Galleria, 100 Cambridgeside Pl., Cambridge, 617-252-3810
Atrium Mall, 300 Boylston St., Chestnut Hill, 617-964-3001
☑ "Who needs entrees" when the cheesecake "is this good?", yet the International menu at these "Disney-esque" chain Americans is so "huge", it "should include a table of contents"; while many detect an "assembly-line" quality to the food and gripe about the "robotic" service, they willingly "wait for hours" for a wedge of the namesake sweet treat.

Chef Chang's House ⓈⓂ | 19 | 12 | 17 | $19 |
1004 Beacon St. (St. Mary's St.), Brookline, 617-277-4226
☑ "Easy to pop in and out of" (an especially important consideration "before a Sox game"), this Brookline Chinese "standby" offers "consistent quality at fair prices", ensuring that it's "always a hit" (the "superb" Peking duck is a must); few mind the "tired setting" because the pace is so quick they're busy wondering "how do they cook it so fast?"

Chef Chow's House ⓈⓂ | 18 | 12 | 17 | $18 |
354 Chestnut Hill Ave. (Cleveland Circle), Brighton, 617-566-2275
230 Harvard St. (Coolidge Corner), Brookline, 617-739-2469
☑ In the "Chef Chang-Chow war" (albeit some call these competing Houses "interchangeable") for dominance in the area, this Chinese duo in Brighton and Brookline wins the "cheap-price" battle by a nose; it's a dubious victory, though, since many say the food is "nothing exceptional."

Chez Henri ⓈⓂ | 23 | 20 | 20 | $35 |
1 Shepard St. (Mass Ave.), Cambridge, 617-354-8980
■ Devotees declare it's "so very Cambridge" of this "dynamic" bistro to spark "innovative French food with Cuban influences", resulting in "clever" combinations that "pack a flavor punch"; the room is "inviting" and "romantic" with an "unpretentious" ambiance, and it boasts the "perfect bar to eat at alone" because "you'll always meet interesting people there."

China Pearl ⓈⓂ | 21 | 11 | 14 | $18 |
9 Tyler St. (Beach St.), 617-426-4338
■ "A long flight of stairs" leads to a "cavernous space" in Chinatown filled with "endless carts" of what many insist is "the best dim sum in town"; at lunch and dinner, there's a two-tiered menu – "one for the Chinese and one for the crowd from the 'burbs", a boon to those who find the food "too authentic"; regulars forgive the "factory-like" room because "so many people serve you" yet a meal won't put a "dent in your wallet."

Christopher's ◗ⓈⓂ　　　16 | 14 | 16 | $18
1920 Mass Ave. (Porter Sq.), Cambridge,
617-876-9180

■ "As Cambridge as can be", this "warm and cheerful" neighborhood place is a "trend-proof" Eclectic in Porter Square that features "upscale hippie food", including "great vegetarian" options; despite service that "runs hot and cold" and a room that "needs a renovation", in winter there may be few better places to "go sit by a fire."

Ciao Bella ⓈⓂ　　　19 | 17 | 17 | $31
240A Newbury St. (Fairfield St.), 617-536-2626

■ Everyone "always gets a warm welcome" from the "wonderful host" at this "premier site" on Newbury Street, which is famed for its "spectacular" chops of veal, swordfish and lamb, though a few "would like to see some new items" on the Italian menu; the space is "crowded" and "cliquey", but most feel it's an "affordable way to be among the beautiful people."

Cityside Bar & Grille ⓈⓂ　　　12 | 11 | 13 | $17
1960 Beacon St. (Chestnut Hill Ave.), 617-566-1002

◪ Pretty "good sandwiches and beers" are the pre-movie attractions at this Cleveland Circle "BC hangout" where the "college crowd" orders a "quick cheeseburger" at a "cheap price" on the "cool" deck; the American menu is "boring and perfunctory" and the "student staff indifferent", so many warn "go only if you are or want to be a student."

Claremont Café Ⓢ　　　23 | 17 | 20 | $30
535 Columbus Ave. (Claremont Park), 617-247-9001

■ "Comfy, homey yet eclectic", this "intimate" bistro is an "unexpected surprise" in the South End, a "great neighborhood eatery" with "always-appetizing", "inventive" fare delivered by an "obliging" staff; "addicted" regulars "could eat here every day and be happy with every bite"; plus, it offers "pleasant alfresco" seating.

Clarke's ⓈⓂ　　　10 | 11 | 11 | $17
21 Merchants Row (State St.), 617-227-7800

◪ Near Faneuil Hall, this American "meet market" is "a fun place for drinks, music and mingling, but eat prior to going" advise experienced barflies, because the "burgers are no longer the best in town" and the rest of the "basic" "bar food" fares no better.

Clery's ⓈⓂ　　　11 | 13 | 14 | $16
113 Dartmouth St. (Columbus Ave.), Back Bay,
617-262-9874

◪ At the intersection of the Back Bay and South End, this "lively" Irish pub is a "popular drinking spot" and it seems to be "one of the few places where you can still smoke"; the "typical" grub "could be better", but "on a cold night", some find it nice to "sit by the fire and have shepherd's pie."

CLIO [S] [M] 26 26 24 $57

Eliot Suite Hotel, 370A Commonwealth Ave. (Mass Ave.), 617-536-7200

■ "Swanky" and "romantic", this petite Eliot Suite Hotel dining room in the Back Bay is "where the chic eat" surrounded by "plush" appointments like cushy banquettes and a leopard-print carpet; "brilliant" chef Ken Oringer (ex SF's Silks) "gets it just right", turning out "divine" interpretations of New French cuisine that are "orgasmic taste sensations"; admirers only wish they'd "consider serving lunch" – and lower the "astronomical" prices.

Club Cafe ◐ [S] [M] 17 16 16 $31

209 Columbus Ave. (Berkeley St.), 617-536-0966

◪ "The vortex of the gay, yuppie Boston world" forms at this South End "scene", a "non-nightclub alternative for the alternative crowd"; the New American "food is hardly better than an airline's, but it's a pleasant gathering spot", with "entertaining" "people-watching" and live jazz.

Colonial Inn [S] [M] 15 20 17 $29

48 Monument Sq. (Rte. 2), Concord, 978-369-2373

◪ In the heart of Concord Center, this "beautiful historic inn" (circa 1760) with "Revolutionary" decor is "all about atmosphere"; the "olde American" menu is "predictable" and the service is "variable", but the "old-fashioned" experience seems to suit the "geezer crowd."

Commonwealth Fish & Beer Co. [S] [M] 13 15 15 $19

138 Portland St. (Causeway St.), 617-523-8383

◪ "A good bet for before or after Fleet Center events", this microbrewery has the largest selection of cask-conditioned ales in New England, all "fresh" and "tasty"; a new focus on fish supplements the American "pub food", and a post-*Survey* redo may outdate the above decor score.

Coolidge Corner Clubhouse ◐ [S] [M] 13 11 13 $15

307A-309 Harvard St. (bet. Babcock & Beacon Sts.), Brookline, 617-566-4948

◪ "What a pleasure to sit at a smoke-free bar, have a great burger and watch the game" say fans of this Brookline sports mecca "with no frills and lots of noise"; the rest of the American menu includes all the usual suspects, and though mostly "nondescript", the food comes in "copious amounts" and there's a fine array of beers on tap.

Copley's Grand Cafe [S] [M] 21 24 22 $40

Fairmont Copley Plaza, 138 St. James Ave. (bet. Dartmouth & Trinity Sts.), 617-267-5300

◪ Adjacent to the Back Bay's Trinity Church, this "elegant" American in the Fairmont Copley Plaza exudes a "wonderful old Boston atmosphere"; it's renowned for its "awesome Sunday brunch" – worth it for a "special occasion."

Cornwall's ●🅂🅜
14 | 16 | 18 | $16

510 Commonwealth Ave. (Kenmore Sq.), 617-262-3749
■ "Simple good times" are on hand at this "welcoming", "cozy" English pub in Kenmore Square, a "fun place for a burger, a beer and a game"; the staff is most "friendly" and "they provide board games and cards", making this "little" "gem" a "great hangout" for a "relaxing" evening; N.B. a move to Beacon Street is scheduled for fall.

Cottonwood Cafe 🅂🅜
19 | 18 | 17 | $27

222 Berkeley St. (St. James Ave.), 617-247-2225
Porter Exchange Mall, 1815 Mass Ave. (Roseland Ave.), Cambridge, 617-661-7440
☑ "Solid" Southwestern fare "as spicy as you like" is the draw at this "casual" Back Bay and Porter Square duo; it's "relaxing" at lunchtime, but an "after-work" crowd turns it into a festive "margaritaville" at night; purists yawn "nothing special, even with low expectations"; N.B. a recent redo at the Boston branch may outdate the above decor score.

Country Life Vegetarian 🅂
18 | 10 | 13 | $12

200 High St. (Rowes Wharf), 617-951-2534
☑ The "vegetarian lunch and dinner buffets" at this cafeteria-style spot with a "utilitarian" atmosphere in the Financial District is a "great value" for "health nuts"; the "varied selection" of "nourishing foods" includes vegan options that fans deem "excellent", but others cry "boring."

Court House Seafood 🅜
▽ 20 | 6 | 17 | $12

498 Cambridge St. (6th St.), Cambridge, 617-491-1213
■ Though this "plain" Cambridge joint keeps "very limited hours, it's a great place for simple seafood", straight from the "fish market next door"; it's all "consistently excellent" and served at "unbeatable prices"; P.S. there's no decor and not many seats, so it's mostly "a take-out place."

Cranebrook Restaurant & Tea Room 🅂
▽ 24 | 25 | 23 | $42

229 Tremont St. (Lakeview St.), South Carver, 508-866-3235
■ For a "romantic, elegant" experience in an "out-of-the-way" location in Carver, this "gracious" American in a "lovely" country setting is a pure "delight" for a "quiet", "delicious dinner by candlelight"; a few quibble about "steep prices", but most think it's "well worth it in every way."

Daddy-O's 🅂
20 | 16 | 18 | $26

134 Hampshire St. (bet. Elm & Norfolk Sts.), Cambridge, 617-354-8371
☑ "Uniquely" tweaking American "comfort foods" into "interesting" "creations", this "gem" in Cambridge "defines funky"; taste how "super" pork chops and meat loaf can be, but save room for the "show-stealing desserts"; though the interior may be a bit "tired", the "heavenly garden" patio allows for an "enchanting meal under the stars."

Daily Catch ⓜ　　　　　22 │ 10 │ 16 │ $25

259-261 Northern Ave. (Fish Pier Rd.), 617-338-3093 Ⓢ
323 Hanover St. (bet. Prince & Richmond Sts.),
617-523-8567 Ⓢ ⊟
441A Harvard St. (bet. Beacon St. & Commonwealth Ave.),
Brookline, 617-734-5696 ⊟

◪ All seafood, all the time is the motto of this "no-frills"
Sicilian trio that lures in patrons with its "black pasta
puttanesca", "outstanding" calamari and the "freshest"
fish, brought to table in the "pot it was cooked in"; those who
aren't hooked by the "well-executed simple concept" carp
about the "humble setting", but defenders insist that the
"anti-decor is its own decor."

Dakota's ⓜ　　　　　18 │ 18 │ 18 │ $30

34 Summer St. (Arch St.), 617-737-1777

◪ Still popular with the "expense-account crowd", this
Financial District American grill remains a "place to be
seen" while "power lunching" on "basic seafood" and "no-
nonsense steak"; be warned, however, that it's so "noisy"
it's "hard to hear yourself think" ("can't they do something
about the acoustics?").

DALI Ⓢⓜ　　　　　24 │ 24 │ 22 │ $29

415 Washington St. (Beacon St.), Somerville, 617-661-3254

■ "A full-sensory experience" awaits at this "wonderfully
funky and romantic" slice of Spain in Somerville that tempts
with more than 40 choices of "authentic", "garlic-laden"
tapas, as well as "fabulous sangria" and an all-Iberian wine
list, delivered by "vibrant" waiters wearing "20 pounds of
glitter on their vests"; aficionados only wish it "wasn't so
popular" (expect "endless waits").

Dalya's ⓜ　　　　　21 │ 20 │ 21 │ $32

20 North Rd. (Rtes. 4 & 62), Bedford, 781-275-0700

◪ "Lovely all around", this "suburban gem" is rated by
admirers as "Bedford's best", an "unexpected find" in a
"warm", "old-style room" with a "romantic" ambiance;
the kitchen turns out Mediterranean fare that many find
"rich" and "delicious", but others complain that the "skimpy
portions" are "unevenly" executed.

Davide Ristorante Ⓢⓜ　　　　　23 │ 20 │ 22 │ $40

326 Commercial St. (bet. Battery & Clark Sts.),
617-227-5745

■ In a "cozy waterfront" setting in the North End, this
"gourmet Italian" with a "classic old-world" sensibility
("complete with tableside" preparations of some dishes)
is a "reliable" option for "excellent" fare that goes well
beyond pasta; the "owner treats diners like old friends",
so "despite being located in a basement, it's always a
pleasurable experience."

Davio's [S] [M] 20 18 19 $34

269 Newbury St. (bet. Fairfield & Gloucester Sts.), 617-262-4810
Royal Sonesta Hotel, 5 Cambridge Pkwy.
(opp. Cambridgeside Galleria), Cambridge, 617-661-4810

◪ "Scrumptious Italian" in "great locations" marks this "satisfying" duo, as does "pleasant" atmosphere; but detractors who cite "food with no spark" and "inattentive" service feel that they're "paying more for the setting" ("stunning river views" in Cambridge) "than for the food."

Delux Cafe ☾ [M] ≠$ 20 18 15 $18

100 Chandler St. (Clarendon St.), 617-338-5258

■ Very South End, this "quirky", "smoky" "retro" "hangout" attracts a "crazy quilt" of regulars with its "creatively homey" Eclectic eats priced "cheap" and served amid "campy" decor that's certainly "entertaining" ("don't miss the busts of Elvis"); be warned that the "tiny and always crowded" room "leads to long waits", so "get there early."

Demo's [S] [M] ≠$ 19 6 14 $12

146 Lexington St. (bet. Main & 128th Sts.), Waltham, 781-893-8359
60-64 Mt. Auburn St. (bet. Main St. & Rte. 16), Watertown, 617-924-9660

■ Feta fans line up for "Greek fast food" at these "no-ambiance" "kitchens" in Watertown and Waltham, famous for skewering "fabulous lamb kebabs"; "tables bolted to the floor" say it all atmosphere-wise, but patrons marvel at "the mystery" of "how they find your table" to bring you the food you ordered "cafeteria-style."

De Pasquale's [S] [M] ▽ 18 11 15 $20

374 Main St. (Harvard St.), Medford, 781-395-9591

◪ "Reliable" pizza and pastas in a "good location" in Medford make this neighborhood Italian "great for families" looking for a "cheap night out"; its basement location and so-called decor beg for a "face-lift", but hey, this "old warhorse" has been kicking since 1939.

Desmond O'Malley's [S] [M] 15 17 17 $20

30 Worcester Rd. (Rte. 9), Framingham, 508-875-9400

◪ Built in Ireland and shipped piecemeal to Framingham, this "authentic pub" provides a cheery "oasis in mall-land"; the grub "standards" come in "heaping portions", but they're "hit or miss", which laddies don't mind because they're here for the "bar scene" and "terrific service."

Dick's Last Resort ☾ [S] [M] 10 10 11 $19

55 Huntington Ave. (Prudential Ctr.), 617-267-8080

■ "Befitting its name", this Prudential Center American "dive bar" reeks of a "frat house" atmosphere, with "loud" live music and a staff whose "shtick" is to be "obnoxious" to the customers, so you better "be in the mood to party"; the eats mostly amount to "so-so" buckets of chicken, ribs and seafood, but food is clearly not the point here.

Dino's Sea Grille [S] [M] ▽ 16 | 12 | 16 | $22
640 Arsenal St. (Coolidge Ave.), Watertown, 617-923-7771
■ Expect "nothing fancy" at this Watertown seafood house, but the menu is "decent, if not very imaginative", focusing on "well-prepared" fish that's "better than expected" and delivered at "reasonable prices" by a "nice" staff.

Dish, The ◐ [S] [M] – | – | – | M
253 Shawmut Ave. (Milford St.), 617-426-7866
This new streetfront cafe in the South End specializes in Eclectic comfort food served in equally comfy, earth-toned digs; it's a fresh face on the popular South End Sunday brunch scene, building its rep with brioche French toast and a frittata du jour.

Diva Indian Bistro [S] [M] – | – | – | M
246 Elm St. (Chester St.), Somerville, 617-629-4963
Davis Square's newest Indian outpost is a spin-off from the owners of Cafe of India and Kashmir; this incarnation features an open kitchen and a more modern look to complement the classic cuisine on the à la carte menu and lunch buffet spread.

Dixie Kitchen [S] [M] 18 | 9 | 15 | $17
182 Mass Ave. (St. Germain St.), 617-536-3068
◪ "Spicy" "bayou flavors" jazz up this "New Orleans–style dive" in the Symphony Hall district (try the "mouthwatering" jambalaya or "jumbo" gumbo); even if it's "not always consistent" and the atmosphere is but "one step up from a cafeteria", there's "plenty to eat" at a "good price."

Dockside [S] [M] 12 | 11 | 13 | $17
229 Centre St. (Rte. 60), Malden, 781-321-3000 ◐
2B Wilson Rd. (Nahant Beach), Nahant, 781-593-7500
◪ Adhering to a "smoky" "bar-meets-sports-meets-ocean" theme, this pair of Americans in Malden and Nahant is filled with "screaming yuppies" "watching a fight" on "too many TVs" while chowing down on "just-ok" pub grub.

Dodge Street Bar & Grill [S] [M] ▽ 16 | 12 | 14 | $18
7 Dodge St. (bet. Lafayette & Washington Sts.), Salem, 978-745-0139
■ "Basically a local bar with good ribs", this "loud" Salem American draws a young crowd with its live nightly bands; this is "certainly not fine dining", but for many it's an "enjoyable", "reasonably priced" evening.

Dolphin [M] 19 | 13 | 17 | $21
1105 Mass Ave. (Remington St.), Cambridge, 617-661-2937
12 Washington St. (Rte. 135), Natick, 508-655-0669
◪ "For seafood that won't break the bank", hit this pair of "dependable" fish houses where you "get your money's worth" of "fresh" fare "simply prepared"; the look is "utilitarian", but the decor score might not reflect a recent renovation and expansion at both branches.

Dom's ⓈⓂ   20 | 16 | 21 | $36
10 Bartlett Pl. (Salem St.), 617-367-8979
◪ Whether you like the "personal attention" or find it "overbearing", you'll have a one-on-one "experience" at this North End Italian where the owner "talks to each customer" and makes "recommendations" ("Dom's routine"), which helps those who find the "gourmet" menu "unusual and confusing"; despite "a stuffy" atmosphere, most feel the "very good" food makes the "kitsch" "worth it."

Donatello Ristorante ⓈⓂ   22 | 20 | 21 | $34
44 Broadway (Rte. 1N), Saugus, 781-233-9975
◪ Dinner at this "roomy", family-run Saugus "favorite" is "like a scene from *The Godfather*", with a glimpse of a varied "Italian world" converging for "delicious" dishes paired with a "daunting wine list"; the "pleasant" ambiance is conducive to conversation too, but some still quibble that the "portions are too small" for the price.

Dong Khanh ⓈⓂ⊅   ▽ 21 | 9 | 15 | $13
81-83 Harrison Ave. (Beach St.), 617-426-9410
◼ This little-known "hole-in-the-wall" wins high praise from a cadre that proclaims the "interesting menu" of "excellent" fare the "best Vietnamese in Chinatown"; plus, the food is served "fast and cheap."

Doyle's Cafe ⓈⓂ⊅   14 | 19 | 17 | $16
3484 Washington St. (Williams St.), Jamaica Plain, 617-524-2345
◼ A "taste of old Boston" lives on at this "legendary" Jamaica Plain "political hangout", renowned for its "folksy" atmosphere and "Irish soul"; in the high-ceilinged rooms that "never change", regulars enjoy a "great selection" of beers and single-malts; the eats are merely "decent", but you can "stay and talk forever without getting pushed out."

Duckworth Lane ⓈⓂ   14 | 16 | 16 | $24
1657 Beacon St. (Washington Sq.), Brookline, 617-730-8040
344 Walnut St. (Washington St.), Newton, 617-244-0004
◪ "Garage-sale art" on the walls gives this duo of Eclectic bistros a "funky" feel, albeit in a "chintzy" way; most are "disappointed" that the "only passable" food isn't as "memorable" as the decor, but the menu tries to offer "something for everyone."

Ducky Wok ⓈⓂ   18 | 10 | 16 | $18
122-126 Harvard Ave. (Commonwealth Ave.), Allston, 617-782-8868
◪ "Goofy name" aside, an "interesting mix of Chinese and Vietnamese" attracts some Allston locals to this "Chinatown alternative" where the menu features "enough choices to last a lifetime"; insiders advise "go for the seafood", which is still "swimming" around in the "exposed fish tank", but critics say this is "the very definition of a generic restaurant."

Durgin Park [S] [M] 16 12 13 $23

Faneuil Hall Mktpl., 30 N. Market St. (Clinton St.), 617-227-2038

◩ "Tourists" come to this 1827 "Boston landmark" in Faneuil Hall to "eat like colonists"; the "solid" New England–style menu includes "standards" such as "excellent" prime rib served in "prolific quantities" at "rustic", communal picnic tables by "surly waitresses"; it may be a "tired" "classic", but most agree it's "a must-do-it-once experience."

Dynasty 🌙 [S] [M] 16 10 12 $18

33 Edinboro St. (bet. Beach St. & Surface Rd.), 617-350-7777

◩ "Till 4 AM" this "cavernous" "Chinatown staple" woos late-nighters with an "interesting variety of dim sum" that's either "great" or "ordinary", depending on how "sober" you are; "purists" say it's "too touristy" and the food's "a bit greasy", but service is "quick" and it's an "inexpensive" "place to go after all the other places are closed."

EAST COAST GRILL & RAW BAR [S] [M] 24 18 20 $32

1271 Cambridge St. (Prospect St.), Cambridge, 617-491-6568

■ Chris Schlesinger's Inman Square "seafood thriller" continues to sizzle with "finger-licking 'cue" and "sensory-overload sides" delivered in an "exuberant" room with a "funky" vibe; heat-chasers urge "come on 'hotter-than-hell' nights" when the "spicy" food is notched up yet a few more degrees; despite a "jammed" site and "long waits", these masters of the grill "know their smoky stuff" – in fact, it was ranked the No. 1 BBQ in Boston.

Eastern Pier Seafood [S] [M] 19 11 17 $21

237 Northern Ave. (Atlantic Ave.), 617-423-7756

■ "Underrated" say partisans of this "excellent Chinese" on the Pier, which aptly "specializes" in "fresh and tasty" seafood (the Cantonese-style "lobster with ginger and scallions rules"); there's "no decor" and no atmosphere, but the dishes are "well executed" and moderately priced.

East Ocean City 🌙 [S] [M] 23 13 17 $21

25 Beach St. (bet. Harrison Ave. & Washington St.), 617-542-2504

■ "Hong Kong expats" gather at this Chinatown late-nighter (till 3:30 AM) that lets you "choose your own fish from the tanks" for the kitchen to "custom-make any dish"; the room could sport "nicer decor", but the food is just about the "best" of its kind in town.

eat [S] [M] 21 17 20 $27

253 Washington St. (Union Sq.), Somerville, 617-776-2889

■ "Making it easy to eat healthy", this "laid-back" Eclectic "scene" in Somerville has convinced more than a few converts that this is "how we should all eat" by turning out "creative" dishes "done well"; "what it lacks in atmosphere, it makes up for in taste", though some commend the "homey" setting – "it's almost like not eating out."

83 Main 🅂🅼 | – | – | – | M |
(fka Duckworth Lane)
83 Main St. (Pleasant St.), Charlestown, 617-242-6009
Despite the new name, funky art and Eclectic eats are still the hallmarks of this popular Charlestown bistro, which continues to draw its faithful followers from the nearby Bunker Hill nabe with dishes like seafood risotto and vegetarian wheatloaf; a rotating roster of local artists showcases work on the walls that's available for sale.

El Cafetal 🅂🅼   ∇ | 16 | 6 | 17 | $16 |
479 Cambridge St. (Brighton Ave.), Brighton, 617-789-4009
■ "Family-run", this "nice little place" in Brighton serves "decent", "very fresh tasting" Colombian specialties ("mostly meat"), along with some vegetarian options and "wonderful fruit shakes"; everything is "really cheap", and it's open for three meals a day, every day.

ELEPHANT WALK 🅂🅼 | 23 | 21 | 20 | $30 |
900 Beacon St. (Park Dr.), 617-247-1500
2067 Mass Ave. (bet. Hadley & Russell Sts.), Cambridge, 617-492-6900
☑ Hordes "stampede" to Kenmore and Porter Squares for the "wonderful juxtaposition" of Cambodian and New French cuisines, which "deliciously" results in "eclectic" dishes such as "phenomenal" *loc lac* (lime-cured beef); the "classy" ambiance is made "exotic" with elephant figurines along the ceiling, and despite "long waits", most urge "run, don't walk" to get in on this "unique" experience.

El Pelon Taqueria 🅂🅼≠   ∇ | 21 | 16 | 18 | $11 |
92 Peterborough St. (Boylston St.), 617-262-9090
☑ "Wow, what a find" enthuse amigos about the "great, authentic" food at this new Fenway Mexican where nothing costs more than $6; the "freshest" "high-quality ingredients" are turned in to "tasty tacos" and the like, but as there are only 16 seats, think "takeout."

Erawan of Siam 🅂🅼 | 20 | 21 | 18 | $21 |
469 Moody St. (High St.), Waltham, 781-899-3399
☑ "Spacious and elegant" ("the fountain is a nice touch"), this Waltham Thai "gem" is a "favorite" "for a quiet meal" – it's "like visiting a beautiful museum", with "dependable" "standards" "done well"; though detractors cite "tired" food and "only ok" service, at least there's "never a wait."

Euno 🅂🅼 | 22 | 21 | 20 | $30 |
119 Salem St. (Cooper St.), 617-573-9406
☑ "Nestled on a stone street" in the North End, this "intimate" Italian "find" is a "romantic" place "for a date", especially if you clinch a table "next to the fireplace" in the "cozy downstairs" room; many praise the "superb", "traditional" fare brought by the "welcoming" staff but knock the "tiny portions on a big plate for a big price."

Evoo Ⓜ
| 23 | 20 | 22 | $37 |

118 Beacon St. (Washington St.), Somerville, 617-661-3866

■ Part of the "chic"-ification of Somerville, this "rising star" with a sassy name (an acronym for "extra virgin olive oil") impresses with "innovative" Eclectic dishes like "duck, duck, goose" served in an "elegantly minimalist" interior that evokes a "beautiful NYC-style converted industrial space"; even if a few nitpick about "disorganization" and overly "complicated" creations, nearly all agree it's "a keeper."

Exchange, The ●Ⓜ
| 16 | 16 | 15 | $35 |

148 State St. (India St.), 617-726-7600

◪ Lunch, dinner and after-hours are the three staples at this New French Downtowner, recently revitalized by a post-*Survey* menu change and renovation that outdate the above scores for food and decor; the expense-account set kicks back in the splashy open space, and there's plenty of room to eat at the bar when the nightlife activity kicks in.

Fajitas & 'Ritas Ⓜ
| 15 | 11 | 14 | $16 |

25 West St. (bet. Tremont & Washington Sts.), 617-426-1222
48 Boylston St. (Harvard & Washington Sts.), Brookline,
617-566-1222 Ⓢ

◪ "Crazy" decor that includes graffiti-covered walls ("feel free to draw") adds to the "casual party atmosphere" at this duo of "cheap and cheerful" Downtown Crossing and Brookline Tex-Mex "dives"; the "large portions" of fajitas and burritos are merely "serviceable" and thus can only be improved by "pitchers of margaritas" – perhaps the "best in town."

Fava
| 22 | 16 | 19 | $35 |

1027 Great Plain Ave. (bet. Chapel St. & Eaton Sq.), Needham,
781-455-8668

◪ "Imagine – this in Needham!" rave gourmands joyfully surprised to find such an "innovative", "really yummy" New American near the train station, making it a "handy" "hideaway" for commuters; but whereas romantics call it "cozy" and "intimate", others find it "dark" and "jammed" with "dense seating"; still, many feel it's "a wonderful addition to the 'burbs."

Federalist, The ⓈⓂ
| – | – | – | E |

XV Beacon, 15 Beacon St. (bet. Bowdoin & Somerset Sts.),
617-670-2515

Perched atop Beacon Hill in the luxe XV Beacon hotel, this elegantly minimalist hideaway is a popular destination for business meals and formal occasions; expect New England cuisine given a modern edge by new chef Eric Brennan (ex Four Seasons Toronto) and backed by an impressive wine collection; as a nod to the power crowd, hidden inside the pillars are dataports so that workaholics need never be disconnected from their e-mail.

57 Restaurant [S][M] 18 | 17 | 19 | $33

Radisson Hotel, 200 Stuart St. (bet. Arlington & Charles Sts.), 617-423-5700

◪ For nearly a half-century, this Continental "throwback" in the Radisson Hotel (a "prime location" for pre-theater dining) has featured "solidly reliable, if unexciting, food; it's "a staple in every way and still seems to maintain its niche" among a "meat-and-potatoes" crowd, especially thanks to a heightened focus on steak; for those who pleaded for a "makeover", the room has finally been redone (not yet reflected in the above decor score).

FIGS [S][M] 21 | 17 | 17 | $25

42 Charles St. (Chestnut St.), 617-742-3447
67 Main St. (Monument Ave.), Charlestown, 617-242-2229
1208 Boylston St. (Hammond St.), Chestnut Hill, 617-738-9992
92 Central St. (Rte. 135), Wellesley, 781-237-5788

◪ Every meal seems like a "pizza party" at Todd English's popular (or "tumultuous"?) Italian quartet where diners can't resist the "exquisite", "unconventional" "thin-crust" pies with "unique toppings"; though some balk at the "long waits" and "shaky" service and others think the chainlet's "overexpansion" has caused the "quality" to suffer, legions of fans swear the "pizzas and pastas will blow your mind."

Filippo Ristorante [S][M] 17 | 17 | 16 | $30

283 Causeway St. (Endicott St.), 617-742-4143

■ There's "never a wait" at this North End Italian, which could make it a convenient option before a game at the "Fleet Center right down the street"; the traditional fare is "consistently" good, if "a bit overpriced."

Finale ◐[S][M] 22 | 21 | 19 | $20

1 Columbus Ave. (Park Plaza), 617-423-3184

■ The sweet of tooth head to this dessert cafe in the Theater District for a "splurge" on "dreamy" and "decadent" but "oh-so-pricey" "works of art", "spectacularly presented"; "save this for a special occasion – the desserts are beyond compare"; P.S. the 'prelude' menu offers a limited choice of "satisfying" small plates.

Fire & Ice [S][M] 17 | 16 | 13 | $20

50 Church St. (Harvard Sq.), Cambridge, 617-547-9007 ◐
31 St. James Ave. (Berkeley St.), 617-482-3473

◪ For the ultimate in "creative control over your food", try this "bright" Mongolian BBQ in Harvard Square where patrons pick from an array of meats, vegetables and sauces and then let a chef grill it all together; beware that with the availability of Asian, Mexican and American ingredients, "you could become your own worst culinary enemy"; N.B. there's a new and unrated branch in Boston.

Fire King Baking Co. & Bistro [S] [M] 21 | 18 | 19 | $24
19 North St. (Rte. 3A), Hingham, 781-740-9400
◪ "Fantastic" artisanal breads and "unsurpassed" pastries put this Hingham bakery on the map as the "funky" sibling of Tosca across the street; the "creative" menu of Eclectic savories, alas, is "ambitious but sometimes falls short"; even so, many think it's "worth the trip", especially for a meal on the patio that's "perfect on a summer evening."

Five North Square [S] [M] 21 | 18 | 20 | $31
5 North Sq. (Prince St.), 617-720-1050
◪ Sentimentalists say that a meal at this "quaint", "old-fashioned" North End Italian is like "eating at grandma's house – delicious and cozy"; detractors shrug "nothing special", but the "plentiful" portions won't leave you hungry.

Five Seasons [S] [M] 18 | 18 | 17 | $23
1634 Beacon St. (Washington St.), Brookline, 617-731-2500
◪ "Appealing to nonvegetarians too", this "haute" health food "hangout" set in an "airy", "soothing" Brookline venue features "delicious" "organic" veggies and wine, as well as "fresh fish" and poultry; dissenters, though, dismiss it as "a cliché of vegetarian cuisine – designed for health without regard for taste" – and gripe about the "slow" service ("it takes about five seasons to get anything)."

Flashes ◐ [S] [M] 🚫 – | – | – | M
310 Stuart St. (bet. Arlington & Berkeley Sts.), 617-574-8888
Flashback is the operative word at this retro rookie, which arrives on the Theater District scene with New American fare and funky style to spare; the innovative menu includes Yankee tapas at dinner, while throwback cocktails like grasshoppers and Singapore slings give the Motown-inspired lounge that extra swing.

Fleming's Prime Steakhouse & Wine Bar [S] [M] – | – | – | E
217 Stuart St. (bet. Arlington & Charles Sts.), 617-292-0808
This town's newest steakhouse debuts in the Theater District with a decidedly nontraditional twist – it's entirely smoke-free; the cherry-wood setting is ideal for tucking into steak, lobster or chops, matched with over 100 wines by the glass and views of the open stone-and-copper kitchen.

Flora [S] 23 | 20 | 20 | $33
190 Mass Ave. (bet. Chandler & Lake Sts.), Arlington, 781-641-1664
■ Credited in part for "Arlington's restaurant renaissance", this "stylish and intimate" American bistro set in an old bank building ("sit in the vault") near the Capitol Theater is a "real find" for its "inventive", "fabulous" seasonal menu, matched with an "interesting wine list"; but be "prepared to wait", and brace yourself for the "incredible noise."

Florentina ⓜ | 16 | 13 | 16 | $23 |
143 Main St. (bet. Broadway & 3rd St.), Cambridge, 617-577-8300

◪ "Filling" "mainstream standards served fast" is the draw of this "dependable" Cambridge Italian; foes yawn "humdrum", but diners who "go back" again and again insist that with "very good food at very reasonable prices" delivered by "the nicest staff", you "can't go wrong here."

Florentine Cafe ⓢⓜ | 21 | 22 | 18 | $30 |
333 Hanover St. (Prince St.), 617-227-1777

■ "The perfect spot on a summer's eve" may be at this North End Italian's "energetic", "beautifully appointed open bar" where patrons can partake in "fabulous people-watching" while enjoying dishes with a "gourmet twist"; the "inventive food and enticing atmosphere" make this a "favorite" of many, so expect a "long wait."

Forest Cafe ⓢⓜ | 19 | 8 | 15 | $19 |
1682 Mass Ave. (bet. Harvard & Porter Sqs.), Cambridge, 617-661-7810

■ Hiding inside this "raunchy, smoky" "dive bar" in Cambridge lurks a "diamond in the rough" that proves there's "more to Mexican food than burritos"; relish "authentic fare filled with flavor", including "zesty grilled fish", washed down by "good margaritas", but "don't look around" because this is "a true hole-in-the-wall."

Franklin Cafe ◖ⓢⓜ | 24 | 18 | 19 | $28 |
278 Shawmut Ave. (Hanson St.), 617-350-0010

■ Visit "Greenwich Village without leaving Boston" at this "lively, swanky" South End bar-cum-bistro that shakes a "fabulous martini" and offers a full menu of "amazingly sophisticated" New American fare till 1:30 AM every night in a "dark" setting that makes "everyone look good"; if only "a few hundred less people knew about it."

Frank's Steak House ⓢⓜ | 17 | 14 | 17 | $21 |
2310 Mass Ave. (Rice St.), Cambridge, 617-661-0666

■ At this "wonderful throwback" in Cambridge, the oldest steakhouse in Greater Boston, chow down on "big portions of good beef"; the surroundings may be "drab", but it's been around since 1938, so for those who like to "reminisce", this piece of Americana is "a remarkably good reminder of the kind of steakhouse you liked as a kid."

Fugakyu ◖ⓢⓜ | 23 | 25 | 21 | $31 |
1280 Beacon St. (Harvard St.), Brookline, 617-738-1268

◪ "Watch how you pronounce the name" of this Japanese – billed as the largest in New England – in Brookline, but otherwise just savor the "awesome", "melt-in-your-mouth" sushi; the bi-level room is most "handsome", with "beautiful private rooms", "intriguing" details such as "booths with sliding doors" and "a bar out of an old James Bond flick."

Full Moon [S][M] — 17 | 14 | 16 | $21

344 Huron Ave. (bet. Chilton & Fayerweather Sts.), Cambridge, 617-354-6699

◪ Have the "best night out with the bambinos" at this "casual" "neighborhood spot" in Cambridge that's suitable "for the family when the parents want a real meal" of "surprisingly good" New American fare while the kids entertain themselves in the mock kitchen in the rear, a "great play space"; childless critics, however, ask why put up with "screaming kids and mediocre food?"

Gala Ristorante [S][M] — 19 | 14 | 18 | $26

138 Mass Ave. (Milton St.), Arlington, 781-646-1404

■ Another "good addition" to Arlington's booming dining scene, this Mediterranean storefront dishes up "interesting" "Italian-Portuguese combinations" (and boasts "the best bread basket around"), served by an "obliging" staff in a "homey" room with an "inviting" atmosphere; though it's "a bit cramped", a post-*Survey* expansion has doubled the capacity to 100 seats.

Galleria Italiana [M] — 24 | 18 | 19 | $40

177 Tremont St. (Boylston St.), 617-423-2092

■ Admirers sing the praises of the "showstopping" "Tuscan experience" at this "chic" Theater District Italian "gem", "a wonderful place to indulge" in "marvelous, inventive" food paired with a "reasonably priced wine list"; N.B. the post-*Survey* departure of the chef and the introduction of a less complicated dinner menu may outdate the above food score.

GALLERIA UMBERTO [M]≠ — 25 | 9 | 14 | $10

289 Hanover St. (bet. Prince & Richmond Sts.), 617-227-5709

■ For the "cheapest good food in Boston" at lunchtime, budget-minded foodies head to this "no-frills" Southern Italian "treasure" in a "cafeteria setting" in the North End for "the real thing" – "excellent pizzas" (rated as the "best" in town) and "tasty" spinach calzone; legions will attest that these eats are "worth the wait in line"; N.B. it closes at 3 PM.

Garden of Eden [S][M]≠ — – | – | – | I

571 Tremont St. (bet. Clarendon & Dartmouth Sts.), 617-247-8377

This garden blossomed recently, bringing its charms to a roomy new location in the heart of the South End; it still serves country French fare with Italian and American twists, including homemade croissants and pastries, creative sandwiches and gourmet takeout; amenities include airy ceilings, wood-block tables and large windows for primo people-watching.

Gardner Museum Cafe S   19 | 19 | 17 | $20
Isabella Stuart Gardner Museum, 280 The Fenway (Huntington Ave.), 617-566-1088

■ "What a surprise" say patrons of the arts startled by the "garden-fresh food" at this International in the Fenway's Isabella Stuart Gardner Museum; the most "delightful" area to enjoy a "light lunch" is on the "lovely patio", but plan on a leisurely meal because there's "usually a line."

Gargoyles on the Square S   24 | 20 | 20 | $34
215 Elm St. (Summer St.), Somerville, 617-776-5300

■ Relocated to "great digs" a couple of doors down, this "innovative" Contemporary American is "a fantastic little restaurant tucked away in Davis Square"; it features a "beautifully balanced menu" of "splendid" dishes (especially "fantastic fish creations") served in an "intimate" room with a "soothing atmosphere."

Geoffrey's Cafe & Bar S M   19 | 16 | 18 | $23
578 Tremont St. (bet. Clarendon & Dartmouth Sts.), 617-266-1122

◪ "Bring on the mashed potatoes" say "repeat customers" who favor this "popular" "upscale diner" in the South End as an "everyday place" that specializes in American "home cooking with a twist"; kudos go to the "grand" weekend brunch and the "great wine list", but "save room for dessert" (you'll see why when you eye the glass case).

Giacomo's S ⊘   23 | 16 | 19 | $28
355 Hanover St. (bet. Fleet & Prince Sts.), 617-523-9026 M
431 Columbus Ave. (Dartmouth St.), 617-536-5723

◪ Bookending the city with branches in the North and South Ends, this family-owned pair of "small, tasty" Italian spots is famed for "truly good pastas" and the archetype of "what *fra diavolo* is supposed to be"; but prepare to feel "rushed" out, even when there aren't the trademark "long lines."

Giannino's S M   20 | 19 | 20 | $31
Charles Hotel, 20 University Rd. (bet. Memorial Dr. & Mt. Auburn St.), Cambridge, 617-576-0605

■ Enthusiasts with small appetites say "thank you for the half-portion option" of "solid" Northern Italian dishes offered in the "beautiful" courtyard of the Charles Hotel; a convenient "pre-theater" or post-shopping "haven" off Harvard Square, it's a "comfortable" "standby."

GINZA S M   25 | 17 | 18 | $29
16 Hudson St. (bet. Beach & Kneeland Sts.), 617-338-2261 ◗
1002 Beacon St. (St. Mary's St.), Brookline, 617-566-9688

■ Rated the No. 1 Japanese in Boston, this "bit of Tokyo" in Chinatown and Brookline will "make you wonder why food should ever be cooked" after just one bite of its "amazing" sushi, "artistically presented"; the "late-night" Hudson Street flagship is "hip and crowded", despite somewhat "sterile" surroundings, so expect "long waits."

Glenn's Restaurant & Cool Bar [S] ▽ 22 | 16 | 19 | $34

44 Merrimac St. (Green St.), Newburyport, 978-465-3811

■ North Shore denizens applaud the "innovative" food at this "fabulously funky" Newburyport Contemporary American where the "nicely presented" "eclectic" fare is prepared with "lots of flair"; live blues and jazz on Sundays and swell "people-watching" add to the "good times."

Glory [M] – | – | – | M

19 Essex St. (Main St.), Andover, 978-475-4811

"Finally, something interesting in Andover" cheer locals about this Eclectic-American, which focuses on seafood accented with Asian touches; most appreciate its "good intentions" but suggest it "needs a little polish" – the kitchen could be "a bit more creative."

Goemon Japanese Noodle & Tapas Restaurant 🌙 [M] 19 | 14 | 16 | $16

189 State St. (Atlantic Ave.), 617-367-8670

◪ "Delicious food in bite-sized portions", along with a "solid cross section" of "good" soups and noodles, has made this "inexpensive" Downtown Franco-Japanese fusion a welcome addition; accompany the "Pan-Asian tapas" with a glass or two from the sake and wine bar.

Golden Palace [S] [M] 20 | 13 | 16 | $19

14 Tyler St. (bet. Beach & Kneeland Sts.), 617-423-4565

■ For "real Chinese food", partisans say "this is it"; it may have all the atmosphere of a "school dinner hall", but this Chinatown Cantonese offers "wonderful food at wonderful value", especially the "yummy dim sum", and service comes with a "friendly face."

Golden Temple 🌙 [S] [M] 19 | 19 | 18 | $24

1651 Beacon St. (Washington Sq.), Brookline, 617-277-9722

◪ In an "attractive" space in Brookline, this "upscale" Chinese prepares food that supporters say is the "best non-authentic" Cantonese, making "excellent" "improvements on familiar favorites"; critics, however, who cite "boring", "Americanized" chow designed for the "BMW crowd", "can't understand why so many people eat here."

Good Life, The 🌙 [S] 19 | 19 | 19 | $35

28 Kingston St. (Bedford St.), 617-451-2622

Good Life Cambridge, The 🌙 [S] [M]

720 Mass Ave. (bet. Inman & Prospect Sts.), Cambridge, 617-868-8800

■ "Lounge lizards rule" at this "trendy", late-night American haunt near Downtown Crossing that "hipsters" put at the "top of the list for martinis", served in a "quirky, retro" room featuring "velvet curtains" and "Sinatra on the jukebox"; throwback eats the likes of meat loaf and "big burgers" are merely "so-so", but most "go for the drinks, not the food"; N.B. the Cambridge branch is new and unrated.

Grafton Street Pub & Grill ◐ [S] [M] 15 | 17 | 15 | $21
1280 Mass Ave. (bet. Linden & Plympton Sts.), Cambridge, 617-497-0400
◪ "Don't expect haute cuisine" at this Irish pub, but do expect a "lively scene", as it's perhaps the "best people-watching spot in Harvard Square"; though the grub may be no "better than average", it comes in portions "big enough to feed a small country"; the real attraction is the "beautiful wooden bar", a most "convivial" spot to meet for drinks.

Grand Canal [S] [M] 16 | 20 | 17 | $20
57 Canal St. (Causeway St.), 617-523-1112
◪ The "great fireplace" at this Victorian-style Irish-American gives it a "comfortably" "warm and cozy" feel, and its location near North Station makes it a convenient "option before a Fleet Center event"; the "bar menu" is "adequate, if unremarkable", but with a choice of 34 beers on tap at the "grand" mahogany bar, "the food is beside the point" here.

Grand Chau Chow ◐ [S] [M] 22 | 11 | 16 | $20
41-45 Beach St. (Harrison Ave.), 617-292-5166
■ "Be adventurous" and "ask them to choose for you" at this "authentic", "bustling" Chinatown Chinese where whatever the "helpful" waiters bring will "always be a feast" – from "steamed oysters the size of your fist" to "crab not to be believed" to "crispy, aromatic shrimp"; "ok, the decor stinks", but the seafood is "top-notch" and it "won't break your budget."

Grapevine, The [S] [M] 24 | 20 | 22 | $33
26 Congress St. (Derby St.), Salem, 978-745-9335
■ Bostonians "wish it were closer", but this "charming" New American belongs to Salem, where it serves some of "the North Shore's most creative" "vegetarian dishes and pastas"; the "dark", "romantic" interior and "lovely garden" make it a "surefire first-date spot", but remember, "reservations are key."

Grasshopper [S] [M] ▽ 19 | 17 | 18 | $17
1 N. Beacon St. (Union Sq.), Allston, 617-254-8883
■ "Dedicated to vegan food" and "serenity", this "creative" Allston tofu haven features a "big menu" of faux meat dishes, noodles and "excellent soups", all boasting "diverse flavors" and Pan-Asian flair; the room's "Zen-like" calm is only enhanced by "easy-on-the-wallet" prices.

Green Dragon Tavern [S] [M] 14 | 18 | 15 | $17
11 Marshall St. (Union St.), 617-367-0055
◪ The "old Boston atmosphere" is the draw at this appropriately "dark and loud" Irish-American pub near Faneuil Hall; it's popular for "drinks and snacks after work", though the "historically important" locale and "cold beers" far outshine the "so-so" "bar food."

Green Papaya 🅂Ⓜ   19   13   17 $19
475 Winter St. (Rte. 128, exit 27B), Waltham, 781-487-9988
◼ Reputedly the "best Thai west of Route 128", this "casual and friendly" Waltham entry is favored for "fresh and tasty" dishes, attracting a sizable "lunch crowd"; even critics who claim the "bright", "sterile" room "isn't inviting" appreciate the "reliable takeout" at a "reasonable price."

Green Street Grill 🅂Ⓜ   21   11   17 $26
280 Green St. (bet. Magazine & Pearl Sts.), Cambridge, 617-876-1655
◼ "They know how to use peppers" at this "creative" Central Square Caribbean where the heat from the "incendiary" fare is best soothed by their "killer planter's punch"; an "offbeat" hot spot, it's a "dark" and "funky" "dive" where diners sit "cheek by jowl" and let the chile-induced "tears" flow; P.S. "go on Mondays for the half-price menu."

Greg's Ⓜ   17   10   18 $19
821 Mt. Auburn St. (Belmont St.), Watertown, 617-491-0122
◼ This Watertown "neighborhood Italian" slings "tasty" "red-sauce" standards in "huge portions", and though it's "a little dark" and could use an "update", the "moderate" tabs keep it packed with all the area's "familiar faces."

Grendel's Bar 🅂Ⓜ   – – –   M
89 Winthrop St. (JFK St.), Cambridge, 617-491-1160
The beloved Harvard Square eatery Grendel's Den is now defunct, but the lower-level bar upholds its bohemian tradition with many of the same menu items, minus the famed salad bar.

Grille at Hobbs Brook 🅂Ⓜ   ▽ 18   18   19 $28
Doubletree Guest Suites, 550 Winter St. (Rte. 128), Waltham, 781-890-6767
◼ Lodged in Waltham's Doubletree Guest Suites, this American grill offers "decent value" and sets up a worthy "Sunday [brunch] buffet"; though the kitchen can be "a bit erratic", the plush setting is "relaxing", and consensus finds the experience on par "for a hotel."

Grillfish 🅂Ⓜ   20   18   17 $27
162 Columbus Ave. (bet. Arlington & Berkeley Sts.), 617-357-1620
◼ "Young adults" frequent this "cavernous" seafooder in the South End where the "fresh fish" is served in "simple but delicious" style; the "neon lights" and "way-loud" room are "not for everyone", but this "scene" is just "what it purports to be" – "funky"; P.S. "be sure to face your mother away" from the "awesome mural" over the bar.

GRILL 23 & BAR S M   25 | 23 | 24 | $49
161 Berkeley St. (Stuart St.), 617-542-2255

■ "Movers and shakers" gather at this "manly" Back Bay steakhouse to "relax and indulge" in chef Jay Murray's "superb" menu, which goes "beyond beef" to highlight "excellent" seafood as well; the historic building boasts a "beautiful", "soaring interior", and thanks to an ongoing expansion, doubled seating on a second floor.

G'Vanni's S M   20 | 16 | 18 | $29
2 Prince St. (Hanover St.), 617-523-0107

◪ A "serviceable" North End "favorite", this "tiny" trattoria is apt to be "crowded" with fans of its "very good" regional cooking; it's known as a "cozy" fixture for "pleasant" dining, though there's room for improvement "service-wise."

Gyuhama ● S M   22 | 15 | 17 | $29
827 Boylston St. (bet. Fairfield & Gloucester Sts.), 617-437-0188

◪ "Still hip after all these years", this classic "rock 'n' roll" Japanese is a "late-night" destination in the Back Bay where the "stellar sushi" is bolstered by "loud music" and a "party-time" atmosphere; maybe the service is "uneven" and a major "decor update" is overdue, but it remains the club-hopper's "sushi fix" of choice.

Halfway Cafe S M   16 | 11 | 17 | $17
174 Washington St. (VFW Pkwy.), Dedham, 781-326-3336
820 Boston Post Rd. (Farm Rd.), Marlborough, 508-480-0688
394 Main St. (Lexington St.), Watertown, 617-926-3595

◪ "Come as you are" to these "'round-the-corner" sports bars with a "roadhouse" look, purveyors of "huge portions" of "tasty" but "typical bar food"; they're the "place to go after a game" – "if you can handle the noise and smoke."

HAMERSLEY'S BISTRO S M   27 | 24 | 24 | $51
553 Tremont St. (Clarendon St.), 617-423-2700

■ Gordon Hamersley's South End namesake is a "stylish yet understated" French-American "phenomenon", with a "versatile", "consistently excellent" seasonal menu offering the likes of bouillabaisse and "jaw-droppingly good" roast chicken to the city's power brokers; along with "impeccable decor", "attentive service" and an "interesting wine list", it "remains a classic" and "every visit reinforces" its rep.

Hard Rock Cafe S M   13 | 20 | 15 | $21
131 Clarendon St. (bet. Boylston St. & Columbus Ave.), 617-424-7625

◪ "Go for the Aerosmith collection" but "leave your eardrums at home"; although the dining experience at this repository of "rock memorabilia" is akin to eating "semi-good" burgers "at an amusement park" where you "can't hear yourself think", it's a perennial "fun spot" in the eyes of tourists and teenagers.

Harry's ●⦻Ⓢ Ⓜ ⌐   ▽ 20 | 10 | 18 | $16
149 Turnpike Rd./Rte. 9, Westborough, 508-366-8302
◪ For "great fried clams" in the Western 'burbs, the Mass
Pike populace heads to this roadside "square box", home to
a cheap menu of American diner classics; the 1 AM closing
time makes it a late-night haunt, but one surveyor's
"landmark" is another's "dull" "suburban standard."

Harry's Too ●Ⓢ Ⓜ   ▽ 19 | 13 | 18 | $20
153 Turnpike Rd./Rte. 9 (directly behind Harry's),
Westborough, 508-898-2200
◪ Harry's "nicer" next-door sib upgrades the formula with
"big portions" of "tasty" American fare from a "surprisingly
varied menu"; supporters welcome it as a "friendly"
"alternative to the chains", though it's "not in a class"
with the high-end houses.

Hartwell House Ⓜ   18 | 20 | 19 | $33
94 Hartwell Ave. (Rtes. 4 & 225), Lexington, 781-862-5111
■ The "nouveau colonial setting" of this "fancy-schmancy"
Lexington Continental-American provides a smart backdrop
for its "traditional" (if "uninspired") fare; the "sophisticated"
feel is a hit with the "over-65" crowd and businesspeople
"on the company dime", though some favor the upstairs
annex for its "casual" atmosphere and "bistro menu."

Harvard Gardens ●Ⓢ Ⓜ   15 | 15 | 17 | $21
316 Cambridge St. (Grove St.), 617-523-2727
■ With nightlife impresario Patrick Lyons at the helm, this
Beacon Hill spot is now "gussied up" with a "more upscale"
look and a "solid" New American menu that works as well
for "family meals" as for a "first date"; early reports confirm
the "makeover" is a success and the "good value" is intact.

Harvest Ⓢ Ⓜ   23 | 22 | 22 | $43
44 Brattle St. (Church St.), Cambridge, 617-868-2255
■ Now run by the Grill 23 & Bar management team, this
revived "Cambridge relic" in Harvard Square is "clubbier
and more mature" than before, with an "outstanding"
American menu showcasing striped bass, grilled rack of
lamb and "one mean chowder"; the "tasteful" layout
features subdued wood with taupe tones, a "lovely
courtyard" and the perfect bar for a "sophisticated drink";
the verdict: "reincarnation works."

HELMAND, THE Ⓢ Ⓜ   25 | 23 | 21 | $29
143 First St. (Bent St.), Cambridge, 617-492-4646
■ "Experience Afghanistan" at this Cambridge "original"
where the "exotic" temptations include "wonderful lamb",
"irresistible breads" and many "unusual" veggie dishes,
served in a "warm and beautiful" interior that provides a
"feeling of luxury" at a "reasonable price"; admirers only
"wish it weren't so popular."

Henrietta's Table 🅂🅼   22 19 21 $31
Charles Hotel, 1 Bennett St. (University Pl.), Cambridge,
617-661-5005
■ A "charming country" ambiance sets the tone for "finger-lickin' home cooking" at this New Englander on Harvard Square, much lauded for its "real produce in season" and other "fresh farmhouse food" – like "grandma would make if she were a yuppie"; "the tab sure adds up fast", but nothing deters the crowds from the "lavish Sunday buffet brunch" or the "power breakfast and lunch" action.

Hill Tavern, The 🅂🅼   15 13 13 $19
228 Cambridge St. (Garden St.), 617-742-6192
☑ Expect an "active bar scene" at this Beacon Hill "hangout" near the junction of Mass General and the State House; the "relaxed atmosphere" draws in the "20s/30s age bracket" for "decent" American "pub grub", and the "great beers" help to offset the "sluggish service."

Hilltop Steak House 🅂🅼   15 10 15 $22
210 Union St. (Rte. 3, exit 7), Braintree, 781-848-3363
855 Broadway/Rte. 1, Saugus, 781-233-7700
☑ "Plastic cows out front" foretell the "kitsch" that endures at these suburban steakhouses where the "hokey" barnlike rooms and abundance of "grandmas with corsages" lend a "'50s throwback" feel; the "overload" of "mainstream beef" can be a "guilty pleasure", though the quality is "uneven."

Himalaya 🅂🅼   19 11 17 $18
95 Mass Ave. (Newbury St.), 617-267-6644
■ This Back Bay Indian is a "true find" for both "standard" Northern fare and "more unusual Southern specialties" marked by a "savory" "balance of flavors"; if the decor is found "lacking", scenesters advise "sit by the window" for nice people-watching near the top of Newbury Street.

Hi-Rise Bread Co. 🅂🅼   ▽ 23 13 13 $12
56 Brattle St. (Church St.), Cambridge, 617-492-3003 ⊄
208 Concord Ave. (Huron Ave.), Cambridge, 617-876-8766
☑ The "endless temptations" at this Cambridge bakery/cafe duo go beyond "delicious breads" and "yummy" pastries to include "fabulous soups" and "fresh, inventive sandwiches"; in spite of a "spacey staff" and steep tabs (wags dub it the "Hi-Price Bread Co."), enthusiasts keep coming back to "watch 'em bake."

House of Blues 🅂🅼   16 20 16 $22
96 Winthrop St. (JFK St.), Cambridge, 617-491-2583
☑ "Hallelujah" cry devotees of the Sunday gospel brunch ("go prepared to sing") at this soulful site in Harvard Square where the "decent Southern grub" focuses on "spicy" Cajun fare; nightly live entertainment and Civil War–era art make for a "very cool" scene, though most grant the sights and sounds top billing and rank the food "secondary."

House of Siam 🖪Ⓜ
22 | 18 | 20 | $22

542 Columbus Ave. (Worcester St.), 617-267-1755
■ Bringing its "delicate" touch to the South End, this "outstanding" Thai is noted for its lengthy menu of "fresh" and "spicy" fare, including an especially "tasty pad Thai"; red walls and Siamese art give the room a "traditional" feel, enhancing the food's "authentic" flavors.

House of Tibet Kitchen 🖪
19 | 14 | 19 | $15

235 Holland St. (Broadway), Somerville, 617-629-7567
■ With its "different" culinary twist, this "tiny" Tibetan is an "inviting" addition to Somerville, presenting "out-of-the-ordinary", "wholesome" fare for those willing "to explore"; the staff is "helpful" and "friendly", though the monastic setting has "scant" decor and there's "no alcohol."

Hungry i, The 🖪Ⓜ
23 | 25 | 22 | $45

71½ Charles St. (bet. Mt. Vernon & Pinckney Sts.), 617-227-3524
■ "Quintessentially romantic", this "cozy", "quaint" Beacon Hill veteran seduces with "delicious" country French cooking and "decor out of *Victoria* magazine"; despite the "limited menu" and "high prices", most find it "*très romantique*" and tout the "incredible" Sunday brunch for the morning after.

ICARUS 🖪Ⓜ
26 | 24 | 24 | $47

3 Appleton St. (bet. Arlington & Berkeley Sts.), 617-426-1790
■ When it's time for a "splurge", the well-heeled wing it to this "sophisticated" South Ender, a "class act" where "superb", "inventive" American fare is delivered by an "A+ staff" amid "stunning decor"; most agree it "lives up to its well-deserved reputation" as a "formal" standout where the extras include live jazz Friday nights and valet parking.

Iguana Cantina 🖪Ⓜ
16 | 16 | 16 | $19

1656 Worcester Rd. (Rte. 9), Framingham, 508-875-1188
66 Chestnut St. (Great Plain Ave.), Needham, 781-444-9976
313 Moody St. (Main St.), Waltham, 781-891-3039
◪ These "campy" Tex-Mexers are spreading like sagebrush, featuring "wacky decor" that provides distraction from the "adequate" but "not exciting" cooking and "entertaining" touches like a "talking iguana at the door"; a "kids' favorite", it's also big with the "college crowd" and anyone else "on a budget."

Il Bacio 🖪Ⓜ
18 | 18 | 16 | $26

226 Hanover St. (Cross St.), 617-742-9200
◪ "Cafe-style" is the way to go at this Mediterranean-Eclectic where doors that "open onto the street" allow for "great people-watching" in the bustling North End; drawing mixed responses, however, are the food (from "just ok" to "fabulous") and the service ("a bit uneven"); N.B. the food rating may not reflect the latest chef's performance.

IL CAPRICCIO Ⓜ   26 | 21 | 23 | $45
888 Main St. (Prospect St.), Waltham,
781-894-2234

■ "Why go to Boston?" suburbanites wonder when there's a "first-class" Northern Italian right in Waltham serving "delicious, innovative" handmade pastas (and a "sublime" porcini soufflé), matched with a "great wine list"; the cognoscenti deem it "elegant", if "noisy", and its status as "Waltham's best" means it can be "difficult to get in."

Il Giardino Cafe Ⓜ   – | – | – | M
132 Brookline Ave. (Kenmore Sq.), 617-267-6124

As a supplier of "quick", "authentic" and "fresh" pastas and light bites, this Italian near Fenway is a "marvelous" stop before a ball game or a movie; boosters kiss their fingertips to the "plentiful servings" (also available for takeout), though the modest decor is less than *bellissimo*.

Il Moro Ⓢ   – | – | – | M
143 Pleasant St. (Washington St.), Marblehead,
781-639-8682

"Specializing in fish", this Marblehead Mediterranean-Italian is noteworthy for its "excellent" coastal cooking; proximity to the Warwick Theater makes it convenient for pre-show meals, though those who grumble that it's "overpriced" would prefer *moro* for the money.

Imperial Seafood House ◗ Ⓢ Ⓜ   ▽ 18 | 10 | 14 | $17
70 Beach St. (Harrison Ave.), 617-426-8439

◨ There's an "emphasis on shrimp", but this long-reigning Chinatown Chinese provides its subjects with a wide "assortment of fish and shellfish", as well as "consistently good" weekend dim sum; it's "a favorite" despite its "shopworn" appearance, and business hours until 4 AM make it a "late-night joint" of distinction.

India House Ⓢ Ⓜ   ▽ 17 | 15 | 17 | $20
239 Harvard St. (Longwood Ave.), Brookline, 617-739-9300

■ This "reliable" Brookline Indian hits the "perfect spice level" with "simple preparations" of "fresh ingredients" that upgrade the "standard" assortment of curries, vegetables and meats; it's no powerhouse, but fans "welcome" it as an option in a "good location" near Longwood Avenue.

Indian Cafe Ⓢ Ⓜ   21 | 15 | 19 | $20
1665 Beacon St. (Winthrop Rd.), Brookline,
617-277-1752

■ Masala mavens call this "relaxing and reliable" Brookline Indian a "favorite" because of its "authentic" approach and "cozy" "neighborhood" feel; it's known for its "rich" and "tasty" cooking, "reasonable prices" and "attentive service."

Indian Club [S] [M] | 20 | 14 | 17 | $19

1755 Mass Ave. (Porter Sq.), Cambridge, 617-491-7750

◪ "Modest" but "dependable", this Porter Square Indian boasts a "broad menu" of "middle-of-the-road" favorites and "South Indian" specialties; citing "quality" and "value", boosters say it "doesn't get its due", but critics find the food only "ok" and the decor "tacky."

India Pavilion [S] [M] | 18 | 12 | 17 | $17

17 Central Sq. (Western Ave.), Cambridge, 617-547-7463

◪ Longevity has made this Indian a Central Square "staple" for its "very tasty" way with "great spices", "yummy, hot breads" and a popular and "inexpensive" lunch buffet; a dissenting minority, however, calls it "uninspiring" and complains of "cramped quarters."

India Quality [S] [M] | 22 | 12 | 17 | $18

484 Commonwealth Ave. (Kenmore St.), 617-267-4499

■ "Back from the ashes" after a fire and now set in "bigger" and (slightly) "fancier" digs, this "bargain" Kenmore Square Indian continues to provide "authentic and delightful" fare and "friendly", "speedy service"; it stays "crowded" with enthusiasts who hail it as "one of the best."

India Samraat [S] [M] | ▽ 19 | 9 | 17 | $18

51A Mass Ave. (bet. Commonwealth Ave. & Marlborough St.), 617-247-0718

■ "Family"-run and "very authentic", this Back Bay Indian offers "tasty" fare ("great *saag* and vegetarian *thali*") at such "good prices" that most are willing to overlook the dodgy decor; N.B. on Saturdays and Sundays, the AYCE feast is a steal at $9.95.

Intrigue Café [S] [M] | ▽ 21 | 23 | 21 | $22

Boston Harbor Hotel, 70 Rowes Wharf (Atlantic Ave.), 617-856-7744

■ "One of Boston's best-kept secrets" is this Downtown American cafe in the Boston Harbor Hotel, serving three "excellent" meals a day from chef Daniel Bruce's kitchen, minus the steep prices of the hotel's Rowes Wharf dining room; a waterside terrace commands a "fab view" too, leading admirers to admonish "don't tell."

Ironside Grill [S] [M] | 17 | 14 | 15 | $28

25 Park St. (Warren St.), Charlestown, 617-242-1384

◪ A "Charlestown alternative" for "huge portions" of American eats (a 26-ounce pork chop, anyone?), this "neighborhood hangout" wins praise for offering "solid fare" and "outdoor seating" just an anchor's toss from the Constitution Marina; however, doubters deem it "a little pricey" given the "tavern" ambiance.

Iruna 🅜
17 | 14 | 17 | $20

56 JFK St. (Mt. Auburn St.), Cambridge, 617-868-5633

■ "Simple Spanish" is the mode at this Harvard Square "hideaway", a "fixture" known for providing "earthy" and "authentic" tastes at "cheap" prices ("best picks" include the "fresh fish" and paella); it's a "perfectly romantic" "retreat", though some suggest this "pocket of the old world" could use a fresh "coat of paint."

Isabella 🅢🅜
23 | 18 | 21 | $30

566 High St. (Eastern Ave.), Dedham, 781-461-8485

■ Judging by the crowds, this "Dedham diamond in the rough" is "worth finding" for the "flashes of excellence" on its "imaginative" and "appealing" New American menu; the "small" room and "funky, artsy decor" lend it a "bistro feel", and though "weekend waits" are standard, "if it was in Boston you'd never get in and it'd be twice as costly."

Jacob Wirth 🅢🅜
14 | 16 | 14 | $21

31-37 Stuart St. (bet. Tremont & Washington Sts.), 617-338-8586

■ While this historic German-American in the Theater District works "for a philosophical talk" over a "great dark beer" or as a pre-theater "standby" for "pretty good" wurst and sauerkraut, it's more the "step-back-in-time" ambiance that leads nostalgic surveyors to "treat it respectfully."

JAE'S CAFE & GRILL 🅢🅜
22 | 19 | 17 | $26

520 Columbus Ave. (Concord Sq.), 617-421-9405
1281 Cambridge St. (Prospect St.), Cambridge, 617-497-8380
Atrium Mall, 300 Boylston St., Chestnut Hill, 617-965-7177
1223 Beacon St. (St. Paul St.), Brookline, 617-739-0000

■ Expect a "fanciful hybrid" of "excellent" Pan-Asian fare, including "the best pad Thai", "great" sushi and "delicious *bibimbop*", at this popular, "reasonably priced" quintet whose "dreamy aquariums entertain you while you wait" for a table; N.B. the Brookline branch is new and unrated.

Jake's Boss BBQ 🅢
22 | 10 | 15 | $15

3492 Washington St. (Williams St.), Jamaica Plain, 617-983-3701

■ "Tender, tender, tender" rave BBQ fans of the "delicious" ribs that "friendly" "Jake himself serves up" at this "cheap" Jamaica Plain cookout near Franklin Park; while a sit-down lunch makes sense "after a visit to the zoo", the place could "use some booze and a face-lift" and therefore some reserve it "for takeout."

Jasmine Bistro 🅢
▽ 23 | 19 | 24 | $23

412 Market St. (Washington St.), Brighton, 617-789-4676

■ Hidden away on the "back side of Brighton" is this French-Hungarian-International "melting pot", a "romantic", "intimate" "gem" that serves "exotic" dishes, including "superb seafood specials"; the "wonderful family" that runs the establishment ensures a pleasant meal.

Jasper White's Summer Shack ⬛Ⓜ – | – | – | M

149 Alewife Brook Pkwy. (Sterling St.), Cambridge, 617-520-9500
Fin fans dive into casual seafood at lobster czar Jasper
White's kitschy newcomer in the Alewife area, where the
family-friendly menu offers everything from chowder and
baked stuffed lobster to corn dogs and fresh-fruit snow
cones; booths and picnic tables fill a huge space featuring
corrugated-tin walls, a raw bar and a giant lobster tank.

Jimbo's Fish Shanty ⬛Ⓜ 15 | 12 | 15 | $22

245 Northern Ave. (Boston Fish Pier), 617-542-5600
■ A location near the Pier allows this "basic roadhouse-
style" seafooder to reel in the "tourists" for a "decent", if
"far from exciting", menu comprised of "lots of fried" stuff;
the decor may be a bit "tacky", but it's a more "casual"
alternative to Jimmy's Harborside, its sibling next door.

Jimmy's Harborside ⬛Ⓜ 19 | 17 | 18 | $34

242 Northern Ave. (Boston Fish Pier), 617-423-1000
◪ "Nostalgic Bostonians", "tourists" and "seniors" continue
to sail into this mammoth, 76-year-old seafood "kingpin of
the Northern Avenue stretch" for a "legendary view" of the
harbor, "good, fresh seafood" and live piano music; critics,
however, think it's "tired" and "running on its reputation."

Jimmy's Steer House ⬛Ⓜ 19 | 13 | 18 | $20

1111 Mass Ave. (Quincy St.), Arlington, 781-646-4450
■ "Travel back to the '40s" at this retro steakhouse in
Arlington, which attracts "lots of elderly patrons" with its
"bargain" plates of "good", if "predictable", fare; while the
lines can be "long", the "attentive" waitresses are swift.

Joe's American Bar & Grill ⬛Ⓜ 15 | 15 | 15 | $23

279 Dartmouth St. (Newbury St.), 617-536-4200
100 Atlantic Ave. (Commercial Wharf), 617-367-8700
South Shore Plaza, 250 Granite St. (Rte. 30), Braintree,
781-848-0200
985 Providence Hwy. (Rtes. 1 & 128), Dedham, 781-329-0800
2087 Washington St./Rte. 53 (Rte. 123), Hanover, 781-878-1234
Northshore Mall, 210 Andover St. (Rte. 128), Peabody, 928-532-9500
311 Mishawum Rd. (Washington St.), Woburn, 781-935-7200
◪ Depending on the time and day, this American chain –
which serves "standard" eats, along with "great chowder" –
functions as a family-type place, a "Howard Johnson's for
yuppies" or a singles' "meet market"; detractors, however,
find the food too "typical."

Joe Tecce's ⬛Ⓜ 16 | 15 | 16 | $27

61 N. Washington St. (Cooper St.), 617-742-6210
◪ "Tourists" and Fleet Center ticket-holders flock to this
North End Italian fronting the Big Dig because of its
"convenient" location and "big portions"; but while it
might be "ok" enough, that doesn't stop bashers from
dismissing it as "ordinary."

John Harvard's Brew House ●⬛Ⓜ 15 16 16 $20
*33 Dunster St. (bet. Mass Ave. & Mt. Auburn St.), Cambridge,
617-868-3585
1 Worcester Rd./Rte. 30 (Rte. 9), Framingham, 508-875-2337*
⬛ A "lively", "fun place" for "young people" to "hang out",
this national microbrewery chain complements its snazzy
suds selection with a "diverse" American menu ranging
from salads and sandwiches to pastas and steaks.

Johnny D's Uptown ⬛ 16 14 17 $18
17 Holland St. (College Ave.), Somerville, 617-776-2004
⬛ Lively bands back up the "cheap" eats at this Somerville
Eclectic, which gets kudos for its "bargain" half-price menu
on Tuesday–Friday and "great" jazz brunch on weekends;
otherwise, many feel "the point here is music", "not food."

Johnny's Luncheonette ⬛Ⓜ 18 16 16 $15
*1105 Mass Ave. (Remington St.), Cambridge, 617-495-0055
30 Langley Rd. (bet. Beacon & Centre Sts.), Newton,
617-527-3223*
■ "Slick back your hair" before heading out to these
'50s-style retro diners, "friendly" places for "awesome
breakfasts", burgers and "delicious" sweet-potato fries;
but beware of "long weekend lines" and lots of "noise."

Joseph's on High Ⓜ ▽ 17 18 17 $30
200 High St. (Atlantic Ave.), 617-523-4000
⬛ Situated on the same waterfront location for 30 years, this
seafood-oriented Traditional American recently moved up
the street to more upscale, modern digs in the Financial
District; find "lobster treated royally", as well as a polished
oak bar that features music Friday–Saturday nights.

Jose's ⬛Ⓜ 15 10 14 $15
*131 Sherman St. (bet. Rindge & Walden Aves.), Cambridge,
617-354-0335*
⬛ "Big portions" of "functional", "homestyle Mexican" is
the word on this "fun" Cambridge cantina frequented by a
"student crowd" that's too busy knocking back the "great
margaritas" to notice that the "cheap" dishes can "taste
the same" or that the service is mighty "slow."

Joy Luck Café ⬛ 20 16 19 $21
*1037 Great Plain Ave. (Chestnut Pl.), Needham,
781-455-8908*
■ For "swanky Chinese in the suburbs", consider this
Needham option not far from Wellesley, which "beautifully
presents" "fresh", "innovative" dishes, as well as "good
sushi", in an "attractive pastel" room; even the few who
find the food "lacks spark" laud the "personal" service.

JP Seafood Cafe [S] [M] 23 | 16 | 19 | $22
730 Centre St. (Seaverns Ave.), Jamaica Plain, 617-983-5177
■ "Connoisseurs" declare it's "worth an excursion" to Jamaica Plain to sample this Japanese-Korean's "solid" food, notably "great scallion pancakes" and "wonderfully fresh" sushi; enjoy your meal in a "low-key atmosphere" that's "nice" to dine in either "solo or with friends."

J.T.K. Grill & Sushi [S] [M] – | – | – | M
617 Main St. (Elm St.), Waltham, 781-894-9783
Stark tones of black and white contrast with traditional Eastern adornments at this new Pan-Asian, setting the stage for cuisine from Japan, Thailand and Korea; the focus is sushi – that is, for those not focused on knickknacks like fans and swords, which serve as decor.

JULIEN [M] 26 | 27 | 26 | $57
Le Meridien Hotel, 250 Franklin St. (bet. Oliver & Pearl Sts.), 617-451-1900
◪ "Civility" defines this "elegant", "formal" New French experience in Le Meridien Hotel where diners savor "perfection" in "every bite"; look forward to a "wonderful wine list", "great" "European-style" service and a "relaxing" ambiance; overall, it's an "awesome place" for a "quiet" "celebration" or a "power lunch", but then again, it "should be at these prices."

Jumbalaya [S] [M] – | – | – | M
174 Sylvan St. (Endicott St.), Danvers, 978-774-6666
This Cajun-Mexican hybrid is no longer part of Joey Crugnale's empire, but it still dishes up spicy enchiladas, fajitas and burritos; crawfish flags and colorful jazz posters convey a New Orleans theme, further seasoned by the wall of herbs and spices.

Jumbo Seafood ◐ [S] [M] ▽ 23 | 12 | 19 | $20
7 Hudson St. (Beach St.), 617-542-2823
■ "The name is accurate" enthuse recipients of the "huge" portions of "delicious" seafood, including "fabulous salted shrimp" and " great fried squid", served at this Chinatown venue, a favorite of discerning locals who appreciate the late-night hours.

Kareem's [M] 💳⃠ 22 | 7 | 14 | $16
600 Mt. Auburn St. (bet. Arlington & School Sts.), Watertown, 617-926-1867
◪ "Lovingly prepared" homestyle Middle Eastern fare, especially "wonderful lamb", makes this Watertown "star" a "superb" "local spot", even if dissenters gripe about the "lousy" atmosphere and "weird hours" (closed weekends).

Karoun
18 | 15 | 17 | $25
839 Washington St. (Walnut Terrace), Newtonville, 617-964-3400
■ Newtonville denizens turn to this "authentic" Armenian for its "wide variety" of lamb dishes and kebabs (the kitchen now also prepares a number of Mediterranean and Asian-influenced dishes); on weekend nights, belly dancers entertain; N.B. a post-*Survey* "rejuvenation" may outdate the decor score.

Kashmir S M
22 | 18 | 17 | $23
279 Newbury St. (Gloucester St.), 617-536-1695
■ A "great location" on Newbury Street, a "nice" outdoor patio, an "elegant interior" and the "perfect" all-you-can-eat buffet are why this midpriced Back Bay Indian is "head and shoulders" above the competition.

Kaya S M
18 | 15 | 16 | $24
581 Boylston St. (bet. Clarendon & Dartmouth Sts.), 617-236-5858 ●
1366 Beacon St. (Harvard St.), Brookline, 617-738-2244
1924 Mass Ave. (Porter Sq.), Cambridge, 617-497-5656 ●
☑ "Get the seafood", "excellent" *bulgoki* or a good-value lunch-box special advise surveyors who like to *bibimbop* over to this Korean-Japanese trio; the sushi and service, however, draw highly mixed responses.

Kebab-N-Kurry S M
21 | 12 | 17 | $20
30 Mass Ave. (bet. Beacon & Marlborough Sts.), 617-536-9835
☑ This "longtime source for Indian" in the Back Bay is praised for "authentic" fare – particularly the chicken *tikka* and vindaloos – that's "cheaper" than others in the neighborhood; but beware the "tiny", "cramped" setting.

Ken's Steak House S M
16 | 12 | 16 | $28
95 Worcester Rd. (Speen St.), Framingham, 508-875-4455
☑ Sure, some still "take grandma and old Rotarians" to this Framingham steakhouse because it's a "standby" for "traditional" beef, but a chorus of critics proclaims that the place has "seen better days" and "needs a good overhaul."

King & I S M
22 | 14 | 19 | $21
145 Charles St. (Cambridge St.), 617-227-3320
■ Beacon Hill residents "pine for" the pad Thai ("still the best") offered at this taste of Bangkok where "delicious, well-prepared" food comes at an "amazingly low cost"; moreover, the staff is "eager to please."

KingFish Hall S M
– | – | – | M
Faneuil Hall Mktpl., South Market Bldg., 617-523-8862
Chef-owner Todd English continues to scatter loaves and fishes, now at this new seafooder in Faneuil Hall; selections range from sushi to a raw bar to whole fish prepared on a 'fish dancer' rotisserie, plus nonaquatic options like rib eye and quail satay, all served in a David Rockwell–designed room where dangling mobiles stick to the marine theme.

Kokopelli Chili Co. [S] [M] 14 | 15 | 15 | $19
1648 Beacon St. (Washington St.), Brookline, 617-277-2880
◪ "I never realized how many kinds of chiles there are" marvel novices at this Brookline Southwestern known for a menu that "allows for a lot of experimentation", as well as a "fun salsa bar" and "dozens" of "pretty mean" margaritas; those who give it a chilly review concede that it's a "good concept" but "wish the food were better."

Kong Luh [S] [M] ▽ 19 | 9 | 14 | $17
Arlington Ctr., 9 Medford St. (Mass Ave.), Arlington, 781-643-2456
◪ "Bring an appetite" to this "unassuming" "mom-and-pop Mongolian" that cooks up Northern Chinese food "unlike anything else" in Arlington; it may well make "the best potstickers in Boston", but be prepared to wait for them, since the "kitchen can be slow."

Koreana ◐ [S] [M] 20 | 11 | 16 | $20
154 Prospect St. (Broadway), Cambridge, 617-576-8661
◪ For "comforting" Korean fare, head to this Central Square venue where "yummy" stews share an "immense" menu with "heavenly" cook-your-own BBQ; quibblers find the decor "depressing" and think the pace of service may require diners to "bring a sleeping bag and shaving kit", but more laud it as an "authentic" "favorite."

Kowloon ◐ [S] [M] 16 | 15 | 15 | $20
948 Broadway/Rte. 1, Saugus, 781-233-0077
◪ "I love how cheesy it is" admit kitsch connoisseurs about this 50-year-old, 1,200-seat Polynesian palace, which features a ship-shaped dance floor, live entertainment and froufrou cocktails; others, however, complain about "mass-produced" Chinese (and slightly "better" Thai) food that's "rushed out" to allow for quick "table turnover."

LA CAMPANIA 25 | 22 | 22 | $35
504 Main St. (bet. Cross & Heard Sts.), Waltham, 781-894-4280
■ Run by a "gracious", "hardworking" family that's "devoted to its food and customers", this "Waltham hot spot" with "charming country decor" wins raves for its "gourmet and traditional" Italian offerings, complemented by a 300-bottle wine list; the only complaint is that its 40 seats are clearly "not enough."

La Famiglia Giorgio [S] [M] 15 | 10 | 15 | $20
112 Salem St. (Parmenter St.), 617-367-6711
250 Newbury St. (bet. Fairfield & Gloucester Sts.), 617-247-1569
◪ Value-minded "gluttons" bring their hearty appetites to this pair of "standard" Italians because the portions are so "ridiculously large" the "doggy bag contains a week's worth of dinners"; but that doesn't entice gourmands who say it merely practices "quantity over quality."

La Groceria ⓈⓂ   19 | 15 | 18 | $25
853 Main St. (Mass Ave.), Cambridge, 617-497-4214
◪ Central Square's nook for "textbook red-sauce dishes",
this "cheerful" 29-year-old Italian also serves commendable
antipasti and risottos; the "homey" atmosphere, however,
only reminds the unimpressed how the food is just "one
step up from what anyone could make at home"; still, it's
"dependable" and the prices are "fair."

Lala Rokh ⓈⓂ   23 | 22 | 23 | $34
97 Mt. Vernon St. (Charles St.), 617-720-5511
■ This "tranquil" "little hideaway" on Beacon Hill tempts
with the "exotic aromas" and "transporting" tastes of
"phenomenal" Persian cuisine, served in "sophisticated"
rooms that exude a "romantic" ambiance; along with
"gracious" owners who "really care" and "knowledgeable"
servers, it's no surprise that for its genre it's "one of the
best in the country."

Landing, The ⓈⓂ   – | – | – | M
81 Front St. (State St.), Marblehead, 781-631-1878
Hoping to capitalize on its "great" waterside view, the new
owners of this nautical-themed Marblehead landmark
have "totally redone" the decor and introduced a more
ambitious Contemporary American menu that includes such
dishes as Caribbean-spiced salmon with mango chutney;
meanwhile, the pub remains a "great place to hang out."

La Paloma Ⓢ   20 | 14 | 18 | $21
195 Newport Ave. (Hobart St.), Quincy, 617-773-0512
■ Despite its "unlikely" strip mall location, this Quincy
Mexican is much "better than your average" burrito joint,
thanks to "excellent salsa" and a "something-for-everyone"
menu highlighted by "wonderful", "interesting" specials;
P.S. "when in doubt", keep in mind that "the chef excels
at fish dishes."

Last Hurrah ◖ⓈⓂ   – | – | – | M
Omni Parker House, 60 School St. (Tremont St.),
617-227-8600
No more subterranean setting for this political hang at the
Omni Parker House; the newly renovated bar/restaurant
is now raised to the ground floor to provide a brighter
schmoozing spot fronting Beacon Street, where pundits
hold forth over drinks, casual American meals and – of
course – Boston cream pie.

La Summa ⓈⓂ   ▽ 21 | 15 | 21 | $28
30 Fleet St. (Hanover St.), 617-523-9503
■ Owner Barbara Summa's North End Italian is a "real
neighborhood place" "off the main drag", distinguished
by "consistent quality" and "handmade pastas like mom
never had time" to make; even if a few find it "expensive"
for what it is, at least there's usually "no wait."

Laurel 🅂🅼   22 | 23 | 22 | $38 |
142 Berkeley St. (Columbus Ave.), 617-424-6711
🔳 "A vast improvement over its predecessor", this "distinguished" New American in the Back Bay is "a real sleeper", with "fabulous"cuisine, an "elegant" interior and "attentive" service; it attracts a "ladies-who-lunch crowd", and its "low noise level" makes it "a great place for a business dinner"; P.S. try the "superb brunch" on Sundays.

Le Bocage 🅼   24 | 21 | 23 | $46 |
72 Bigelow Ave. (Mt. Auburn St.), Watertown, 617-923-1210
🔳 "Well-spaced tables" help create an "unhurried" ambiance at this "adorable" Watertown charmer whose French cuisine scores highly but garners mixed comments; while some find it "overpriced for the quality", others consider it an "oldie-but-goodie" for a "fancy night out."

LEGAL SEA FOODS 🅂🅼   21 | 15 | 18 | $30 |
Long Wharf, 255 State St. (Court St.), 617-227-3115
Prudential Ctr., 800 Boylston St. (bet. Fairfield & Gloucester Sts.), 617-266-6800
Copley Pl., 100 Huntington Ave. (bet. Dartmouth & Exeter Sts.), 617-266-7775
26 Park Sq. (Columbus Ave.), 617-426-4444
South Shore Plaza, 250 Granite St., Braintree, 781-356-3070
Burlington Mall, 1131 Middlesex Tpke. (Rte. 128), Burlington, 781-270-9700
Kendall Sq., 5 Cambridge Ctr. (bet. Ames & Main Sts.), Cambridge, 617-864-3400
43 Boylston St. (Hammond Pond Pkwy.), Chestnut Hill, 617-277-7300
Miltons Plaza, 1400 Worcester Rd. (bet. Rte. 126 & Speen St.), Natick, 508-820-1115
Northshore Mall, Rtes. 114 & 128, Peabody, 978-532-4500
🔳 A "local legend" that's "gone national", Roger Berkowitz's ever-expanding fleet of fish houses owes its "hall-of- fame" status to "impeccably fresh" seafood; while detractors carp about "pricey" yet "boring" preparations and "plain" settings, they're outvoted by schools of fin fans.

Le Gamin ⬤🅂🅼   19 | 16 | 17 | $19 |
550 Tremont St. (opp. Boston Ctr. of Arts), 617-654-8969
⬛ You'll "feel like you're in Paris" at this "casual", "cheery", South End crêperie, which may be the "biggest bargain" in a neighborhood that sorely needs one; in addition to the "delicious" sweet or savory signature item, there are also salads, soups and "light" entrees.

Le Lyonnais 🅼   ▽ 21 | 21 | 23 | $36 |
416 Great Rd./Rte. 2A, Acton, 978-263-9068
🔳 This "charming", "cozy house" in the Acton 'burbs attracts a "classy" crowd that "loves its atmosphere" and "delicious" French standards; others note it's "almost the only game in town" and a "pricey" one at that.

L'ESPALIER Ⓜ   28 | 27 | 27 | $69

*30 Gloucester St. (bet. Commonwealth Ave. & Newbury St.),
617-262-3023*

■ Count the accolades: Frank McClelland's "world-class"
Back Bay New French ranks No. 1 for Food, No. 2 for
Decor and No. 3 for Service; revel in "sheer bliss" with
a "sumptuous" three-course prix fixe or seven-course
degustation meal served in a "gorgeous" townhouse setting
by an "outstandingly" "gracious" staff; the tab is definitely
"not for the faint of heart", but this is a "perfect experience
from coat check to goodbye."

Les Zygomates Ⓜ   22 | 20 | 21 | $36

129 South St. (bet. Beach & East Sts.), 617-542-5108

☑ "Bring your cell phone" to this "hip" French bistro and
wine bar in the "chic" Leather District where 40 selections
by the glass and 150 international choices by the bottle
leave "young" oenophiles in ecstasy (plus, the "great"
weekday prix fixe is a "best-kept secret"); N.B. a recent
renovation (which outdates the decor rating) has enlarged
the dining areas and added a small stage to highlight the
bistro-cum-club's increased emphasis on jazz.

Library Grill Ⓢ   ▽ 24 | 29 | 25 | $37

*Hampshire House, 84 Beacon St. (bet. Arlington &
Charles Sts.), 617-227-9600*

☑ Adjacent to the Bull & Finch Pub (aka *Cheers*), this
recently renovated Back Bay New American continues to
be "a relatively unknown gem", despite its "cozy" 19th-
century vintage-library decor, "romantic" atmosphere and
lovely view of the Public Garden; take "your out-of-town
guests" here for a "nice brunch", the only meal available
to the general public.

Linwood Grill & BBQ Ⓜ   – | – | – | I

81 Kilmarnock St. (Queensberry St.), 617-247-8099

Southern flavors in a sassy, smokin' setting characterize
this BBQ joint in the Fenway where Texas smokers and
grills turn out pork, brisket, sausage and dry-rub ribs from
the capable tongs of Todd Carey; the hip decor includes
retro-style booths and metal-trimmed concrete bars.

Locke-Ober Cafe Ⓜ   20 | 22 | 23 | $47

*3 Winter Pl. (bet. Tremont & Washington Sts.),
617-542-1340*

☑ "Tradition triumphs" at this 1875 "time capsule", a
"dark", "clubby" Downtown Crossing Continental where
"old-style waiters" serve the "classics" (notably "great
hunks of meat") to a mostly "masculine" crowd of "blue
bloods"; younger critics call it "stuffy" and "sadly *ober*
the hill" but are heartened by a "new trend" here – "women
at the bar"; N.B. jacket recommended.

L'Osteria [S] [M] 22 | 15 | 19 | $24

104 Salem St. (Cooper St.), 617-723-7847

◪ "Unassuming from the outside", this North End Italian offers "reliable", "robust" "red-sauce" dishes prepared by an "accommodating chef" who will make dishes "off the menu"; P.S. the entire restaurant is "quiet" and "conducive to conversation", but picky types prefer a street-level table ("beware the basement").

Lotus Blossom [S] [M] 23 | 19 | 20 | $24

394 Boston Post Rd./Rte. 20 (Sudbury Farms), Sudbury, 978-443-0200

■ A "savior in the suburbs" is how reviewers describe this "classy" Sudbury Chinese (the sibling of Changsho), which satisfies a Cantonese itch with "excellent", "very fresh" dishes that "never taste heavy or greasy"; be warned, it can "get crowded", but the takeout is always an easy option.

L Street Diner [S] [M] ▽ 17 | 10 | 14 | $15

108 L St. (bet. 4th & 5th Sts.), South Boston, 617-268-1155

■ "If you're in the neighborhood", consider visiting this "solid" South Boston diner, which features "big portions" of "cheap" Traditional American eats, along with pizzas, pastas and a "nice", hearty Irish breakfast.

Lucia's Ristorante [M] 18 | 16 | 18 | $30

415 Hanover St. (Harris St.), 617-367-2353 [S]

53 Mt. Vernon St. (bet. Main & Washington Sts.), Winchester, 781-729-0515

◪ Patrons like that they can "usually get in" to this pair of North End and Winchester Italians, which feature homestyle fare prepared with "a special flair" and delivered by an "attentive" staff; while both branches boast fresco renditions of the Sistine Chapel's ceiling, Winchester has the added allure of an enoteca (wine cellar).

Lucky Garden [S] [M] ▽ 12 | 7 | 13 | $16

282 Concord Ave. (Huron Ave.), Cambridge, 617-354-9514

◪ "Very basic" is about the best respondents can say about this plain-Jane Cambridge Chinese noted more for its "family-friendly atmosphere" and "fast delivery" than for its "mediocre" dishes.

LUMIÈRE [S] 26 | 24 | 25 | $44

1293 Washington St. (Waltham St.), West Newton, 617-244-9199

■ "The brightest light" in the suburbs may well be this "small", cozy Contemporary French bistro in West Newton that turns out "straightforward", "absolutely delicious" cuisine ("try the sea scallops"), paired with a "dynamite" wine list and served by an "excellent" staff; the "upbeat" interior features cream-colored walls, whimsical light fixtures and an open kitchen that "radiates warmth."

Lyceum Bar & Grill 🅂🅜   22 | 20 | 20 | $30
43 Church St. (Washington St.), Salem,
978-745-7665
■ Quite possibly "Salem's best", this "comfortably elegant"
Contemporary American delivers "consistently delicious"
victuals, including an "awesome" portobello signature
appetizer, to locals who appreciate the "gracious" staff
that "aims to please" and the "moderate prices."

Maddie's Sail Loft 🅂🅜⇗   ▽ 13 | 10 | 15 | $20
15 State St. (bet. Front & Washington Sts.), Marblehead,
781-631-9824
◩ "Famous" for its potent "monster cocktails" mixed at a
"comfortable bar" that attracts "friendly people", this
"old Marblehead hangout" is less renowned for its "large
portions" of "simple" (often fried) seafood, though tipplers
who are "pleasantly drunk" don't much mind.

Maggiano's Little Italy 🅂🅜   – | – | – | M
4 Columbus Ave. (Arlington St.), 617-542-3456
Red-and-white checked tablecloths and Sinatra-esque
background music set the Mulberry Street tone at this new
Theater District link in the Italian chain; the large room is
made warmer with oversized booths and a homey approach,
meaning all the staples arrive in bountiful portions.

Ma Glockner's 🅂   ▽ 18 | 11 | 16 | $18
151 Maple St. (Rtes. 126 & 140), Bellingham, 508-966-1085
◩ This "cheap" "old favorite" in Bellingham is famed for
two things on its "family-style" Traditional American menu –
namely, the "hallmark" 'birched chicken' and the "excellent
cinnamon buns" ("just thinking about them puts on the
pounds"), reason enough for most to conclude that this
place is "still aging well."

Magnolia's Southern Cuisine   21 | 17 | 20 | $28
1193 Cambridge St. (Tremont St.), Cambridge, 617-576-1971
■ "Rhett Butler would surely give a damn" about the
"unusual combinations" of "Southern comfort food" at
this "small", recently redecorated Cambridge "sleeper",
which specializes in New Orleans–style cuisine; it's a
"welcoming" "change in Yankee country", especially
"during crawfish season" (January–June).

Maharaja's 🅂🅜   ▽ 16 | 7 | 16 | $15
2088 Mass Ave. (Walden St.), Cambridge,
617-492-9538
◩ A modest "storefront setting" in a "slightly off-the-beaten-
path" location in Cambridge means this Indian usually
"doesn't get crowded", which is just fine with those who
count on it as a "cheap", "reliably good" choice.

MAISON ROBERT Ⓜ 24 | 24 | 24 | $48
Old City Hall, 45 School St. (bet. Tremont & Washington Sts.),
617-227-3370
◪ "*C'est magnifique!*" declare devotees of this Old City Hall
Classic French where Jacky Robert crafts "top-notch"
preparations, the "professional" staff "pampers" all and the
"magnificent" peach-colored, crystal chandelier–graced
"formal" room exudes pure "elegance"; dissenters,
however, cite a "stodgy" ambiance, but they're far outvoted
by those who relish it as a special-occasion "favorite."

MAMMA MARIA Ⓢ Ⓜ 25 | 23 | 23 | $42
3 North Sq. (bet. Little Prince & North Sts.), 617-523-0077
■ "Talk about a deceptive name" – there's "nary a straw
Chianti bottle" in sight at this North End Italian, which
"deserves all its accolades" on the strength of "flawlessly
executed" cuisine, "regal" service and a "romantic"
atmosphere (especially if you "try the upstairs porch");
moreover, they "honor reservations to the minute."

Manhattan Sammy's Deli Ⓜ ▽ 18 | 7 | 13 | $12
1 Kendall Sq. (bet. Broadway & Hampshire St.),
Cambridge, 617-252-0044
◪ "Like a classic NYC deli", this Cambridge shop delivers
"great" pickles, big sandwiches and "terrific" knishes;
but unlike many of its Big Apple counterparts, it also
features healthier stuff like veggie burgers, grilled on the
warm-weather outdoor patio.

Marcellino Ⓜ 19 | 15 | 18 | $29
16 Cooper St. (Pine St.), Waltham, 781-647-5458
◪ A "convenient" location "near the movie theater" and a
"nice terrace" make this Waltham Italian a "popular place"
for "exceptional wood-fired specialties", particularly the
"excellent lamb and beef"; the unimpressed, however,
feel the "open" interior is "somewhat austere."

Marché Boston ◖ Ⓢ Ⓜ 16 | 18 | 13 | $20
Prudential Ctr., 800 Boylston St. (Huntington Ave.), 617-578-9700
◪ This multilevel Swiss import in the Prudential Center
allows patrons to "take a trip around the world" with an
International array of "jazzed-up" food stations that stock
everything from sushi to "yummy" crêpes; while this
"gimmick works" for some, others find the setup "confusing"
and "not worth" the self-service "hassle."

Marcuccio's Ⓢ Ⓜ 24 | 20 | 21 | $36
125 Salem St. (bet. Parmenter & Prince Sts.), 617-723-1807
◪ "One of the top restaurants in the North End", this "slightly
hidden" Italian features an "innovative" menu that goes from
"strength to strength", notably "signature dishes that are off
the chart" (don't miss the "heavenly sea bass"); factor in
a "nice view" of the open kitchen and a "perfect, leisurely
ambiance" and you have a "trendy" crowd "favorite."

Marino Ristorante [S] [M] 21 | 19 | 19 | $30
2465 Mass Ave. (bet. Porter Sq. & Washburn St.), Cambridge, 617-868-5454
◪ "Really fresh" organic vegetables grown on the owner's farm are one reason why this "loud", "hectic" Cambridge Italian is "worth a detour" from the North End; P.S. reward yourself with the "to-die-for tiramisu."

Marketplace Cafe & Grill [M] – | – | – | M
300 Faneuil Hall Mktpl. (Quincy Mkt.), 617-227-1272
Reverting back to a former name and menu format, this bi-level Contemporary American located in the North building of bustling Faneuil Hall attracts both tourists and natives with a pleasant cafe on the ground floor and a trendier grill upstairs; expect a lively crowd at happy hour.

Marrakesh [S] 18 | 15 | 19 | $21
561 Cambridge St. (7th St.), Cambridge, 617-497-1614
◪ The no-shoes policy in the back room means you should "wash your socks" before dining at this "colorful" Cambridge Moroccan, which "lives up to its authentic" billing and "should be better known" according to insiders who've sampled the *b'steeya* and "sensational *tagines*."

Mary Chung [S] [M] ≠ 20 | 8 | 15 | $17
464 Mass Ave. (Central Sq.), Cambridge, 617-864-1991
■ "Spicy is for real" at this Central Square Chinese "institution", which gets kudos for its "awesome" noodles and weekend dim sum; the "cramped" "basement location" isn't a selling point, but that doesn't deter supporters from calling this "one of the best" outside of Chinatown.

Masa [M] – | – | – | E
(fka South End Grill)
439 Tremont St. (Appleton St.), 617-338-8884
This newcomer adds Southwestern flair to the South End with Mexican-inspired dishes (e.g. tequila-marinated Gulf shrimp, salmon with chipotle) spicing up the menu; earth tones and mahogany beams contribute to the rustic charm, and the lounge is one of the area's finest.

Ma Soba [S] [M] – | – | – | M
156 Cambridge St. (Hancock St.), 617-973-6680
The name means 'my noodle', and this Beacon Hill rookie lives up to it with a menu encompassing noodles of the Japanese, Thai, Korean and Chinese varieties; also on offer are sushi and dim sum, all designed to popularize Pan-Asian for the Mass General and State House clientele.

Massimino's Cucina Italia [S] [M] 22 | 14 | 18 | $26
207 Endicott St. (Commercial St.), 617-523-5959
■ Arrive early to "beat the rush" at this "great little" family Italian located at the "edge of the North End"; the "modest" *cucina* offers an extensive "variety of dishes", but first-timers should consider the veal chop, the house specialty.

Matteo's S – – – M
51 Lincoln St. (Columbus St.), Newton Highlands,
617-965-3100
This cozy streetfront cafe on a Newton Highlands corner
focuses on modern Italian with a vigorous nod toward the
classics; specialties like pizza, winter lasagna and grilled
steaks are complemented by a Tuscan-accented wine list.

Matt Murphy's Pub S M ⊘ 21 17 16 $19
14 Harvard St. (Kent St.), Brookline, 617-232-0188
■ "On a cold winter's night", stop by this "small", "authentic
Irish pub" in Brookline and soak in the "warm, friendly"
atmosphere while enjoying the "perfect pint" of Guinness
and "unexpectedly" "great food" – "earthy" housemade
bread, "fantastic" soups and "the best shepherd's pie
anywhere"; N.B. it's smoke-free too.

MAURIZIO'S S 25 16 21 $30
364 Hanover St. (Clark St.), 617-367-1123
■ "Bring a date" to this "first-rate" North End Italian-
Mediterranean where chef Maurizio Loddo is "actually at
the stove," preparing the "world's best bruschetta" and
appetizers "so huge you have to make room" for his "terrific
Sardinian" specialties; it's "cramped", but the "attentive"
staff helps compensate, and they "accept reservations."

Medieval Manor ◐ S M 9 17 14 $30
246 E. Berkeley St. (bet. Albany St. & Harrison Ave.),
617-423-4900
■ "Go for the entertainment, not the food" at this medieval-
themed dinner theater in the South End; the Traditional
American fare is pretty "lousy", but some say the "engaging
show" makes for a "fun outing" "with a group"; even so, "if
you've seen the show once, there's no reason to go back."

Metropolis Cafe S M 24 19 21 $36
584 Tremont St. (bet. Clarendon & Dartmouth Sts.),
617-247-2931
■ Chef-owners Seth and Shari Woods garner heaps of
praise for their "quintessential" New American–Eclectic in
the South End, which highlights "fantastic", "creative" fare
at dinnertime (including "heavenly" pastas), a "wonderful"
weekend brunch and an "excellent" wine list; though the
"tiny", "funky", boutique-style storefront is "cramped", this
"neighborhood gem" warrants a visit.

Middle East ◐ S M 15 12 13 $16
4 Brookline St. (Central Sq.), Cambridge, 617-354-8238
472 Mass Ave. (Brookline St.), Cambridge, 617-492-9181
▨ An "under-30" crowd grooves to the "quirky" combination
of "quick", "cheap" Middle Eastern fare and "great bands"
offered at these "late-night" Cambridge clubs with lots of
"rock 'n' roll atmosphere"; critics, however, gripe that the
food is a "perfunctory" "afterthought" to the music.

Midwest Grill ◐ [S] [M] — 19 | 11 | 19 | $23

1124 Cambridge St. (bet. Elm & Norfolk Sts.), Cambridge, 617-354-7536

■ Cambridge residents are more than willing to forgive this rodizio-style Brazilian's "misleading name" once they sample the extensive variety ("BBQ chicken hearts", anyone?) and "endless" parade of "delicious" meats; solid service and live music help offset the unimpressive decor.

Mike's City Diner [S] [M] — 18 | 11 | 18 | $14

1714 Washington St. (Mass Ave.), 617-267-9393

■ A "great mix of people" flocks to this three-meal-a-day South End "greasy spoon", "one of a handful of true diners left", for "massive portions" of "basics" including hand-carved "ham as it should be"; but "beware of long lines" because more and more locals are discovering it.

Milano's Italian Kitchen [S] [M] — 14 | 13 | 15 | $23

47 Newbury St. (Berkeley St.), 617-267-6150

◪ This Newbury Street Italian serves standard "boilerplate" fare, but its prices are "moderate" and it also features "sidewalk seating that's ideal for people-watching."

Milk Street Cafe [M] — 17 | 10 | 13 | $13

Post Office Sq. (bet. Congress & Franklin Sts.), 617-350-7275
50 Milk St. (Devonshire St.), 617-542-3663

◪ "Good" dairy kosher food can be hard to find, but some surveyors recommend these "quick" Downtown lunch spots, which offer a rotating roster of "high-quality" sandwiches, soups and salads.

Ming Garden [S] [M] — 16 | 13 | 15 | $19

1262 Boylston St. (opp. Star Mkt.), Chestnut Hill, 617-232-4848

◪ For those who want to fill up on Asian chow cheaply and "don't want to go to Chinatown", consider this Chestnut Hill Chinese for the "all-you-can-eat dim sum buffet" on weekends; otherwise, the food is just "average."

Miracle of Science Bar + Grill [S] [M] — 18 | 17 | 16 | $17

321 Mass Ave. (State St.), Cambridge, 617-868-2866

■ This "MIT bar" and grill near Central Square attracts a "scholastic but hip" "twentysomething" crowd with "après-research drinks" and a "limited (though high-quality)" menu, particularly a burger that "deserves Nobel consideration."

MISTRAL [S] [M] — 25 | 25 | 23 | $54

223 Columbus Ave. (Berkeley St.), 617-867-9300

◪ Straddling the Back Bay and the South End is this "electric" Provençal destination, often "filled at midnight on a Wednesday" with a "trendy" "power" crowd, thanks to a room that's "one of the most beautiful in Boston", as well as "excellent" cuisine prepared by "talented chef" Jamie Mammano; so "dress to impress", "bring $$$" and prepare for a major "people-watching" "scene."

Montien SM
21   17   19 $23
63 Stuart St. (bet. Tremont & Washington Sts.),
617-338-5600
■ "Glad they rebuilt after the fire" declare the many fans
of this "friendly", smartly refurbished Thai "conveniently"
located in the Theater District; it remains a "reliable" choice
for a "very good" weekday lunch or pre-performance dinner.

Moon Villa ●SM
14   8   14 $18
19 Edinboro St. (bet. Essex & Kingston Sts.), 617-423-2061
◪ It's 3 AM, "you've had a long night" of drinking and now
you have the munchies — so follow partiers in the know to
this "cheap" Chinatown Chinese that's "always packed";
the food might be merely "decent" during the day, but at
this hour "everything tastes good."

MORTON'S OF CHICAGO SM
25   19   23 $50
1 Exeter Plaza (Boylston St.), 617-266-5858
■ "Perfectly grilled steaks" draw in the "expense-account"
set to this Back Bay chain meat emporium; even though
critical carnivores complain about the "dark", "smoky" and
"claustrophobic" "basement-level" venue, that doesn't
prevent them from lingering over the Godiva cake, "a
chocolate lover's dream."

Mother Anna's SM
20   14   18 $26
211 Hanover St. (Cross St.), 617-523-8496
■ "Old and wise" is how pasta *paesani* refer to this longtime
North End Italian known for housemade favorites including
manicotti and "must-try" lobster ravioli; detractors insist
the room needs a "complete makeover", but the "personal"
service and "cheery" atmosphere more than compensate.

Mr. & Mrs. Bartley's Burger Cottage M≠
20   12   14 $12
1246 Mass Ave. (bet. Bow St. & Plympton Ave.),
Cambridge, 617-354-6559
■ "Awesome", "greasy" burgers (one of the "best in
Boston"), "fab onion rings" and "great lime rickeys" make a
visit worthwhile to this "cheap" Harvard Square American
"institution", which attracts a "student-oriented" crowd that
feels right at home in the "dark", "college-hideout" digs.

Museum of Fine Arts Restaurant SM
19   21   17 $30
Museum of Fine Arts, 465 Huntington Ave. (Museum Rd.),
617-369-3474
◪ The "interesting" New American menu "changes along
with the exhibits" at this second-floor room at the MFA,
which now sports a "refreshing new look", making it more
than ever a "convenient", "pleasant respite"; while some
feel it's become "pricey for the teeny portions", more think
that they do a "fine job for a captive audience."

Naked Fish S M   – – – M

Faneuil Hall Mktpl., 16-18 North St. (Union St.), 617-742-3333
48 Whiting St./Rte. 53 (bet. Accord Ln. & Pond St.),
Hingham, 781-740-0880
215 Broadway/Rte. 1 N. (bet. Carpenter & Daly Rds.),
Lynnfield, 781-586-8300
1114 Beacon St. (bet. Acacia & Reservoir Aves.), Newton,
617-965-0110
516 Adams St. (Furnace Brook Pkwy.), Quincy,
617-745-9700
455 Totten Pond Rd. (3rd Ave.), Waltham, 781-684-0500
95A Turnpike Rd. (Rte. 9), Westborough, 508-366-5959
This fishy chainlet launched by Joey Crugnale specializes
in wood-fired seafood and meats grilled with Latin flair;
spawning throughout the region, five new branches opened
post-*Survey*, from Lynnfield to Hingham.

Nara M   ▽ 20 12 18 $22

85 Wendell St. (Broad St.), 617-338-5935
◪ This "homey sushi nook" in the Financial District is
"hidden" in an alley off Broad Street, but some say it's
"worth the effort to find" because of its "good, traditional
Japanese fare"; "fast service" counts as much as "location"
when you're doing a quick "business lunch."

Narita Japanese Restaurant S M   ▽ 20 14 17 $22

18 Eliot St. (JFK St.), Cambridge, 617-868-2226
◪ Sushiphiles submit mixed reports on this Harvard Square
Japanese – "passable" vs. "outstanding"; what's certain is
that it's a "quiet place" with an "innovative" selection and
"fun staff", leading some to consider it a find in Cambridge.

Neighborhood Restaurant &   19 9 14 $14
Bakery S M ⇼

25 Bow St. (Union Sq.), Somerville, 617-623-9710
■ "Ridiculously large breakfasts" are the forte of this Union
Square Portuguese diner famous for its "fluffy eggs" and
waffles; "no decor" means the only ambiance is found
outdoors "under the grape arbor", which many laud as
"lovely" "in the summertime."

New Asia S M   15 11 15 $16

194 Mass Ave. (Lake St.), Arlington, 781-643-6364
93 Trapelo Rd. (Common St.), Belmont, 617-484-7000
180 Endicott St. (opp. Liberty Tree Mall), Danvers,
978-774-8080
211 Mass Ave. (Park Ave.), Lexington, 718-863-5533
328 Somerville Ave. (Union Sq.), Somerville, 617-628-7100
◪ In the 'burbs, this chain of "basic Chinese" satisfies
with a "buffet for big eaters" that's a "reliable standby";
dishes are "hit or miss", but "the price is right" if your
"expectations aren't too high."

New Bridge Cafe [S] [M] ≠ 20 | 7 | 13 | $17

650 Washington Ave. (Woodlawn Ave.), Chelsea, 617-884-0134

■ In spite of the "roughing-it" atmosphere, Chelsea steak hounds stand by their cafe ("I don't care what you say, I love it and have for 22 years"); even though the "no-class" service runs neck-and-neck with the "seedy" decor, devotees can't say enough about the "simple" BBQ and "best steak tips in the world."

New Mother India [S] [M] 21 | 16 | 19 | $21

336 Moody St. (Main St.), Waltham, 781-893-3311

◪ Decor "more Waltham than Bombay" sets this suburban Indian kitchen squarely on Moody Street, where patrons show equal enthusiasm for the "delicately spiced" food (especially the "great lunch buffet") and "huge beer selection"; even if the staff can be "slow", it's "always gracious", leaving "problem" parking as the only drawback.

New Shanghai [S] [M] 23 | 14 | 19 | $21

21 Hudson St. (bet. Beach & Kneeland Sts.), 617-338-6688

■ "Tablecloths in Chinatown?" marvel surveyors who line up at lunchtime for "addictive" eggplant and "many lobster selections"; any questions about authentic "tradition" amid the relative "sophistication" are resolved when you look at the menu that's "not translated for you."

New Yorker Diner [S] [M] ≠ ▽ 14 | 9 | 14 | $12

39 Mt. Auburn St. (Summer St.), Watertown, 617-924-9772

◪ "Everybody's got to love a diner like this" predict fans who place short orders for "short money" at this "cheerful" Watertown joint with "great breakfasts" and jukeboxes that add to the "classic diner experience"; N.B. it closes at 2 PM daily but reopens Thursday–Saturday from 10:30 PM–4 AM.

Nicole Ristorante [S] ▽ 20 | 17 | 19 | $28

54 Salem St. (bet. Cross & Parmenter Sts.), 617-742-6999

■ "Home cooking par excellence" distinguishes this "splendid little" North Ender known for "traditional Italian" ("actually, too traditional" for a few) where the owner "comes to your table" and "makes you feel like family"; a "pleasant atmosphere" and "accommodating" staff help diners overlook tables "too close for comfort."

Noble House [S] [M] 19 | 18 | 18 | $24

1306 Beacon St. (Harvard St.), Brookline, 617-232-9580

◪ This "noble but pricey" Brookline Chinese earns kudos for cooking that's "fairly creative" and "flavorful"; the owner "takes care of his regular customers", and the "civilized" Coolidge Corner setting and "soothing service" ensure that most patrons are "always content", although a few naysayers find it "wonderful sometimes, indifferent others."

No Name [S][M]⊘ 15 | 8 | 13 | $19

15 Fish Pier (Northern Ave.), 617-338-7539

◪ "No frills, no fuss", "no decor, no name" sum up this "cheap" "relic" of a waterfronter that draws "busloads of tourists"; reactions to the "everything-is-fried" seafood range from "disappointing" to "delicious."

NO. 9 PARK [M] 25 | 22 | 23 | $52

9 Park St. (bet. Beacon & Tremont Sts.), 617-742-9991

■ A "smashing success" is how fans of chef Barbara Lynch (ex Galleria Italiana) characterize this "serene", "tastefully understated" European set in a "charming" parkside location by the State House, where "movers and shakers" congregate and ponder whether the "original and tempting" menu is more "French or Italian"; a minority throws darts at "tiny portions" and "so-so service."

North East Brewing Co. [S][M] 16 | 17 | 17 | $20

1314 Commonwealth Ave. (Harvard St.), Allston, 617-566-6699

◪ The "great selection" of brews "is the star" at this Allston suds house that also features "pretty good basic food" and live entertainment, making it a "fun twentysomething hangout"; many praise the "ski-lodge" setting, but some sniff it's "a beer joint trying to be a gourmet restaurant."

Not Your Average Joe's [S][M] 16 | 16 | 16 | $21

1138 Worcester Rd./Rte. 9 (Temple St.), Framingham, 508-875-9929

105 Chapel St. (bet. Great Plain Ave. & May St.), Needham, 781-453-9300

15 Mazzeo Dr. (Rte. 6), Randolph, 781-986-2900

55 Main St. (Galen St.), Watertown, 617-926-9229

◪ Despite its name, "very average" is the consensus on this "funky", colorful suburban minichain that has a "diverse menu" noted for its "good variety of pizzas"; it's "decent for families" and it's a popular "place to meet after work", so don't be surprised if it's "crowded" and "loud."

OAK ROOM, THE [S][M] 25 | 27 | 25 | $55

Fairmont Copley Plaza, 138 St. James Ave. (bet. Dartmouth & Trinity Sts.), 617-267-5300

■ "Classic steak" is the forte of this "pricey", "traditional favorite" in Copley Square, set in an "elegant", "old-world" room that's "one of the most beautiful spots in the city"; "gracious service" is another reason it's popular for "special occasions" among an "older" crowd.

Ocean Wealth ◐[S][M] 21 | 10 | 14 | $22

8 Tyler St. (Beach St.), 617-423-1338

◪ "What they do with lobster and shrimp is amazing" marvel admirers of this Chinatown Chinese known for "good, fresh fish" and "unusual selections from a huge menu"; "don't be bashful" about testing the "imaginative seafood", even if you find it tough to "ignore" decor that "could use sprucing up."

O'Fado 🅂🅜   ▽ 17 | 13 | 16 | $22
72 Walnut St. (Harris St.), Peabody, 978-531-7369

◪ Some surveyors call this Peabody Portuguese an "excellent" "find" that's "nice for a change", with "good fish dishes" and "reasonable" prices; but a vocal minority grouses that the fare is "too heavy" and the room "too dark"; your call.

Olé, Mexican Grille 🅜   21 | 16 | 17 | $19
203A Broadway (bet. Adams & Foster Sts.), Arlington, 781-643-2299 🖃
11 Springfield St. (bet. Beacon & Cambridge Sts.), Cambridge, 617-492-4495 🅂

■ These "hopping" fiesta spots in Arlington and Inman Square are making their marks with "cliche-free", "tasty, healthy Mexican" that's "more interesting" than most others of the genre; the "low-key setting" has a "funky" feel, but as the room's "a little small", expect a wait.

OLIVES 🅜   27 | 22 | 22 | $48
10 City Sq. (bet. Main & Park Sts.), Charlestown, 617-242-1999

◪ "Every bite introduces something new" at the popular Charlestown headquarters of chef Todd English, whose unique brand of Mediterranean involves an "enormous menu" of "complex combinations", resulting in "layers and layers of flavors" that most call "exquisite" but a few find "over the top"; the "casual", "beautiful" room is another crowd-pleaser, though even devotees are irked by the "no-reservations" policy (for parties fewer than six) that creates "mob-scene" waits.

Omonia 🅂   18 | 16 | 19 | $26
75 S. Charles St. (Stuart St.), 617-426-4310

◪ This "undiscovered" gem in the Theater District is a "great Greek find" in a city with "too few" places for "classy" yet "down-home" standards like moussaka; the "range of choice is not great", but the cooking is "solid."

On The Park 🅂   22 | 17 | 20 | $28
1 Union Park (Shawmut Ave.), 617-426-0862

■ "Get in line" for the weekend "pilgrimage" to this "colorful" neighborhood Eclectic bistro near Union Park in the South End for what admirers claim is "the best brunch in the city"; the "limited" dinner menu is "upscale but not too expensive", and the "warm decor" and "intimate" ambiance make it a "perfect date restaurant."

Original Sports Saloon ◖🅂🅜   16 | 12 | 15 | $20
Copley Square Hotel, 47 Huntington Ave. (Exeter St.), 617-536-1904

◪ Sports and 'cue fans cheer for the "good" ribs and brisket at this Back Bay hotel, though spoilers say if you're "not here to watch sports on TV, you may be disappointed."

Oskar's Ⓜ　　　　18　19　16　$30
107 South St. (Kneeland St), 617-542-6756

◪ A "tasty", "creative" midday "winner" for Leather District lunchers, this New American transforms at nightfall to a "place to see and be seen", where a tattooed "Generation X hangs out" in a "great pool room" with a "New Yorkey feel"; but don't overlook the "unexpectedly good food" and "private booths" in the dining room.

Other Side Cosmic Cafe Ⓢ Ⓜ ⊘　　17　15　11　$13
407 Newbury St. (Mass Ave.), 617-536-9477

◪ There's "crunchy food for the Urban Outfitter set" at this Newbury Street haunt where an "eclectic crowd" hangs out for sandwiches "the size of your head" and "interesting people-watching"; some denounce it as an "overpriced deli" with a "poor selection", but free spirits celebrate a "surviving independent coffee shop."

Pagliuca's Ⓢ Ⓜ　　　　22　13　19　$22
14 Parmenter St. (Hanover St.), 617-367-1504

◪ Visitors to the North End appreciate this Southern Italian "family place" where they can always get a "real old-fashioned" meal (don't miss the "best white clam sauce around"); it's not much to look at, but the occasional accordion player is "great" and adds a "romantic" note.

Palenque Ⓢ　　　　　19　13　20　$20
300 Beacon St. (Eustis St.), Somerville, 617-491-1004

◪ This Somerville Mexican delivers a "special experience" in a "hidden away" location that promises "very good" south-of-the-border staples; generous patrons praise the "quaint", "soothing room" with "unique decor", though perhaps they've been charmed by a staff that "cares for you like family", because others cite a merely "dark" space.

Palm Restaurant Ⓢ Ⓜ　　　19　17　19　$47
Westin Hotel, 200 Dartmouth St. (bet. St. James Ave. & Stuart St.), 617-867-9292

◪ "Caricatures on the wall" reflect the city's "very male" "power brokers" who frequent this Copley branch of the national steakhouse chain in the Westin Hotel; the buzz is that it's "best for a business lunch", with "good, basic" carnivorous standbys, as well as "a lot of non-meat options", though its "sterile decor" (with booths like "cubicles") denies it placement in the "top tier of steak rooms."

Pandan Leaf Ⓢ Ⓜ　　　18　15　18　$22
250 Harvard St. (Coolidge Corner), Brookline, 617-566-9393

◪ "Lucky Coolidge Corner" say fans of this Malaysian offering "a nice alternative" to the mundane with "sizzling tastes" and "unusual flavors"; although "crowded", the ambiance is "pleasant" thanks to "enthusiastic service", but experienced patrons advise "it can be a gamble" – so "go with someone who knows the menu."

Pandorga's S   ▽ 18 | 12 | 21 | $19
170 Willow St. (bet. Main & River Sts.), Waltham,
781-647-9270
■ Go figure – an "Ecuadoran hideaway" has won over
Waltham with "great South American" home cooking in a
"wonderful, warm, family-run place"; but while decor scores
indicate that "ambiance is lacking", the "charming staff"
and "terrific" owners create a "quaint and cozy" feel.

Papa Razzi S M   16 | 16 | 17 | $25
271 Dartmouth St. (bet. Boylston & Newbury Sts.),
617-536-9200
2 Wall St. (Rte. 3A), Burlington, 781-229-0100
Cambridgeside Galleria, 100 Cambridgeside Pl. (Memorial Dr.),
Cambridge, 617-577-0009
Chestnut Hill Mall, 199 Boylston St. (Rte. 9), Chestnut Hill,
617-527-6600
768 Elm St. (Baker Ave.), Concord, 978-371-0030
16 Washington St. (Rte. 16), Wellesley, 781-235-4747
■ Expect "basic Italian" at this "good-value" minichain with
branches in Boston and the 'burbs that delivers "consistent
pizzas and pastas" in "simple yet modern" settings that
are "pleasant", if "kinda boring"; the upshot: the "price is
right" for "pedestrian Italian."

Parker's Restaurant ● S M   18 | 22 | 20 | $39
Omni Parker House, 60 School St. (Tremont St.),
617-227-8600
■ Set in the Omni Parker House, this "old, traditional
restaurant" is long renowned for classic New England fare
like lobster, Boston cream pie and "tons of Parker House
rolls" (legend has it that the latter two items were invented
here); the "dignified setting" received a boost from a recent
rehab, leading loyalists primarily of a certain age to assert
"when you want good and fancy, go here."

Parrish Cafe ● S M   20 | 14 | 15 | $19
361 Boylston St. (Arlington St.), 617-247-4777
■ A "must-stop for sandwich aficionados", this Back Bay
cafe offers what fans swear is the "best selection on the
East Coast", with recipes contributed from some of the
city's top chefs; "cramped seating is a drawback" (as is
"slow service"), but patrons applaud the "cool concept"
and "yummy combinations."

Passage to India S M   ▽ 16 | 11 | 15 | $17
Porter Sq., 1900 Mass Ave., Cambridge, 617-497-6113
■ The "friendly staff" and "good, consistent Indian" food are
the hallmarks of this "nice curry house" in Porter Square,
but the "bright white" decor is not especially enhanced
by the "random yard-sale art" on the walls; though it may
be "typical", it's a "safe bet for a decent meal."

Pat's Pushcart | 20 | 12 | 20 | $23
61 Endicott St. (Cross St.), 617-523-9616
◪ You can "smell the garlic before you even walk in the door" at this "crowded", "homey" North End Italian "hole-in-the-wall" with a "family feel" where there's "always a good meal" to be had; "if you can get there" past the Big Dig, it's "worth the hike."

Peach Farm ◐ [S] [M] | 21 | 7 | 14 | $20
4 Tyler St. (Beach St.), 617-482-1116
◪ "Good food, no atmosphere" is the consensus on this Chinatowner that's "as hot to locals as [it is to] outsiders" thanks to specialties like "fresh and tasty" fried squid and "sublime" ginger lobster; though a few "don't get the hype" and pan the "lousy decor", it's "always crowded" with those hungry for "excellent" Cantonese seafood.

Peking Cuisine [S] [M] | ▽ 19 | 14 | 18 | $20
10 Tyler St. (Kneeland St.), 617-542-5857
870 Walnut St. (Beacon St.), Newton, 617-969-0888
◪ "Dumplings to die for" warrant repeat visits to both the "authentic" Chinatown hub and its Newton spin-off; night owls who like the "fresh-tasting" fare and "fun, eclectic atmosphere" have basically one gripe – it "closes too early", unlike most other Downtowners.

Pellino's [S] [M] | ▽ 24 | 18 | 23 | $34
261 Washington St. (bet. Atlantic Ave. & Pleasant St.), Marblehead, 781-631-3344
■ "Maybe the best restaurant in Marblehead", this "consistent local favorite" wins over the North Shore set with modern Italian specials like garlic-crusted rack of lamb and "fresh" ravioli; an "outstanding wine list" and "friendly, knowledgeable staff" further secure its status, though a few feel it's "worthy of a better space" than this "crowded, noisy" locale.

Penang ◐ [S] [M] | 22 | 19 | 17 | $22
685 Washington St. (Kneeland St.), 617-451-6373
◪ A "Malaysian Disney World" is how some characterize this "hip" "gift from NYC to Boston" serving "mildly to wildly exotic" fare in a "cool", "jazzy space" in Chinatown; though "daring" diners (the majority) praise the menu as "dead-on authentic", "outstanding and affordable", a timid few find it "too adventurous", with service that runs hot and cold.

P. F. Chang's [S] [M] | 19 | 20 | 19 | $25
8 Park Plaza (bet. Boylston & Stuart Sts.), 617-573-0821
◪ "Filling a void in the Theater District", this "new twist on Asian cuisine" offers a "large" selection of "surprisingly tasty", "hearty and exotic" Chinese fare in a "spectacular room" that draws a Commons-area "after-work crowd", as well as "tourists"; but the unconvinced growl "phoney" – "why bother when Chinatown is three blocks away?"

Phoenicia [S] [M] ▽ 17 | 10 | 17 | $22

240 Cambridge St. (Garden St.), 617-523-4606

◪ Tucked into the side of Beacon Hill, this "good Lebanese" specializes in "yummy" "Middle Eastern comfort food" like "always-fresh tabbouleh"; for many it's a "very acceptable supper spot", although a "disappointed" few find it "tired."

Pho Pasteur [S] [M] 21 | 12 | 16 | $17

682 Washington St. (Beach St.), 617-482-7467
119 Newbury St. (bet. Clarendon & Dartmouth Sts.), 617-262-8200
123 Stuart St. (Tremont St.), 617-742-2436
137 Brighton Ave. (Harvard Ave.), Allston, 617-783-2340
35 Dunster St. (Mt. Auburn St.), Cambridge, 617-864-4100

■ When you "don't feel like cooking", head to one of these "incredibly fresh" Vietnamese eateries for "heaping bowls" of "delicious, addictive" soups; if the setting is "utilitarian", whaddaya want when it's so "unbelievably cheap"?

Pho République ◐ [S] [M] 20 | 17 | 17 | $21

1415 Washington St. (Union Park), 617-262-0005

◪ Though its "cool" Cambridge digs were destroyed by a fire, this "funky" French-Vietnamese lives on in a "quirky" storefront in the South End where the "creative appetizers" rival the "tasty" *pho* and noodle dishes; the "phun setting" bubbles with "dramatic effects", but cynics who find the fare "bland" insist it "should be called Faux Republic."

Piccola Luna [S] 21 | 17 | 19 | $30

(fka Moon Woman Cafe)

108 Oak St. (bet. Chestnut St. & Highland Ave.), Newton, 617-630-9569

■ Newton fans call the "renovation a success" at this Stellina sibling earning bravos for "great, healthy" Italian dishes such as "incredible risottos" and "tasty pastas"; regulars advise "go early."

Piccola Venezia [S] [M] 17 | 15 | 17 | $24

263 Hanover St. (bet. Cross & Richmond Sts.), 617-523-3888

◪ "Stop – too much food!" cry diners stuffed by the "abundant portions" of "reliable" standards dished out at this "unassuming" North End Italian; still, nostalgists "long for the low-brow appeal of the old location."

Piccolo Nido [M] ▽ 20 | 18 | 22 | $30

257 North St. (Lewis St.), 617-742-4272

◪ The "nicest staff and owner" make this a "great North End secret" where an "accommodating kitchen" turns out fare that's "always good", if "nothing fancy"; but those looking for complexities deem it "not too interesting."

Pignoli [S] [M] 25 | 24 | 22 | $47

79 Park Plaza (Arlington St.), 617-338-7500

◪ For "sophisticated" pre-theater dining in Park Square, head to Lydia Shire's "imaginative Italian" for "great risottos" off a "whimsical" menu; many admire the "artistic use of wood" in the "sleek" dining room, but those who find the decor "weird" may opt to "sit on the terrace in the summertime"; a few think it "tries too hard to be clever" and warn of "spotty" service, but overall, it's "a treat" for most.

Pillar House [M] 22 | 23 | 23 | $41

26 Quinobequin Rd. (bet. Rtes. 16 & 128), Newton, 617-969-6500

◪ An "old" "gloves-and-hat" clientele remains loyal to this "staid dowager" in Newton with "just enough formality to make it special"; but whereas veterans laud the American fare as "impeccable", detractors find it "predictable" and scoff "who ever heard of a restaurant not open on Saturday or Sunday?"

Pit Stop Bar-B-Q ◐ ≠ ▽ 24 | 8 | 21 | $12

888 Morton St. (Evan St.), Mattapan, 617-436-0485

■ Chow down on the "best barbecue around" at this little Mattapan joint famed for its "yummy" ribs, "great pork", "excellent brisket" and peculiar hours ("open only Thursday–Saturday"); there's barely a dining room, so plan on getting your "quick, tasty meal" to go.

Pizzeria Regina [S] [M] ≠ 21 | 9 | 13 | $14

Faneuil Hall Downstairs, 226 Faneuil Hall Mktpl., 617-227-8180
11½ Thatcher St. (N. Margin St.), 617-227-0765
Auburn Mall, 385 S. Bridge St., Auburn, 508-721-0090
South Shore Plaza, Braintree Food Court, Braintree, 781-848-8700
Burlington Mall, Burlington Food Court (Rte. 128), Burlington, 781-270-4212
Solomon Pond Mall, Marlboro Food Court, Marlboro, 508-303-6999

■ According to many connoisseurs, this "classic institution" "brings you back to the North End of the past" with "amazing" "traditional" pies – the "best thin crust" topped with "perfect sauce"; the "surly service" and "sub-shop atmosphere" don't deter those who proclaim this chain "the standard-bearer for pizza", so "get in line early."

Pizzeria Uno ◐ [S] [M] 13 | 12 | 14 | $16

731 Boylston St. (Dartmouth St.), 617-267-8554
1 Brookline Ave. (Kenmore Sq.), 617-262-4911
Faneuil Hall, 22 Clinton St. (North St.), 617-523-5722
280 Huntington Ave. (Gainsborough St.), 617-424-1697
1230 Commonwealth Ave. (Harvard Ave.), Allston, 617-739-0034
250B Granite St. (I-93S, exit 6), Braintree, 781-849-8667

Pizzeria Uno (Cont.)
22 JFK St. (Harvard Sq.), Cambridge, 617-497-1530
820 Somerville Ave. (Porter Sq.), Cambridge, 617-864-1916
194 Endicott St. (Independence Way), Danvers,
978-777-6385
287 Washington St. (Centre St.), Newton, 617-964-2296
Additional locations throughout the Boston area
◪ Specializing in Chicago-style deep-dish pizzas that
regulars insist are "satisfying" even as critics sniff "a long
way from the original", this chain is at least "convenient"
for "decent" "standards"; the "generic" decor, however,
leads some wags to dub it the "Holiday Inn of Italian."

Plaza III - The Kansas City　　21 | 19 | 20 | $37 |
Steakhouse 🆂🅼
Fanueil Hall, 101 S. Market Bldg. (Merchants Row),
617-720-5570
◪ Despite "its touristy location" in Faneuil Hall, this
chophouse "knows how to grill a steak"; head for the
"relaxing" upstairs room (with comfy, oversized booths
and Western decor) to best enjoy "great beef" with all
the trimmings; dissenters, though, cite "ordinary" stuff
and "mixed" service.

Polcari's 🆂🅼　　　　　　17 | 15 | 16 | $23 |
92 Broadway/Rte. 1N, Saugus, 781-233-3765
◪ North Shore supporters find it easy to "pretend they're in
the North End" at this "good all-around Italian" in Saugus,
where the "excellent variety and prices" compensate for
the "warehouse"-like room; others, though, say the pizza is
"good", but the rest of the menu is "nothing special"; still,
it often "gets crowded."

Pomodoro 🆂🅼⇆　　　　24 | 13 | 17 | $31 |
319 Hanover St. (bet. Prince & Richmond Sts.),
617-367-4348
◪ Even though there's "no AC and no bathroom" at this
"tiny" North End Italian, the "cramped" room is "always
packed" ("be prepared to sit on someone's lap") with
regulars who can't get enough of its "outstanding home-
cooked food"; prepare "to wait longer" than estimated by
the "laid-back" staff, but the "phenomenal" fare is "worth it."

Ponte Vecchio 🆂🅼　　　　23 | 18 | 21 | $39 |
435 Newbury St. (Topsfield Fairgrounds), Danvers,
978-777-9188
◪ "Giving strip malls a good name", this "pricey" Danvers
Italian features "consistently" "top-notch" fare (notably a
"great veal chop"), accompanied by a fine wine list; marring
the experience for some, however, is the staff's tendency
to "condone smoking."

Poppa & Goose Ⓜ
17 | 11 | 13 | $16

69 First St. (Spring St.), Cambridge, 617-497-6772

◪ In Cambridge this "good-value" Asian nourishes the MIT crowd with an "exotic and tasty" lunch buffet that offers a "variety" of "great noodle dishes" and vegetarian options; but the "spartan" setting and "almost nonexistent" service lead foes to gripe that it's all about "quantity, not quality."

Porters Bar & Grill Ⓜ
– | – | – | M

173 Portland St. (Causeway St.), 617-742-7678

Upscale for a bar and sporty for a grill, this new Fleet Center–area pub draws an after-work and arena-bound crowd with beer (12 on tap) and American bites; the brick-walled setting serves as a venue for local bands most Friday and Saturday nights.

Pravda 116
– | – | – | E

(fka Mercury Bar)

116 Boylston St. (bet. Charles & Tremont Sts.), 617-482-7799

An alluring Russian vibe predominates at this velvet-curtained Theater District entry with a happening dance club in the rear; the New American menu hints at Slavic chic with sevruga, osetra and beluga by the ounce, while offering mostly the westernized likes of wood-grilled rib eye and Maine lobster.

Prose
▽ 18 | 9 | 16 | $30

352A Mass Ave. (Wyman Terr.), Arlington, 781-648-2800

◪ Arlington admirers are confident that the Eclectic–New American fare "will always be great" at this teeny storefront with an "elegant", if "limited", menu that "varies" daily; but the fact that there's "absolutely no atmosphere" "dampens" the experience for those who wonder whether it warrants the "nervy" prices.

Purple Cactus Burrito & Wrap Bar Ⓢ Ⓜ
17 | 10 | 14 | $11

674 Centre St. (Seaverns Ave.), Jamaica Plain, 617-522-7422

■ While it may be "hard to eat gracefully" at this Jamaica Plain Tex-Mex joint because the "great, fat burritos and wraps" require some heavy lifting, the "fresh and filling" eats are light on the wallet; "when you need good food that's good for you – fast", this mostly take-out bar fits the bill.

RADIUS Ⓜ
26 | 25 | 25 | $57

8 High St. (bet. Federal & Summer Sts.), 617-426-1234

■ Among "the best places in town" is this Financial District "power scene" where chef-partner Michael Schlow (ex Cafe Louis) makes his mark with "daring", "indescribably delicious" Contemporary French fare, "magnificently presented" and served by one of "the best staffs in the city" in an "amazing space" with an "energized atmosphere"; even though it's "obscenely expensive", most rave that "everything is wonderful."

Raffael's S   – | – | – | E

State Street Complex, 1 Enterprise Dr. (Newport Ave.),
North Quincy, 617-328-1600

The panoramic view attracts as much attention as the food at this Quincy penthouse perch with floor-to-ceiling windows overlooking the city skyline; the Continental fare has an Italianate edge, and sleek banquettes and chrome fixtures put deco in the decor; N.B. dinner and Sunday brunch only.

Rangoli S M   22 | 15 | 19 | $19

129 Brighton Ave. (Harvard Ave.), Allston,
617-562-0200

■ "Pick anything on the menu – you can't go wrong" swear advocates of this "superior" Southern Indian in Allston, though the "pleasant" staff will gladly "help you decide" ("don't miss the *dosas*"); a few nitpick about the "too-bright" setting, but most don't mind because this "real taste treat" rewards with "fascinating flavors."

Rasol S M   ▽ 19 | 14 | 18 | $23

308 Main St. (Rte. 60), Malden, 781-388-2448

■ "Better than most Indian restaurants", this Malden "find" is popular for its "excellent lunch buffet", a "tasty" bargain deal at "$5.95 for all you can eat"; furthermore, the service is "quick."

Rattlesnake Bar & Grill ● S M   12 | 11 | 12 | $20

384 Boylston St. (bet. Arlington & Berkeley Sts.),
617-859-8555

☑ "If you're over 22, you may be too old" for the "active" "singles' scene" at this "late-night" Back Bay bar that's more appealing for its "great margaritas" than for its "hit-or-miss" Tex-Mex grub; most "don't go for the eats" but rather for the "fun atmosphere and rooftop deck."

Rauxa S M   22 | 17 | 21 | $36

70 Union Sq. (Washington St.), Somerville,
617-623-9939

☑ "Forget you're in Somerville" and take a "mini-vacation to Spain" at this "mellow" Catalan establishment that delivers "luscious", "unusual" fare; the basement room is either "darkly romantic" or "depressingly cellarlike", but the staff is "warm and genuine"; P.S. "be warned the food is authentically salty."

Rave S M   – | – | – | M

(fka Mildred's)

552 Tremont St. (Clarendon St.), 617-426-0008

The local coffee klatch goes upscale and mod at this South End java junction, which appeals to the trendy with clusters of tables and couches, splashy hues and assorted funky touches; in addition to pastries, the kitchen now supplies breakfast frittatas, soups, salads and other agreeable eats.

Redbones BBQ S M ⊭   22 | 14 | 17 | $20
55 Chester St. (Elm St.), Somerville, 617-628-2200
■ "Don't be afraid to sit up front near the kitchen" advise "addicts" of this "finger-lickin' BBQ joint" in Somerville that's "straight out of the South", because that's the perfect spot to watch the cooks "carve slabs of ribs", "awesome" and "messy"; the room is "no-frills", but it's a "fun dive" that's "a must" for carnivores.

Red Clay S M   ▽ 23 | 26 | 23 | $31
The Atrium, 300 Boylston St. (Rte. 9), Chestnut Hill, 617-965-7000
■ Courtesy of chef Jody Adams (of Rialto), this "classy" Mediterranean addition in the Chestnut Hill Atrium appeals with hearty, gourmet comfort food that's cooked in terra cotta pots; her accessible fare is served in an earth-toned room with an open view of the kitchen, as well as a separate area designed to look like a sidewalk cafe.

Red Raven's Love Noodle ⊭   ▽ 20 | 21 | 19 | $26
75 Congress St. (Derby St.), Salem, 978-745-8558
◪ "Kinky and different", this Salem eatery is "a surprise gem" on the North Shore, turning out "excellent" Eclectic–New American cuisine in an "offbeat setting"; without a doubt, the ambiance here is a "funky" one – "a brassiere marks the door to the women's room."

Restaurant Bricco S M   – | – | – | M
241 Hanover St. (Atlantic Ave.), 617-248-6800
In a sophisticated room with windows that open onto busy Hanover Street and an equally bustling bar, this North End newcomer goes beyond just pastas; expect eclectic, modern Italian-Mediterranean dishes such as grilled octopus, portobello carpaccio and ricotta gnocchi.

Rhythm & Spice S M   18 | 14 | 16 | $20
315 Mass Ave. (Main St.), Cambridge, 617-497-0977
■ "Hey mon, have some conch fritters" say fans of this Central Square Caribbean who like the "friendly" island feel as much as the "scrumptious" jerk chicken and "spicy, spicy, spicy" specials; even if the "decor could be improved", no one minds when the "great" reggae plays.

✱ RIALTO S M   26 | 25 | 24 | $53
Charles Hotel, 1 Bennett St. (Harvard Sq.), Cambridge, 617-661-5050
■ Chef "Jody Adams' jewel", this Cambridge "heavyweight" boasts an "elegant setting that's a perfect foil for the bold flavors" of her "dynamite" Mediterranean interpretations; a "beautiful" venue that's as "high energy" as it is "formal" makes it "the ultimate" "special-event destination"; though it's "getting to be an expense-account type of restaurant", most insist this sheer "bliss" is "worth every penny."

Ristorante Toscano [S] [M] — 22 | 19 | 20 | $45

41-47 Charles St. (Chestnut), 617-723-4090

◪ Voters who "can't get to the North End" go to this "noisy" Charles Street Northern Italian and enjoy a "festive meal" of "superior antipasti" and "perfectly done pastas"; but wallet-watchers feel "you can do much better" elsewhere.

Rita's Place [M] — ▽ 22 | 11 | 19 | $30

88 Winnisimett St. (Williams St.), Chelsea, 617-884-9010

■ "Homemade everything" is the hallmark of this Chelsea Italian that makes you feel "like you're dining in someone's home"; "still great after all these years", this "friendly hole-in-the-wall" offers "wonderful" food, making it a "favorite" among many locals; N.B. beware its limited hours.

Ritz-Carlton Cafe [S] [M] — 23 | 24 | 25 | $40

Ritz-Carlton, 15 Arlington St. (Newbury St.), 617-536-5700

■ "Comforting tradition" is the calling card of this "casual" cafe at the Ritz-Carlton in the Back Bay where proper Bostonians come to appreciate "fine" ("if a bit boring") New American fare delivered in "delightful surroundings" by an "impeccable" staff that "pampers" all diners; pleasant touches like "fresh flowers" and soft music provided by the "great harpist" make "it easy to enjoy an evening" here.

RITZ-CARLTON DINING ROOM [S] — 25 | 27 | 27 | $59

Ritz-Carlton, 15 Arlington St. (Newbury St.), 617-536-5700

■ An "old Boston" legacy lives on at this "classic" bastion of Back Bay society dining, which reaches "the pinnacle" of French cuisine; the "world-class" fare, matched with an "outstanding" wine list, is proffered by an "extraordinary" staff in a "country-club setting" that provides a "great view of the Public Garden", as well as a glimpse into how "the other half lives"; in sum, most purr "it's the Ritz – what do you expect except the best?"

Rod Dee [S] [M] 💳̸ — 22 | 5 | 13 | $12

1430 Beacon St. (Summit Ave.), Brookline, 617-738-4977

■ "One of the best hole-in-the-wall places ever", this "tiny" piece of "Bangkok in Brookline" dishes up "huge portions" of "authentic" Thai food "with tons of flavor" "fast and cheap"; insiders advise try any "special of the day" or just point to something on the "Thai menu"; this "no-decor" "Formicaville" is always "packed to the gills, yet somehow you never have to wait long for a table."

Roggie's ☾ [S] [M] — 14 | 10 | 15 | $15

356 Chestnut Hill Ave. (bet. Beacon St. & Commonwealth Ave.), Brighton, 617-566-1880

◪ If you "don't mind lots of college students", this "BC hangout" in Brighton is a "decent neighborhood bar" that has virtually "any beer you want on tap" and "better-than-expected" American grill items; the atmosphere may be akin to that of a "fraternity house", but at least it's "upbeat."

Roka §Ⓜ 21 | 15 | 17 | $24
1001 Mass Ave. (bet. Central & Harvard Sqs.), Cambridge, 617-661-0344

◪ "Convenient for good sushi", "excellent tempura" and "solid" noodle dishes, this "homey" Cambridge Japanese between Harvard and Central Squares is a "quiet and reliable" "standby"; the room is "no-frills", but the "sweet" staff and "fair prices" more than compensate.

Rosebud Diner ●§Ⓜ 15 | 17 | 18 | $14
381 Summer St. (Elm St.), Somerville, 617-666-6015

■ Enjoy a "nostalgic" "experience in boxcar dining" at this "cute" "little" "old-time" American diner in Somerville that slings "traditional" "basics" ("great eggs", "good burgers"); a few fault it for "disappointingly ordinary" eats, but most "spin the clock back 50 years and have a ball."

ROWES WHARF §Ⓜ 24 | 27 | 24 | $53
Boston Harbor Hotel, 70 Rowes Wharf (Atlantic Ave.), 617-439-3995

■ In a "beautiful" space with "magnificent waterfront views", this "fabulous" restaurant in the Boston Harbor Hotel showcases the works of "remarkable chef Daniel Bruce", "a great interpreter of New England–style cuisine" (don't miss the "awesome brunch"); indeed it's "very expensive, but what a treat!", and in the summertime, the outdoor cafe is a swell spot to "watch the yachts go by."

Royal East §Ⓜ 19 | 12 | 18 | $18
782 Main St. (Windsor St.), Cambridge, 617-661-1660

■ "Tons of regulars" gladly overlook the "shabby" decor at this Chinese seafood house in Cambridge, a haunt made by "MIT brains" into an "institution"; it "does a good job on all the standards", providing a "wonderful selection" of "quality Cantonese dishes" at "cheap" prices.

R Place §Ⓜ 24 | 15 | 22 | $38
312 Washington St. (Rte. 9), Wellesley, 781-237-4560

■ "A gem" in Wellesley, this "innovative" New American is worth discovering for its "nice twists on Southwestern cuisine", especially the "awesome grilled Caesar salad", paired with a "good wine list"; P.S. a recent move from its original "hole-in-the-wall" location in Waltham outdates the decor score.

Rubin's §Ⓜ 18 | 9 | 15 | $17
500 Harvard St. (bet. Beacon St. & Commonwealth Ave.), Brookline, 617-731-8787

■ "Large portions" of "old-fashioned Jewish food" make this Brookline deli "a good place to get heartburn" from "oversized, tender corned beef sandwiches"; while some mavens predict it "wouldn't last in NYC", most concede that "for kosher meats" in this area, "it can't be beat."

Ruby's ●ⓈⓂ　　　　　　　▽ 14 │ 6 │ 10 │ $12
280 Cambridge St. (opp. Mass General), 617-367-3224
☑ "Cheap, fast breakfasts", with the emphasis on cheap, are the main reason to visit this neighborhood diner opposite Mass General; but as it's "one of the few" 24-hour (on Thursdays–Saturdays; it closes at 9 PM on other nights) "greasy spoons around", even critics admit that the "passable food gets better when it's 2 AM."

Rudy's Cafe ⓈⓂ　　　　　　17 │ 13 │ 16 │ $17
248 Holland St. (Broadway), Somerville, 617-623-9201
☑ "Decent Mexican" at "bargain" prices attracts "poor college students" to this "popular" place in Somerville near Tufts; aficionados like the "extensive selection" of grub and the "fantastic margaritas" (though they "need to give out free chips and salsa"), but wags quip "can you say mediocre?", citing "food as bland as the atmosphere."

Ruggieri's Happy Haddock ⓈⓂ　15 │ 11 │ 15 │ $19
491 Riverside Ave. (Wellington Circle), Medford, 781-395-6785
☑ A longtime "senior citizens' haven", this Italian-American seafood house in Medford is a "middle-of-the-road place" that veterans say offers "reliable" "basics" at "good value"; dissenters, however, find it a "dive" with "pedestrian fish dishes" and wonder if you "must be at least 65 to get in."

R. Wesley's Ⓢ　　　　　　　23 │ 16 │ 20 │ $33
31 Cambridge St. (Sullivan Sq. Rotary), Charlestown, 617-242-7202
■ Expect "great personal attention" at this "innovative" Charlestown "hideaway", a "favorite" destination for "huge portions" (it's "not for the diet set") of "exciting" Eclectic fare based on "interesting food combos"; repeat guests only "wish they'd expand" the "too-small" room.

Sablone's　　　　　　　　　20 │ 13 │ 18 │ $30
107A Porter St. (Chelsea St.), East Boston, 617-567-8140
■ This old-time (1947) East Boston Italian is famous for its clown decor and "small menu" of "great food", especially the "wonderful" *vitello limone*; a few cynics, however, think there are "too many clowns for anyone but Barnum & Bailey" – "time to redecorate."

Sabra ⓈⓂ　　　　　　　　　15 │ 10 │ 14 │ $18
45 Union St. (Langley Rd.), Newton, 617-964-9275
☑ Despite some reports of "run-of-the-mill" food and "tired" decor, this "homey" Middle Eastern spot in Newton is defended by admirers who appreciate "all the basic staples" and "great lunch buffet" at "easy-on-the-budget" prices.

Saffron ⓈⓂ — — — M
279A Newbury St. (Gloucester St.), 617-536-9766
Indian goes contemporary at this Back Bay main-drag
newcomer, home to dishes like tandoori-marinated rack
of lamb and wrapped red snapper; the interior features
custom-made teak furnishings from Thailand, though fair-
weather fans favor the sidewalk cafe.

SAGE Ⓜ 26 18 23 $35
69 Prince St. (Salem St.), 617-248-8814
■ An "adorable", "surprisingly sophisticated" "little place"
in the North End with a "limited menu" of "innovative"
contemporary Californian-Italian specialties "cooked to
order" ("homemade pastas are the way to go") and served
by a "delightful staff"; seating is "limited" too, and it's
always "crowded", so "reservations are a must."

Saigon ⓈⓂ⊄ 21 15 20 $16
431 Cambridge St. (Harvard Ave.), Allston, 617-254-3373
■ This "mom-and-pop" "hole-in-the-wall" is a "sweet
spot" for "fresh, delicious and inexpensive" Vietnamese
in Allston; "incredible" service from a "friendly staff"
helps surveyors overlook the fact that there's no liquor
license and the decor's merely "passable" – two reasons
it's a "favorite" for takeout.

SAKURABANA Ⓜ 25 14 19 $25
57 Broad St. (Milk St.), 617-542-4311
■ "Great maki" and bento boxes, and what many maintain is
the "best sushi in Downtown Boston", draw flocks of
followers to this "genuine Japanese"; regular lunchers
recommend "getting there early" because they "pack 'em
in like sardines."

SALAMANDER Ⓜ — — — E
Trinity Place, 25 Huntington Ave. (Dartmouth St.), 617-451-2150
Chef-owner Stan Frankenthaler is on the move from
Cambridge to Copley Square, where his creative Asian-
Eclectic fare is due to find a new home this November in the
luxury residential development Trinity Place; the standout
kitchen will retain its focus on locally grown organic
produce, and the room will see the addition of a satay bar
and private dining spaces beneath its 14-foot ceilings.

Salts 24 20 23 $41
*798 Main St. (bet. Central & Kendall Sqs.), Cambridge,
617-876-8444*
■ Named after the symbol of hospitality, this "quiet, elegant"
New American bistro on a site that "carries a great dining
legacy" (formerly Panache and the original Anago Bistro) is
a "fantastic addition to Central Square", serving "superlative
food" that's a "contemporary take" on the "old-world"
"Eastern European style"; "cozy and romantic", it is
"delightful to look at" and has "attentive service" too.

Salty Dog Seafood Grill & Bar [S] [M] 13 | 11 | 11 | $22

206 Faneuil Hall Mktpl. (bet. Congress & North Sts.), 617-742-2094

■ Though scores suggest this "overpriced" Faneuil Hall "tourist trap" leaves "much to be desired in food and service", fans feel it's "good" for "basic seafood" like fish 'n' chips and "a drink on a Friday afternoon" – especially on "a warm, sunny day" when you can sit on the patio and "watch the crowd."

Sam's [S] [M] – | – | – | M

100 City Hall Plaza (bet. Cambridge & Congress Sts.), 617-227-0022

This new Downtowner is a yup magnet with an American menu featuring eclectic specials (e.g. scallops with tropical salsa atop mashed potatoes); it's cafeteria-style during the day and full service at dinner, with modern decor made cozy by oversized cranberry-colored banquettes.

Samuel Adams Brewhouse ◐ [S] [M] 12 | 13 | 13 | $19

Lenox Hotel, 710 Boylston St. (Exeter St.), 617-421-4961

■ "If you want to go downscale", this "pretty touristy" Back Bay brewpub attached to the chic Lenox Hotel "is as good as any"; just be sure to "go for the beer" and "fun atmosphere", since the "standard pub fare" "doesn't live up to the quality" of the suds.

Sandrine's [S] [M] 21 | 20 | 20 | $39

8 Holyoke St. (Mass Ave.), Cambridge, 617-497-5300

◪ A "small menu" of "rich", "interesting Alsatian food" from Raymond Ost (ex Julien) served in a "very civilized" setting keeps "natty professor types" coming to this French bistro "with a German accent" in Harvard Square; from a pickier perspective, the fare can be "uneven" – perhaps this "gem" is "still finding its niche."

S&S Restaurant & Deli [S] [M] ≠ 18 | 13 | 16 | $16

1334 Cambridge St. (Inman Sq.), Cambridge, 617-354-0777

◪ This "big and busy" "Cambridge fixture" since 1919 is "a great dive" and a "favorite for brunch", doling out "wonderful challah French toast" and "solid deli food until midnight" amid "people-watching galore"; critics claim it's "overrated", but they're outvoiced by regulars who "hope it never changes" ("except for better parking") and advise "don't let the lines fool you – they move quickly."

Santarpio's Pizza ◐ [S] [M] ≠ 22 | 8 | 13 | $14

111 Chelsea St. (Porter St.), East Boston, 617-567-9871

◪ "Classic" East Boston pizza joint that's "worth a run if you're stuck at the airport" for its fast, cheap and easy slices that some swear are the "best in Boston – hands down"; sure, it's "a dump" with "no-nonsense" (aka "rude") service, but "every neighborhood should have a place like this" (for "takeout").

SAPORITO'S S
26 | 17 | 23 | $37
11 Rockland Circle (George Washington Blvd.), Hull, 781-925-3023
■ It's a "small, plain beach cottage" "far off the beaten path" in Hull, but reviewers report this "creative" Italian is "worth the drive from anywhere" for its "tasty, fresh, carefully prepared dishes" and "excellent daily specials" at "half the price of in-town restaurants"; enthusiasts are convinced it's an "institution in the making."

Sapporo S M
– | – | – | M
81 Union St. (Beacon St.), Newton, 617-964-8044
This recent Pan-Asian arrival offers an extensive Japanese and Korean menu that satisfies appetites for the traditional with everything from sushi to noodle dishes to specialties like *bi bim bah* (vegetables, beef and rice marinated in sesame oil); the authentic look comes complete with kimonos and bonsai trees.

Saraceno S M
23 | 20 | 23 | $32
286 Hanover St. (bet. Parmenter & Prince Sts.), 617-227-5353
■ "Bring an appetite and leave your conscience at the door" of this "classic" North End Italian that's an "exquisite find" but "often overlooked" in the neighborhood; while "not cheap", the food is "great", the service "superb" and the "romantic" setting succeeds in "transporting you to Italy."

Sawasdee Thai Restaurant S M
20 | 16 | 19 | $21
320 Washington St. (Holden St.), Brookline, 617-566-0720
■ "A keeper" is what Brookliners call this "out of the ordinary" Thai, touting "unique selections" (like "spicy squid") that satisfy when "Chinese just won't do the trick"; a "gracious staff" and "quiet", "attractive setting" add to the "consistently enjoyable" experience.

Scandia S M
23 | 19 | 21 | $30
25 State St. (bet. Pleasant & Water Sts.), Newburyport, 978-462-6271
■ With its "romantic" ambiance, "pleasant service" and "well-prepared" New England–style seafood (including "delicious chowder"), this "intimate storefront" in the heart of Newburyport is "great for relaxed dining", a "special occasion" or Sunday brunch.

SEASONS S M
25 | 25 | 24 | $52
Regal Bostonian Hotel, 9 Blackstone St. N. (North St.), 617-523-4119
☑ "Creative, tasty" food "impeccably served" in a "quiet, handsome room" with a "wonderful view" of Faneuil Hall makes this "pricey" New American at the Regal Bostonian a "great" choice for "special celebrations" or business meals; even if a few voters with long memories say the "quality has declined", most insist it should "not be overlooked" as "one of the best gourmet restaurants in Boston."

Sel de la Terre 🖪Ⓜ　　　　　– | – | – | E |
255 State St. (Atlantic Ave.), 617-720-1300
A Gallic haven on the waterfront, this French bistro is the
new offspring of chef-partners Frank McClelland (L'Espalier)
and Geoff Gardner, who match their Provençal cooking
with artisanal homemade breads (also sold in the vestibule
boulangerie); although it's nestled near ground zero of the
Big Dig project, the interior sets a tranquil tone with a slate
tile floor, wrought-iron chandeliers and leather banquettes.

75 Chestnut 🖪Ⓜ　　　　　19 | 22 | 21 | $40 |
75 Chestnut St. (bet. Brimmer & River Sts.),
617-227-2175
◪ "Only locals can find" this "lovely, little" New American
"sleeper" tucked in the flats of Beacon Hill; it has earned a
rep as a "great yuppie date place" with a "delightful menu",
"excellent wine list" and "cozy to the max" atmosphere,
but "outrageous prices" for food that's "good, not great"
lead some to sigh it's a "pity."

Shalimar of India 🖪Ⓜ　　　18 | 12 | 16 | $18 |
546 Mass Ave. (Central Sq.), Cambridge, 617-547-9280
◪ "A star among the Central Square Indian crowd" vs. "your
average high-volume Indian restaurant" sums up the debate
about this "comfortable" Cambridge Indian; regardless,
the buffet is "better than the rest" – "and cheap too."

Shalom Hunan 🖪Ⓜ　　　　13 | 11 | 14 | $19 |
92 Harvard St. (School St.), Brookline, 617-731-9760
◪ "It smells great outside" say fans of the "surprisingly
authentic taste without pork" at this glatt kosher Chinese;
but most call it "passable" and "too salty", concluding
"unless you keep kosher, stick to regular Chinese."

Sherborn Inn 🖪Ⓜ　　　　19 | 21 | 19 | $32 |
33 N. Main St. (Rtes. 16 & 27), Sherborn, 508-655-9521
◪ "In an area starved for good restaurants", this "delightful"
Sherborn American has developed a following for its
"beautiful country inn setting" and "dependable" New
England cuisine served in both the "pretty dining room"
and "terrific tavern"; insiders say the "warm, cozy" tavern
is "especially appealing on a fall or winter day" and the
dining room is the place to be on Tuesday nights when there
are "hoppin' jazz bands."

Shilla ●🖪Ⓜ　　　　　17 | 12 | 16 | $20 |
57 JFK St. (Winthrop St.), Cambridge, 617-547-7971
◪ "Good noodles", "quick sushi", late-night hours and
wallet-friendly prices add up to a "nice evening out"
"with friends" at this Japanese-Korean in Harvard Square; if
there's "no atmosphere", at least the "friendly staff"
provides "explanations and advice when asked."

Shogun S
21 | 13 | 18 | $24

1385 Washington St. (Elm St.), West Newton, 617-965-6699

■ "You can't beat the freshness" of the sushi "for the price" at this "tiny" West Newton Japanese, a "favorite" "neighborhood spot" sought after by suburbanites for its "great food" and "very friendly" (but "not fast") service.

Siam Cuisine S M
21 | 17 | 19 | $19

961 Commonwealth Ave. (Gaffney St.), Allston, 617-254-4335

◪ Fans feel this Allston Thai is "terrific in all regards" – from the "flavorful dishes" to the "beautiful setting" to the "great value at lunch" – while less-impressed diners deem the grub merely "good" and the decor and service "basic"; still, solid food scores suggest it's worth a try.

Siam Garden S M
17 | 14 | 15 | $17

45½ Mt. Auburn St. (Harvard Sq.), Cambridge, 617-354-1718

◪ This "tried-and-true Thai friend" is a good "cheap date" option for "solid" but "not especially exceptional" Asian fare in Harvard Square; depending on your perspective, the "laid-back" service can either be a positive or a negative.

Sichuan Garden S M
20 | 16 | 19 | $18

295 Washington St. (Beacon St.), Brookline, 617-734-1870

■ While it "lacks the glitz of its neighbors", this "authentic" Brookline Chinese "stands above the sea of mediocre Szechuan" with its "fabulous" fare and "plentiful buffet"; "affordable" prices and "generous owners" are bonuses.

Sidney's Grille S M
▽ 18 | 20 | 17 | $32

University Park Hotel, 20 Sidney St. (bet. Franklin & Green Sts.), Cambridge, 617-494-0011

◪ This "funky", "stylish" Cambridge New American earns applause for its "cool" space and "surprisingly very good", "high-end" food; critics, however, declare the "beautiful room is not enough to make up for play-it-safe food."

SILKS S M
25 | 25 | 25 | $52

Stonehedge Inn, 160 Pawtucket Blvd. (Rte. 113), Tyngsboro, 978-649-4400

■ It's "worth the ride" to this "lavish country manor" in Tyngsboro, a "special" inn restaurant boasting a "superbly prepared", if "limited", New French menu, "knock-out wine list", "lovely decor" and "marvelous service"; a few feel it's "pretentious for the suburbs", but many more deem it "dining at its finest" – "Four Seasons North."

Silvertone Bar & Grill M
– | – | – | I

69 Bromfield St. (Tremont St.), 617-338-7887

This lower-level Downtown storefront is a site for sipping as much as for supping (and smoking isn't restricted), but lunchtime and after-five regulars do appreciate the homestyle American cooking and fresh salads; the room is jazzed up with sepia-toned photos and a lively buzz during happy hour.

Siros 21 | 20 | 20 | $31 |
307 Victory Rd. (Boardwalk), North Quincy, 617-472-4500 **S M**
1217 Main St. (Rte. 53), Hingham, 781-749-4500
■ "Elegantly prepared" Med-Italian food paired with a "relaxing atmosphere" and a "wonderful view of the marina at sunset" make this "gorgeous" "summer spot in Marina Bay" a "nice date place"; now "if only the noise could be reduced inside"; N.B. there's a new and unrated branch in Hingham.

6 Burner Urban Diner **S M** 17 | 19 | 18 | $19 |
151 Brighton Ave. (Harvard Ave.), Allston, 617-782-5660
■ "Funky" and "hip" are the watchwords for this "trendy", "reasonably priced" Allston diner where "the lack of alcohol keeps the crowds away" and the "interesting" New American menu includes "lots of pasta", "creative" dishes and a "great brunch with unique options."

Skewers, The **S M** 15 | 7 | 14 | $13 |
92 Mt. Auburn St. (JFK St.), Cambridge, 617-491-3079
☑ Students seeking a "good, fast meal" head to this "hole-in-the-wall" Harvard Square Middle Eastern for "generous portions" of "basic", "cheap", "filling food"; the lack of atmosphere prompts some patrons to "get it to go."

Skipjack's **S M** 18 | 15 | 17 | $28 |
199 Clarendon St. (St. James Ave.), 617-536-3500
2 Brookline Pl. (Brookline Ave.), Brookline, 617-232-8887
55 Needham St. (Boylston St.), Newton, 617-964-4244
☑ "Good", "fresh" fish at "moderate prices" and an annual crabfest that's "like being in Baltimore" are the signatures of these "informal" seafooders that invite comparison to Legal Sea Foods; regardless, regulars recommend the Clarendon Street location for a "nicer" experience; N.B. the Needham Street branch is new and unrated.

Sol Azteca **S M** 20 | 18 | 18 | $23 |
914A Beacon St. (bet. Park Dr. & St. Mary's St.), Brookline, 617-262-0909
75 Union St. (Beacon St.), Newton, 617-964-0920
■ "You can't go wrong" at these "friendly", "authentic" Mexicans that are "better than anything in Oaxaca", especially given the "great patio dining" (at the Newton branch) and "excellent" sangria and margaritas that seem to "taste best when seated outside"; longtime loyalists have only one request: add "some new dishes" to the menu.

Sonsie ● **S M** 19 | 20 | 16 | $32 |
327 Newbury St. (bet. Hereford St. & Mass Ave.), 617-351-2500
☑ "Beautiful people" flock to this "trendy", "smoky" International "hangout" on Newbury Street for the "great people-watching" and "amazing weekend brunch"; cynics "stick to the drinks", but even they admit this "pretentious" place can be "fun when the doors open out onto the street."

Sophia's ◐ Ⓢ　　　　　▽ 19 | 23 | 20 | $24

1270 Boylston St. (bet. Ipswich St. & Park Dr.),
617-351-7001

■ "Great late-night dancing" to Latin bands, a "fantastic tapas selection" and a "beautiful bar area" add up to a "good time" at this "romantic" Fenway-area Spanish-Continental; but would-be diners are advised to "go early" because it gets "crowded after 10:30."

Sorella's ◐ Ⓢ Ⓜ ⇄　　　▽ 23 | 13 | 20 | $13

386-388 Centre St. (Perkins St.), Jamaica Plain,
617-524-2016

■ "Delicious breakfast joint" in Jamaica Plain doling out "inventive omelets" and creative pancakes along with your "perpetually full cup of coffee" — all courtesy of the "earth-mother waitresses" who "call you 'honey'"; lunch is served every day, but early-rising regulars report "breakfast is the reason to go"; P.S. a recent expansion may reduce the "long wait."

Sorento's Ⓢ Ⓜ　　　　　21 | 15 | 18 | $21

86 Peterborough St. (behind Star Mkt.),
617-424-7070

■ Hidden away in the Fens, this "local Italian favorite" proffers pasta "as reliable as your mother's" plus "good cheap wine" and "perfect" pizza that some say is the "best" in town; it's your call whether the setting is "romantic" or "bland", but if it's candlelit intimacy you're after, "avoid game nights" when Red Sox fans show up in force to dominate this "wonderful find."

Sound Bites Ⓢ Ⓜ ⇄　　　22 | 11 | 17 | $11

708 Broadway (Boston Ave.), Somerville,
617-623-8338

■ Breakfast is "fast and cheap" at this "funky" Somerville American famous for its "incredible scones", "popular eggs Benedict" and "home fries so good you could eat them for breakfast and lunch"; some sigh it's "not what it used to be" now that the "secret" is out, but the "long wait" seems to suggest otherwise.

South End Galleria Ⓢ Ⓜ　　　– | – | – | M

(fka La Bettola)
480A Columbus Ave. (bet. Rutland Sq. & W. Newton St.),
617-236-5252

Accessible neighborhood dining is the aim of this renamed, revamped South End Italian, still owned by the Galleria Italiana folks, with co-owner Marisa Iocco taking over the stoves; midpriced dishes such as zuppa di mussels and handmade gnocchi characterize the casual cuisine, which is complemented by a cozied-up room with plush furniture and exposed brick walls.

SPINNAKER ITALIA [S][M] 18 | 25 | 19 | $31

Hyatt Regency Cambridge, 575 Memorial Dr. (Amesberry St.), Cambridge, 617-492-1234

◪ "Go for the view" from this revolving restaurant atop the Hyatt Regency; it's a "perfect spot to bring out-of-towners" to scope the city skyline, with "wonderful" decor, a "relaxing" ambiance and Northern Italian fare that's "better than expected" from one viewpoint and "mediocre" from another; "you pay for the atmosphere."

Sports Depot ◐ [S][M] 11 | 14 | 12 | $17

353 Cambridge St. (Harvard Ave.), Allston, 617-783-2300

◪ This "always-packed" Allston pub with "TVs all around" (including the rest rooms) is "heaven on earth for sports freaks" who don't seem to mind that the eats are "below average" – "who cares about the food when there are this many TVs showing sports of all sorts?"; nonathletic types advise "eat beforehand" or "bring in takeout."

Stars [S][M] 17 | 14 | 17 | $21

2-4 Otis St./Rte. 3A (North St.), Hingham, 781-749-3200

■ "Stars doesn't pretend to be anything but the great diner it is" say surveyors about this "hometown" South Shore Traditional American; while "not exciting", the food is "solid", the beer selection is noteworthy, "children are welcome" and the price is right; "may it twinkle on."

Stellina [S][M] 23 | 17 | 20 | $31

47 Main St. (Rtes. 16 & 20), Watertown, 617-924-9475

■ "Artful combinations" of "quality, ingredients" keep customers coming back to this "cozy and comfy" Watertown Italian where the "warm tomato salad is a must" and the roasted garlic spread could "make a whole meal" by itself; the one major complaint is it's "much too noisy for polite conversation" – regulars recommend dining in the "charming garden" to escape the "wall of noise."

Stephanie's on Newbury [S][M] 18 | 18 | 15 | $29

190 Newbury St. (Exeter St.), 617-236-0990

◪ "The place to grab a bite when doing the Newbury thing", this "trendy" New American offers "great people-watching" via the "best view on the street" and fare that can be "surprisingly good"; but diners could definitely do without the "outrageous prices" and waiters with "terrible 'tude."

Stockyard [S][M] 15 | 13 | 16 | $23

135 Market St. (N. Beacon St.), Brighton, 617-782-4700

◪ "Attentive", "cordial" service "without frills" is the hallmark of this "reasonably priced" Brighton beefery plating "huge portions" of "plain American food" like steaks, chops, mashed potatoes and other "hearty" "low-key" staples; a few pickier palates, however, claim it's "going downhill" while prices are rolling upward; N.B. the decor score may not reflect a recent renovation.

Suishaya ◐ⓈⓂ   ▽ 20 | 10 | 13 | $23
2 Tyler St. (Beach St.), 617-423-3848

◪ The few who commented on this Japanese-Korean in Chinatown rave about the "outstanding all-you-can-eat sushi", including spicy octopus "to die for" and the "best lunch box in Boston"; though there's no decor to speak of and "slow service", devotees declare "this is the place" for sushi lovers.

Sultan's Kitchen Ⓜ   23 | 9 | 14 | $13
72 Broad St. (bet. Franklin & Milk Sts.), 617-338-7819

■ "No wonder the Ottomans had an empire" enthuse supporters of this chef-owned Financial District "refuge for lunch" in "the land of chain food" where "long lines" form for the "healthy Turkish fare"; regulars only wish "they would open for dinner" and find a "better venue" since the current street-level locale can be "a little dispiriting."

Sunset Cafe ⓈⓂ   17 | 15 | 17 | $22
851 Cambridge St. (Inman Sq.), Cambridge, 617-547-2938

◪ This "casual", "fairly priced" East Cambridge Portuguese is known for its "great shellfish" and "good fish stew", but it's the "lively, entertaining" "fado singing on Friday and Saturday nights" that really draws the crowds; former fans feel the menu selections have been "disappointing lately" and fear its best days are "fading into the sunset."

Sunset Grill & Tap ◐ⓈⓂ   16 | 14 | 15 | $18
130 Brighton Ave. (Harvard Ave.), Allston, 617-254-1331

■ "Beer, beer, beer" is what this "fun, young" Allston American is all about, offering more than 100 taps and 400 microbrews, the "best selection this side of Germany"; all agree the "zillions" of varieties are a good enough reason to put up with the "standard pub food" and "ex frat boys with day jobs."

Sweet Basil ⌀   23 | 12 | 19 | $23
942 Great Plain Ave. (Highland Ave.), Needham, 781-444-9600

■ Needham-area foodies dream of the "exquisite", "zesty, lusty Italian" food created at this "totally fantastic" little "jewel" box; the "small and cramped" setting makes *amici* beg "please expand" so they can "get inside to try it" – in the meantime, "takeout is a good idea"; P.S. one caveat: "no coffee or dessert."

Taberna de Haro Ⓜ   21 | 17 | 20 | $26
999 Beacon St. (St. Mary's St.), Brookline, 617-277-8272

◪ "Very friendly owners" who are "successful transplants from Madrid" have infused this "festive" Brookline Spanish with "infectious personality", an "amazing" wine list and "authentic" tapas for "great grazing", especially when ordering is aided by the "caring" staff; cynics squeal about "high prices" for "tiny portions" and a place whose popularity makes it "too hot for its own good."

Tacos El Charro ◐ [S] [M] — 18 | 11 | 16 | $15

349 Centre St. (Jackson Sq.), Jamaica Plain, 617-983-9275

■ This "lively little Mexican" in Jamaica Plain earns olés for its "authentically delicious" dishes ("try the funky goat tacos") at peso-pinching prices and mariachi band on weekends that "makes you forget" the "diner atmosphere" and "slow-paced service."

Takeshima [S] [M] — 22 | 14 | 19 | $26

308 Harvard St. (Beacon St.), Brookline, 617-566-0200

◪ "You'll be happy" if you hit this "underrated", "reasonably priced" Brookline Japanese where the "consistently good sushi" and "very good cooked food" have strong supporters; the "decor could be improved" and the "tables are a little too close together" for the comfort of some surveyors, but others say it adds to the "neighborhood feel."

Tandoor House [S] [M] — 19 | 12 | 18 | $18

569 Mass Ave. (bet. Essex & Norfolk Sts.), Cambridge, 617-661-9001

■ At this upstairs Central Square Indian, the "best tandoori chicken" and other "wonderful authentic" options are presented by an owner who's "almost always present" to "ensure great food and service"; "if you can park" and can deal with the "rather plain decor", it's an "interesting place to eat."

Tanjore [S] [M] — 23 | 17 | 19 | $20

18 Eliot St. (Bennett St.), Cambridge, 617-868-1900

■ "Wonderfully different", this Harvard Square Indian "reigns supreme" with "delicious" "dishes from many regions" ("don't miss the dosas") brought to table by a "friendly staff" in a "good-looking" space; it's "unbeatable for the price."

Tapeo [S] [M] — 23 | 21 | 19 | $28

266 Newbury St. (bet. Fairfield & Gloucester Sts.), 617-267-4799

■ Fashionable strollers along "the Newbury Street runway" pause their posing to sample "terrific tapas" and "luscious sangria" at this "festive" Back Bay Spanish; though there's debate about whether it's equal to its Somerville sister Dali, all agree that dining on the patio is "just heavenly", even if some are "shocked" at how the "delectable morsels" "add up."

Taqueria la Mexicana [S] [M] — ▽ 21 | 8 | 15 | $11

247 Washington St. (Union Sq.), Somerville, 617-776-5232

■ For "fantastic cheap" Mexican in Somerville, amigos head to this "hole-in-the-wall" that's "a cut above" its genre, especially for "tamales, tamales, tamales", "awesome burritos" and "fresh and delicious chalupas"; there's "absolutely no atmosphere", and service can be as "slow as molasses", "but who cares?"

Taqueria Mexico ⓈⓂ　　　　18 | 10 | 12 | $12
24 Charles St. (bet. Main & Murray Sts.), Waltham,
781-647-0166
■ "Excellent, basic Mexican grub" is dished out at this "*muy*
authentic" Waltham "favorite", which is why most don't
mind the "cheesy decor" and "slow" waiters who "do
not speak English"; boosters also tip their sombreros to
the "fantastic value."

Tasca ⓈⓂ　　　　22 | 20 | 22 | $25
1612 Commonwealth Ave. (Washington St.), Brighton,
617-730-8002
■ With its "awesome tapas", "great wine" and "delightful
atmosphere created by live guitar music", this "romantic,
sexy" Brighton Spaniard provides patrons with "an escape
to the Mediterranean"; the latest chef has "a different style",
but most report it "seems to just get better" and rave about
"the most knowledgeable staff around."

Taste of India ⓈⓂ　　　▽ 19 | 14 | 20 | $18
91 Bigelow Ave. (Mt. Auburn St.), Watertown, 617-926-1606
■ This Watertown Indian boasts "great food", leading
loyalists to wonder why it's "always empty" (perhaps
because it's "off the beaten path"); expect "no surprises"
and no atmosphere to speak of, just "delicious", "authentic"
meals and "attentive service."

Tatsukichi ⓈⓂ　　　　22 | 18 | 20 | $32
189 State St. (Atlantic Ave.), 617-720-2468
■ "An oldie but still goodie," this "convenient" Financial
District Japanese continues to appeal with its "superb
sushi", "comfortable" setting and "accommodating" staff;
"lots of lunch business" leads cunning customers to "get
there by noon or wait."

Tavern on the Water ⓈⓂ　　　12 | 16 | 13 | $20
Charlestown Navy Yard, 1 Pier 6 (8th St.), Charlestown,
617-242-8040
◪ "The water's the thing" at this Charlestown Navy Yard
seafooder, a "summer favorite" for its "million-dollar view"
of the city and outdoor deck that "can't be beat"; "too bad
you have to eat" is the consensus on the "just ok" food.

Temple Bar ◖ⓈⓂ　　　　– | – | – | M
1688 Mass Ave. (bet. Martin & Shepard Sts.), Cambridge,
617-547-5055
In Cambridge this Eclectic-American hottie dishes up food
and bevvies for hipsters seeking sophisticated comfort
food with their martinis; soups, salads, pizzas and pastas
meet with snazzier dishes like grilled lamb tenderloins and a
warm pear tart for lunch, dinner and late-night dining.

Ten Center St. [S] [M] ▽ 19 | 19 | 17 | $29
10 Center St. (bet. Liberty & Water Sts.), Newburyport, 978-462-6652
◪ A "great place for a family get-together", this Eclectic-American set in a 1793 Newburyport building offers plenty of "fine" menu options; those in the know declare "the downstairs pub is best", where it's "cozy by the fire", though crowds at times can make it "tough to even get a drink."

TERRAMIA [S] [M] 25 | 16 | 20 | $38
98 Salem St. (Parmenter St.), 617-523-3112
■ "Put yourself in the hands of Mario Nocera" advise the many fans of this "intimate North End" Italian that's "as good as it gets", with "fresh, delicate, creative" fare and a staff "right out of central casting"; the sweet of tooth moan about the lack of desserts, but others "go out for cannoli" afterward and stretch their legs after sitting in a room that "walks a fine line between cozy and cramped."

Thai Basil [S] [M] 21 | 15 | 18 | $21
132 Newbury St. (bet. Clarendon & Dartmouth Sts.), 617-424-8424
■ There's "never a bad meal" at this "friendly" Newbury Street Thai serving "scrumptious" selections from a "small but wonderful" menu; while aesthetes complain that the "awful black tile detracts from the food", everyone else opts to savor the "bold, fresh flavors" and ignore the rest.

Thai's [S] [M] ▽ 17 | 17 | 15 | $20
1 Kendall Sq. (bet. Broadway & Hampshire St.), Cambridge, 617-577-8668
◪ Fans appreciate this Kendall Square Thai for its "amazing spring rolls", "good pad Thai" and "relaxing atmosphere", while critics feel the food "used to be better" and now "does not match what you can get at other places"; your call.

1369 Coffee House [S] [M] ⊘ 16 | 15 | 16 | $9
1369 Cambridge St. (bet. Hampshire & Springfield Sts.), Cambridge, 617-576-1369
757 Mass Ave. (bet. Inman & Prospect Sts.), Cambridge, 617-576-4600
■ "Write your manifesto" at these "trendy, upbeat" coffee shops in Inman and Central Squares where the "Cambridge crowd sips coffee for hours on end" and occasionally samples the "fantastic soups" and "fab scones"; there's "so much facial jewelry it must be dangerous during lightning", but it's a "blessed alternative" to Starbucks.

Tiernan's [M] ▽ 14 | 16 | 13 | $18
99 Broad St. (Franklin St.), 617-350-7077
◪ The few surveyors who've sought out this "decent" Financial District American call it a "very Irish" "bar serving mussels steamed in Guinness" and jambalaya that's "a pleasant surprise"; detractors deem it "mediocre" but admit it "sure beats potatoes."

Tiger Lily ◗ⓈⓂ
18 | 18 | 18 | $24

8 Westland Ave. (Mass Ave.), 617-267-8881

■ Located in "a restaurant-deprived area" convenient to Symphony Hall, this new Pan-Asian is a "welcome addition" for "pre-symphony" sampling of "offbeat" but "tasty" fare amid "interesting decor"; while it may "still be working out some of the kinks", the majority maintains it's "worth trying"; N.B. the large bar is a plus.

Tim's Tavern Ⓜ⇗
21 | 8 | 15 | $13

329 Columbus Ave. (Dartmouth St.), 617-437-6898

■ "Obscene" "hamburgers the size of football fields" are the attraction at this "no-frills" "local institution" that's perhaps the "South End's best-kept secret"; even those who adore the "best damn ribs" that "melt in your mouth" concede it's a "dive", but the "great home cooking at a great price" keeps them taking the plunge.

Tokyo ⓈⓂ
19 | 15 | 16 | $27

307 Fresh Pond Pkwy. (Lakeview St.), Cambridge, 617-876-6600

◩ "Always kid-friendly" West Cambridge Japanese known for its "good simple seafood" ("sparkling fresh fish") and "great (yes, it's true) brunch" on weekends; the "slow, slow, slow" service, however, gets little praise from those who find this "popular" place "not as good as it used to be."

Tom Shea's ⓈⓂ
20 | 19 | 19 | $30

122 Main St. (Rte. 133), Essex, 978-768-6931

■ "Worth a detour if you're in the North Shore area", this "romantic" Essex New Englander with a seafood emphasis has a following for its "super" "family salad bowls" and "favorite" beer-battered coconut shrimp; but the big attraction is the "great view of Essex Marsh" and the "winding Ipswich River" – "ask for a window seat."

Top Kat Lounge Ⓜ
– | – | – | M

(fka Cosmopolitan)
54 Canal St. (Friend St.), 617-720-2889

This North Station–area New American has a fresh name but a familiar look – dark wood paneling, floor-to-ceiling windows and leather sofas – along with upscale cuisine; the nightclubby ambiance is defined by premium martinis and themed party nights.

Top of the Hub ◗ⓈⓂ
20 | 25 | 20 | $42

Prudential Ctr., 800 Boylston St. (Huntington Ave.), 617-536-1775

◩ The "food has returned to match the breathtaking view" from atop the Prudential Tower at this "reborn", late-night American that many feel "doesn't get the credit it deserves" for its recently revitalized menu; even critics who claim it's "pricey" concede it's a "special" place for "guests and out-of-towners", given the "spectacular ambiance", "amazing martinis" and "live jazz" every night.

Torch S　　　　　　　　　– | – | – | M
26 Charles St. (Beacon St.), 617-723-5939
This Contemporary French on Beacon Hill near the Public
Garden, courtesy of Evan and Candice Deluty (formerly of
Bistro Five in Medford), tweaks modern dishes with Asian
touches (expect salmon tartar with Japanese rice and a
wasabi soy reduction or foie gras with green apple and
juniper); crimson accents and copper sheeting add richness
to the small, boxy room, and bright, primary-hued draperies
give colorful flair to the window fronting Charles Street.

Tosca S M　　　　　　25 | 23 | 22 | $39
14 North St. (Rte. 3A), Hingham, 781-740-0080
■ "Suburbanites wouldn't need to come to Boston" if there
were more places like this South Shore Northern Italian
where "well-presented", "exquisite" "seasonal" selections
are served in an "inspired setting" by an "excellent
young staff"; though chef Joe Simone's reign has ended,
replacement chef Kevin Long was under his tutelage,
which should satisfy devotees of this "hip and urbane oasis"
in tranquil Hingham.

Trattoria A Scalinatella S M　24 | 22 | 21 | $39
253 Hanover St., 2nd fl. (bet. Cross & Richmond Sts.),
617-742-8240
■ Ascend "the stairs to culinary heaven" (literally – it's on
the second floor) at this "cozy" North End Sicilian where the
"delicious food" ("more than just pastas"), "reasonable
wine prices" and "warm hospitality" rate raves; the "high
romance factor" and "blazing" fireplace in winter inspire
admirers to "take someone special."

Trattoria Il Panino S M　　20 | 17 | 17 | $28
120 S. Market St. (Faneuil Hall), 617-573-9700
295 Franklin St. (Broad St.), 617-338-1000
11 Parmenter St. (Hanover St.), 617-720-1336
1001 Mass Ave. (Dana St.), Cambridge, 617-547-5818 ⊅
126 Washington St. (Pleasant St.), Marblehead,
781-631-3900
☑ This often "crowded", "trendy" Italian chain is "always
reliable", with "something for everybody" on the menu;
but detractors wonder "did success go to their heads?",
claiming these upscale eateries have gone "from good
to tourist traps in two years"; P.S. consensus is that the
"original on Parmenter Street" is "the best."

Trattoria Pulcinella S M ⊅　21 | 17 | 20 | $42
147 Huron Ave. (Concord Ave.), Cambridge, 617-491-6336
■ With its "low-key atmosphere", "friendly" service and
"huge menu for such a tiny place" ("bring paper to write
down all the specials"), this "romantic" West Cambridge
"find" is "what an Italian bistro should be"; just make note of
the no-plastic policy and "beware high prices on specials" –
"be sure to ask" before you order.

Tremont 647 S M   22 | 19 | 20 | $37

647 Tremont St. (W. Brookline St.), 617-266-4600

■ The "grill is the centerpiece" of chef-owner Andy Husbands' "cutting-edge" New American in the South End where "imaginative" fare prepared "with zip" and accompanied by an outstanding wine list are served by an "accommodating staff"; a handful feels the fare is "uneven" and "overpriced", but the majority maintains it's a "real treat"; N.B. scheduled to open in the adjacent space is Sister Sorel (named after the chef's sister), which will offer light cafe fare.

Truc S   23 | 20 | 21 | $44

560 Tremont St. (Clarendon St.), 617-338-8070

☑ "Within the French bistro craze, Truc gets it right" rave Francophiles who flock to this subterranean "South End charmer" sporting a "small but well-executed" and "wonderfully inventive" menu; reviewers also talk up the "romantic" "back-room greenhouse" – like a "winter garden" – but quite a few find the selection "entirely too limited"; N.B. they no longer serve brunch, but they do take reservations.

Tullio's Restaurant & Grotto S M   22 | 18 | 19 | $23

150 Hancock St. (½ mi. from Neponset Circle), North Quincy, 617-471-3400

■ A "nice variety" of "consistently delicious" fare including "well-done" specials and "great brick-oven pizza" attracts aficionados of the red, white and green to this "noisy and crowded" Quincy Italian; locals label it a "reliable neighborhood standby" for "good food at a good price."

Turner Fisheries of Boston S M   21 | 19 | 20 | $36

Westin Hotel, Copley Pl., 10 Huntington Ave. (Dartmouth & Stuart Sts.), 617-424-7425

☑ "Excellent clam chowder", a Sunday brunch that's "worth every dime" and "great jazz" in the lounge distinguish this "elegant" seafooder from the competition and make it a "good alternative to Legal"; a dissenting school, however, carps "not bad for a hotel" but "not worth going out of your way for."

TUSCAN GRILL S M   25 | 19 | 20 | $37

361 Moody St. (bet. Spruce & Walnut Sts.), Waltham, 781-891-5486

☑ One of "the jewels of suburban dining", this "casually elegant" Northern Italian rates a round of applause for its "cutting-edge" "seasonal menu" (courtesy of new chef Joshua Ziskin) including "delicious grilled meats"; despite reports of "crowds", "noise", "rushed service" and the "oddest reservation system ever", fans still feel this "foodie's must-try spot" "gets better every year" and is "worth the drive to Waltham."

29 Newbury ⓈⓂ   19 | 17 | 17 | $36
29 Newbury St. (bet. Arlington & Berkeley Sts.), 617-536-0290
☑ "Wear black" to this "image-conscious" Newbury Street Regional American (with global accents) where the food is "not excellent, but always pleasant and sophisticated" and "dining alfresco" is a "must"; though the staffers may seem "more worried about their hair" than their service, many don't mind since it's the "active bar scene" that's the primary draw for "Newbury groupies"; N.B. new chef William Park's seasonal menu arrived post-*Survey* and is not reflected in the food score.

224 Boston Street ⓈⓂ   21 | 17 | 22 | $32
224 Boston St. (Andrews Sq. & Mass Ave.), Dorchester, 617-265-1217
■ This "clever", "gay-friendly" Eclectic-American strikes surveyors as "something from Amherst in Dorchester", a "crowded and noisy" "neighborhood place" with a "creative menu", "very friendly staff" and "offbeat clientele" that claims it's "worth it for the scene" alone.

Uncle Pete's Hickory Ribs ⓈⓂ⊄   23 | 10 | 19 | $18
309 Bennington St. (Chelsea St.), East Boston, 617-569-7427
■ Carnivores ignore the "cheap diner" decor and descend upon this family-run East Boston 'cue joint where the "service is always friendly", the prices are "extremely reasonable" and the eats are "phenomenal" – "Pete cares and his BBQ is real."

Union Oyster House ⓈⓂ   16 | 19 | 16 | $28
41 Union St. (bet. North & W. Hanover Sts.), 617-227-2750
☑ "Visit history" at this "charming", circa-1826 seafood "landmark" near Quincy Market that reels in "tourists" but holds "some nostalgia for natives" too; nearly everyone agrees the "great raw bar" is worth a trip, but cynics insist it's "not aging well."

Union Street ◗ⓈⓂ   14 | 13 | 15 | $19
107R Union St. (bet. Beacon & Centre Sts.), Newton, 617-964-6684
☑ "Good for a quick bite or to meet for a drink" is the line on this "casual" Newton American known more for its live music, outdoor seating and "pick-up" possibilities than its "average food"; of course, the crowd is "young and hip."

UP STAIRS AT THE PUDDING ⓈⓂ   24 | 24 | 23 | $46
10 Holyoke St. (Mass Ave.), Cambridge, 617-864-1933
■ "Dine under the stars in the roof garden" at this "brilliant" Harvard Square New American, "still one of the grande dames" that "continues to delight" with "ambiance to the ceiling", "exquisite food" and "even better desserts"; though a few feel the atmosphere is "stuffy" and the fare "overpriced", the consensus is that it "feels like a perfectly catered dinner in your country mansion."

Vault Bistro & Wine Bar Ⓜ

22 | 21 | 21 | $40

105 Water St. (Liberty Sq.), 617-292-9966

☑ "Bring your cell phone or you won't fit in" at this "chic", "sleek" Downtown New American, "a place to be seen at lunch"; expect a "limited menu" of "sophisticated" food and a "cool bar scene"; detractors dis it as "pretentious" and "pricey", but many more bank on it as the "best investment in the Financial District."

Verona Ⓢ

▽ 16 | 10 | 17 | $20

18 Mt. Auburn St. (Main St.), Watertown, 617-926-0010

■ "Seniors love" this "no-frills", "old-fashioned" Watertown Italian for "ample portions" of "homestyle food" at "bargain" prices; "friendly" "waitresses that have been there forever" add to the "neighborhood tradition."

Veronique Ⓢ Ⓜ

20 | 23 | 22 | $36

Longwood Towers, 20 Chapel St. (Longwood Ave.), Brookline, 617-731-4800

☑ "Gorgeous" decor, "gracious service" and live harp music make fans feel like they're "eating in a castle" at this Brookline New French–American, a "perfect" place to take "your valentine" for an "elegant night out"; while the food is "not extraordinary", reviewers report it "has improved"; N.B. a new chef came on board post-*Survey*, possibly outdating the food rating.

Vicki Lee Boyajian Ⓢ

22 | 15 | 16 | $17

1019 Great Plain Ave. (Chestnut St.), Needham, 781-449-0022

☑ "Superb pastries", "works-of-art" cakes, "muffins of love" and "melt-in-your-mouth scones" are standouts at this bakery that's also known as a "trendy lunch spot in not-so-trendy Needham"; though the staff is "snotty" and some say the "pricey" portions are for "small appetites only", the "wonderful food forces you back."

Victoria ● Ⓢ Ⓜ

▽ 18 | 13 | 18 | $18

1024 Mass Ave. (New Market Sq.), 617-442-5965

☑ This "blue-collar drop-in diner" in New Market Square offers a "step back in time" that's "great for the soul" plus "honest" eats "like mom used to make" ("but no lumps") against a background of "fun Abba music"; it may be "nothing special", but locals with "truck-driver appetites" like it just fine.

Vidalia's Truck Stop Ⓢ Ⓜ

12 | 15 | 14 | $16

13 Central St. (Abbott St.), Wellesley, 781-431-0011

☑ "If you like to color" and "you like 'cute'", you might consider this "regular stop for Wellesley families" "nostalgic and fun" for "decent" "old-fashioned food" at a "decent price" ("try the sweet-potato fries"); if you don't, you might decide to "drive on by" this "faux diner" with a "truck theme" and "slow" servers doling out "boring" food.

Viet Hong 🅂⌀   ▽ 25 | 8 | 19 | $11
182 Brighton Ave. (Allston St.), Allston, 617-254-3600
☑ "Great luncheon specials" that are "enough for two meals" and leave you "change from a $10 bill" win admirers at this "very small" Allston "mom-and-pop Vietnamese" and appear to be adequate compensation for the "poor atmosphere" (communal tables, bright lighting); "sweet service" is an added attraction.

Villa Francesca ➊🅂Ⓜ   20 | 18 | 18 | $30
150 Richmond St. (bet. Hanover & North Sts.), 617-367-2948
☑ "Enormous portions" of "delicious" Italian dishes (lots of "garlic in everything"), "beautiful" "open dining" and a "great table-to-table [opera] singer" make this a "key North End experience" for some surveyors; others, however, call it a "tourist trap", but even they concede the food is "solid."

Village Fish, The 🅂Ⓜ   20 | 12 | 17 | $23
22 Harvard St. (Brookline Village), Brookline, 617-566-3474
☑ Fans of fin fare head to this "inexpensive and informal" Brookline Village Italian-style seafooder for "big helpings of very fresh fish" "cooked just right" and served "without pretense" on "checkered tablecloths"; however, they're countered by critics who cite the "serious lack of side dishes" and "bland atmosphere" as reasons why it's "not worth the effort."

Village Smokehouse 🅂Ⓜ   19 | 13 | 16 | $21
1 Harvard St. (Rte. 9), Brookline, 617-566-3782
☑ BBQ buffs find "love in a slab o' meat" at this "friendly" joint that brings "a bit of Texas", complete with "a pit in the middle of the floor", to Brookline; while dissenters declare "this ain't real BBQ" and are turned off by the "family-style tables", this "pig-out" place "still packs 'em in", so they "must be doing something right."

Vin & Eddie's 🅂   22 | 17 | 22 | $31
1400 Bedford St./Rte. 18 (bet. Rtes. 58 & 139), Abington, 781-871-1469
■ This "super" South Shore Northern Italian has "been around a long time [since 1955] because the food is good" and "reasonably priced"; devotees adore the "hearty portions", "unusual offerings" and "great wine list", proclaiming "this is a steal!"

Vinny's at Night Ⓜ   ▽ 24 | 13 | 22 | $22
76 Broadway (Hawthorne St.), Somerville, 617-628-1921
■ "Keep it a secret" beg boosters of this Somerville Southern Italian "treasure" that voters only "wish fewer people knew about"; though it's in a "strange location" in "the back of a convenience store", the fact that it's perhaps "the best meal for the money" keeps regulars coming back.

Vinny Testa's Bar Ristorante [S] [M] 13 | 13 | 16 | $21

867 Boylston St. (opp. Hynes Auditorium), 617-262-6699
1700 Beacon St. (Washington Sq.), Brookline, 617-277-3400
Liberty Tree Mall, 100 Independence Way (Endicott St.), Danvers, 978-762-3500
Comfort Inn, 320 Elm St. (Rte. 1), Dedham, 781-320-8999
20 Waltham St. (Mass Ave.), Lexington, 781-860-5200
801 Worcester Rd. (Rte. 9), Natick, 508-655-8787

◪ Critics line up to fire barbs at this "boisterous" Southern Italian chain famous (or infamous) for its "superhuman portions" "overloaded with garlic", calling it the "McPasta of Boston"; yet there are defenders who deem it "decent for what it is" – a "popular" "place to go with the kids."

V. Majestic [S] [M] ≠ ▽ 21 | 5 | 19 | $13

164 Brighton Ave. (Harvard Ave.), Allston, 617-782-6088

■ "The 'V' is for 'value'" at this "small, family-run" Allston Vietnamese serving "excellent food" – "so fresh, so delicious" – on the "cheap"; "bring your own wine", "ignore the decor" and dig into the "healthy" "home cooking."

Vox Populi [S] [M] – | – | – | M

(fka Back Bay Brewing Company)
755 Boylston St. (bet. Exeter & Fairfield Sts.), 617-424-8300

Once a brewpub, this roomy Back Bay locale now houses a New American newcomer; exec chef Michael Burgess remains on hand to dish up his popular fare, but the beer vats are gone and the dining room and dual lounge areas are now done in deep Roman reds and purples.

Walden Grille [S] [M] 16 | 15 | 16 | $27

24 Walden St. (Main St.), Concord, 978-371-2233

◪ "Surprisingly good" contemporary fare vs. "a missed opportunity to spice up the Concord restaurant wasteland" sums up the debate about this New American near Walden Pond; kinder souls admit it's "not worth a long drive", but if you're in the area it can be a "wonderful lunch spot."

Warren Tavern [S] [M] 15 | 20 | 16 | $21

2 Pleasant St. (Main St.), Charlestown, 617-241-8142

■ "An absolute classic", this circa-1780 Charlestown "watering hole" is beloved for its "history, beer and ambiance" as well as its "good burgers" and "Yankee food"; though "they haven't changed the menu since Paul Revere drank here", most maintain it's "worth the trip for the atmosphere alone."

Watch City Brewing Co. [S] [M] 14 | 14 | 15 | $19

256 Moody St. (Pine St.), Waltham, 781-647-4000

◪ Some swear the food at this "upbeat brewpub" has "improved greatly", calling it a "rising star in Waltham", while others still insist the "best thing is the beer"; they're "trying to be imaginative", but it remains to be seen if this "hangout" will become more than a "typical brewery."

Water Club [S] – | – | – | M

319 Victory Rd. (Marina Dr.), Quincy, 617-328-6500

The tropical motif suits the oceanfront boardwalk location at this casual Key West–inspired New American in Quincy, where the laid-back outlook extends from the island interior (complete with potted palms) to the easygoing menu of salads and sandwiches; N.B. DJs and dancing dominate Thursday–Sunday nights.

Wayside Inn [S] [M] 18 | 24 | 21 | $30

Wayside Inn Rd., Sudbury, 978-443-1776

◪ "Lovely" Sudbury American that "takes you back to colonial times" with "always charming" "waiters in period costumes" serving "classic Yankee food" (crab cakes, chicken pot pie, etc.) to "parents and visitors"; as scores suggest, however, the "historic atmosphere" "outweighs everything else" – "go for the ambiance."

West Side Lounge [S] [M] – | – | – | M

1680 Mass Ave. (bet. Harvard & Porter Sqs.), Cambridge, 617-441-5566

Lounge meets fine dining at this Mediterranean-tinged spot in Cambridge where chef Tim Partridge (ex The Back Eddy) prepares rustic Italian fare with French influences; enjoy dinner in the earth-toned dining room appointed with cushy banquettes or at the 25-foot-long bar with a nightclub feel; N.B. Mondays are movie nights – ask about the theme du jour.

West Street Grille [M] 19 | 17 | 16 | $26

15 West St. (bet. Tremont & Washington Sts.), 617-423-0300

◪ "Surprisingly good food" coupled with a "great location" make this "creative" Downtown Crossing New American a "nice business lunch alternative"; though some snarl over the "amateurish staff", most don't mind given the "good-looking crowd after 11 PM" enjoying the "bar scene."

Whiskey's [S] [M] 12 | 11 | 12 | $17

885 Boylston St. (Gloucester St.), 617-262-5551

■ Everyone agrees this "cool" Back Bay BBQ joint is "like a frat party all the time" where "you can't miss with even the worst pickup line"; a few believe it also doles out "the best pulled pork north of the Mason-Dixon line", but the vast majority cautions "don't go for the food."

White Rainbow [S] ▽ 24 | 21 | 22 | $38

65 Main St. (Rogers St.), Gloucester, 978-281-0017

■ An "unexpected delight", this Continental seafooder "tucked away in Downtown Gloucester" boasts "the longest run of quality" in town, serving "probably the best food north of Boston" in a "romantic" setting; locals dub it an "old reliable", while city folk feel it's "worth the ride."

White Star Tavern ◐ [S] [M] — – | – | – | M

(fka Small Planet Bar & Grill)

565 Boylston St. (bet. Clarendon & Dartmouth Sts.), 617-536-4477

A new look and menu are brightening up this family-owned Copley Square staple; the lengthy New American menu is paired with a wine list that does justice to half-bottles, and it's all on offer in either the downstairs bar or the upstairs dining room.

Wonder Bar ◐ [S] [M] — 16 | 19 | 15 | $21

186 Harvard Ave. (bet. Brighton & Commonwealth Aves.), Allston, 617-351-2665

■ "Toto, we're not in Allston anymore" cry admirers of this "upscale" hangout for "second-generation Sinatra fans" and "yuppie jazz" lovers who dig the live music and "trendy" atmo; most concur the International fare is just "decent" and the "staff thinks too much of themselves", but if the scene's your thing "dress in black at all costs."

Woo Chun [S] [M] — ▽ 21 | 12 | 16 | $21

290 Somerville Ave. (Cambridge St.), Somerville, 617-623-3313

■ Loyalists "love the kimchi" at this Union Square Korean touting "nice appetizers" and "more side dishes" than the norm even for this genre; "decent quality at reasonable prices" keeps 'em coming back.

Woodman's [S] [M] 🚫 — 20 | 10 | 11 | $20

121 Main St. (Rte. 133), Essex, 978-768-6057

◪ "The cathedral of the fried clam", this "down and dirty" Essex seafooder "gives grease a good name" with its "classic clambake fare" that comes "out of paper boxes on picnic tables"; some gripe it's "not as great as its reputation leads you to believe", but those in the "long lines" insist "summer isn't complete" without a visit.

Woody's ◐ [S] [M] — ▽ 16 | 12 | 18 | $14

58 Hemenway St. (Westland Ave.), 617-375-9663

◪ This "great neighborhood pizza joint" near Fenway has a "friendly, relaxing atmosphere" and an open hearth; pie partisans say it's "awesome", while skeptics feel the food "fails to deliver" – unless it's a "pre–Red Sox game dinner."

Wrap, The [M] — 16 | 11 | 14 | $10

82 Water St. (bet. Congress St. & Liberty Sq.), 617-357-9013
137 Mass Ave. (Boylston St.), 617-369-9087 [S]
247 Newbury St. (Fairfield St.), 617-262-2200 [S]
Cleveland Circle, 1940 Beacon St., Brighton, 617-739-0340 [S]
278 Harvard St. (Beacon St.), Brookline, 617-566-9700 [S]
71 Mt. Auburn St. (Holyoke St.), Cambridge, 617-354-5838 [S]

◪ "Good and healthy 'on-the-go' food" is the hallmark of these "simple" wrapperies that whip up "interesting sandwich alternatives" for a "quick" lunch; diners divide on the cost, however, with yeas maintaining it's "cheap" and nays asserting it's "expensive for what it is."

Yama 🆂Ⓜ   21 | 16 | 19 | $24
245 Washington St. (opp. Bread & Circus), Wellesley,
781-431-8886
■ With its "fresh, high-quality food" (including "great sushi"), "calm and relaxing" atmosphere and "friendly service", this BYO Wellesley Japanese is seen by surveyors as "a savior in the suburbs"; now if only they would "expand" and "get a liquor license."

Yangtze River 🆂Ⓜ   17 | 13 | 16 | $19
21-25 Depot Sq. (Mass Ave.), Lexington,
781-861-6030
☑ It may be "nothing special", but it's the "best Chinese" in Lexington – "pleasant", "dependable" and "consistently good"; "best bet": "don't pass up the green beans" ("you'll never forget them") or the "excellent buffets."

Yenching Palace 🆂Ⓜ   ▽ 12 | 6 | 12 | $18
671 Boylston St. (Copley Sq.), 617-266-9367
1326 Mass Ave. (Harvard Sq.), Cambridge, 617-547-1130
☑ Though a few feel for the "sweetest guys on earth" who run this "disappointing" duo in Copley and Harvard Squares, "passable Chinese" is the highest compliment most voters can muster up; still, they might be good if you need a "fast" fix.

Yerardi's 🆂Ⓜ   14 | 11 | 17 | $18
418 Watertown St. (Rte. 16), Newton, 617-965-8310
☑ "Affordable early-bird meals" "straight out of the '50s" accompanied by "great service" are the draw at this "time-warp" Newton Italian replete with a courtyard and authentic bocce court; while "not excellent", "there's definitely love in the food."

Yokohama 🆂Ⓜ   ▽ 20 | 14 | 19 | $22
238 Washington St. (Harvard St.), Brookline, 617-734-6465
■ "A tiny gem", this "very friendly" Brookline Village Japanese-Korean serves up a "clean, lean meal" that's "fresh, well prepared and delicious", causing the handful who commented to wonder "why isn't there a line out the door?"

Zaatar's Oven 🆂Ⓜ   17 | 11 | 13 | $12
242 Harvard St. (Coolidge Corner), Brookline, 617-731-6836
■ "Cafeteria-style kosher" Middle Eastern in Coolidge Corner that earns praise for its "fun" fast food – "excellent" flatbreads with a variety of "tasty" toppings plus soups, salads and such; there's "not much atmosphere" and the staff can be "unfriendly", but it's an "inexpensive" "favorite for a healthy, flavorful lunch"; P.S. "they've expanded" and now offer "table service for dinner."

Zaftigs Delicatessen S M
| 17 | 15 | 17 | $16 |

335 Harvard St. (Coolidge Corner), Brookline, 617-975-0075

☑ "Bubbie and Zaydie would love" this "upscale" Coolidge Corner deli touting "classic menu items enhanced by unique twists" and "the best brunch around"; fans feel it's the "closest thing to a New York deli that Boston has to offer" – complete with "poor service" – but matzo mavens who "had huge hopes" kvetch "it promises more than it delivers"; if you go, "get there early" to avoid the "long weekend waits."

Zuma Tex-Mex Cafe S M
| 14 | 13 | 15 | $19 |

Faneuil Hall Mktpl., 7 N. Market St. (Clinton St.), 617-367-9114

☑ "Generous portions" of "decent" grub washed down with "colored margaritas" in a "lively atmosphere" make this Faneuil Hall Tex-Mex "adequate for a casual lunch" or dinner; some gringos grumble "bland and unimaginative" and ambiance-seekers say "they need to move out of the basement", but most maintain it's "just fun."

Cape Cod, Martha's Vineyard and Nantucket

CAPE COD

F	D	S	C

Abbicci 🅂🅼
24 | 21 | 22 | $42

43 Main St./Rte. 6A (Willow St.), Yarmouth Port, 508-362-3501
■ "I can't drive by without eating there" say reviewers of this Yarmouth Italian-Mediterranean noteworthy for "creative pastas" and "inventive meat dishes and salads"; the "quaint" house is "beautiful" and "romantic", and the few critics irked by the "too-close" seating and the staff's "lack of attention" are outnumbered by those who applaud the "early-bird special" as "a real bargain."

Adrian's 🅂🅼
▽ 18 | 15 | 15 | $25

Outer Reach Motel, 535 Rte. 6, North Truro, 508-487-4360
◪ "Good simple Italian" ("fresh seafood", wood-fired pizzas) and "very satisfying" breakfasts are the forte of this "pleasant" North Truro eatery overlooking the bay, though a few disappointed diners feel it's "gotten too big and popular" and "the decor could use an upgrade."

Aesop's Tables 🅂🅼
22 | 20 | 19 | $39

316 Main St. (next to Town Hall), Wellfleet, 508-349-6450
■ This "intimate" Wellfleet New American seafooder in a white clapboard house is "an oasis in the land of fish and chips", offering a "fair variety" of "delicious" dishes ("the oysters are divine") that make for a "hearty, satisfying" meal; devotees note the "pretty setting" is especially "romantic" if you're "sitting by a window" or on the patio.

Ardeo ◐🅂🅼
– | – | – | M

23 Whitespath Rd., South Yarmouth, 508-760-1500
Casual Mediterranean is the motif at Yarmouth's newest destination for panini, homemade pasta, brick-oven pizza and Mideastern bites; 30 wines by the glass and 20 varieties of martinis make for a spirited dining experience.

Barley Neck Inn 🅂🅼
20 | 21 | 20 | $38

5 Beach Rd. (Barley Neck Rd.), East Orleans, 508-255-0212
■ "Charming" ex–New Yorkers have turned this old sea captain's house into what some say is the "best dining experience" in East Orleans; expect "scrumptious" regional American fare "beautifully presented", "friendly service" and "lovely decor" (thanks to a recent redo).

Bubala's by the Bay 🆂Ⓜ   17 | 14 | 16 | $23

183 Commercial St. (Court St.), Provincetown, 508-487-0773
◪ P-towners looking for "an antidote to fried fisherman's platters" come to this sassy seafooder as much for the "best people-watching" on the outdoor patio as for the "interesting menu" of "fresh" fish and "modern cuisine" at a "good price"; the accolades aren't unanimous, however, with some preferring the "great martinis" over the "fair fare" and others slamming the service as "rude in that distinctly P-town way."

Cafe Edwige ◗🆂Ⓜ   22 | 16 | 18 | $28

333 Commercial St. (bet. Freeman & Standish Sts.), Provincetown, 508-487-2008
■ "Go for breakfast" urge boosters of this "trendy" P-town New American popular for its "brilliant baked goods" and faves like broiled flounder and eggs; a cathedral ceiling tops the "hippie-style" room adorned with "illuminating art", creating an "elegant" setting for dinner as well.

Cape Sea Grille 🆂Ⓜ   ▽ 25 | 21 | 22 | $36

31 Sea St. (Rte. 28), Harwich Port, 508-432-4745
■ In a seaside setting that's "a perfect slice of Cape Cod", this "seasonal goodie" in Harwich Port offers "innovative" New American food including "very good fish"; a handful of penny-pinchers find it "a bit pricey for the Cape" – perhaps they haven't tried the "excellent early-birds."

Chillingsworth 🆂   26 | 25 | 25 | $57

2449 Main St./Rte. 6A (Rte. 124), Brewster, 508-896-3640
■ "Five stars" rate fans of this Contemporary French that tops all *Survey* categories in Cape Cod for its "simply fabulous" multicourse "gourmet spectaculars", "exceptional service" and "rarified atmosphere" that includes antique-filled rooms; there's a casual bistro option for those stung by the "astronomical prices", but enthusiasts insist "you get what you pay for" here – the "ultimate dining experience."

Christian's Restaurant 🆂Ⓜ   19 | 18 | 18 | $32

443 Main St. (Chatham Bars Ave.), Chatham, 508-945-3362
◪ There are "two experiences" to be had at this "Cape Cod classic" in Chatham – "casual fun" in the piano bar upstairs and "innovative, delicious" regional American fare in the main dining room; critics claim the "food has slipped a notch", but most still consider it "a good repeater."

Christopher's American Rib & Seafood Eatery 🆂Ⓜ   – | – | – | M

Rte. 28, South Yarmouth, 508-394-8006
The name leaves no room for mystery – BBQ ribs and deep-fried lobster are indeed the headliners at this American newcomer in South Yarmouth, a beachy, family-friendly hang with fish mounted on the walls; for variety, the menu includes a supporting cast of burgers and surf 'n' turf.

Contrast [S] [M] ▽ 22 | 19 | 17 | $23
605 Rte. 6A (bet. Antonelli Ct. & New Boston Rd.), Dennis, 508-385-9100
■ "All ages" hang out at this "hip" Eclectic-French bistro in Dennis with a rep for cooking "city food on the Cape"; admirers adore the "innovative preparations of traditional comfort food" served in "funky surroundings"; N.B. they've increased seating and expanded their dinner menu.

Dancing Lobster [S] 24 | 19 | 18 | $37
371 Commercial St. (Johnson St.), Provincetown, 508-487-0900
◪ "All the seafood dances" at this "trendy" Italian seafooder with the "dumbest name" but some of the "best" food and views in Provincetown; decor scores have risen since its relocation to "bigger quarters", but the waits are still "very long on summer weekends", despite "too much attitude" and food that some say is "not as good as it was at the original teensy location."

Fish Landing Bar & Grill [S] [M] – | – | – | M
290 Iyanough Rd., Hyannis, 508-775-1045
This hip Hyannis seafooder flaunts its theme with glass fish dangling above the bar and custom-made tables etched with aquatic designs; crab cakes are the signature dish, and the menu features a 'go fish' option that allows patrons to pair their choice of fin fare with a style of preparation, from grilled to blackened to fra diavolo.

Flume [S] 21 | 14 | 18 | $27
13 Lake Ave. (Rte. 130), Mashpee, 508-477-1456
◪ "Excellent chowder and fried oysters" are what reviewers remember about this "interesting place" in Mashpee serving "simple", "wholesome" Northeast "comfort food" with Wampanoag touches like Indian pudding (the chef is a tribe chief); it's "not a fancy place" and service can be "weak", yet this "family restaurant" is always "busy in season."

Front Street [S] [M] 25 | 20 | 22 | $41
230 Commercial St. (Masonic Pl.), Provincetown, 508-487-9715
■ "Year after year", this "creative" P-town Mediterranean tucked in the brick-walled cellar of a Victorian mansion "never changes" – and loyalists "like it" that way, sighing over the "simply sensational offerings"; most don't mind the "cavelike atmosphere", but a few feel it's "time to update."

Gallerani's Cafe [S] [M] 22 | 15 | 21 | $31
133 Commercial St. (bet. Mechanic & Montello Sts.), Provincetown, 508-487-4433
■ One of the few P-town places open year-round, this "wonderfully warm" Italian-American "gem" wins support for its "great range of good food", "friendly feel" and prime "people-watching"; if you have any doubts, trust the crowd: "it must be good . . . that's where the locals go."

High Brewster Inn [S] [M] | 24 | 25 | 24 | $50

964 Satucket Rd. (Stony Brook Rd.), Brewster, 508-896-3636

◪ "A great country inn" dating back to 1738 houses this "beautiful", "innovative" American in Brewster; most call it a "wonderful vacation treat" with "memorable food", "superb service" and an "enchanting atmosphere", but a few dissenters think the "menu needs reinvention."

Inaho [S] | ▽ 24 | 20 | 19 | $32

157 Rte. 6A (bet. Minden & Sandyside Lns.), Yarmouth Port, 508-362-5522

■ "New Yorkers crowd" into the "only place to get good sushi on the Cape", a Yarmouth Port Japanese famous for its "wonderful cuts of fish" that are "expensive but worth it"; the "serene atmosphere" "in an old sea captain's house" and an Asian garden behind the restaurant complete the bonsai bonhomie; no wonder "there's always a wait."

Martin House [S] [M] | 23 | 23 | 22 | $42

157 Commercial St. (Atlantic St. Landing), Provincetown, 508-487-1327

■ A "grand old house" (circa 1740) in P-town is the domicile of New England cuisine that's been "consistently excellent for years"; the "fetching decor" includes "delightful private rooms", a beamed loft and garden terrace "perfect for a romantic dinner"; the "superb" presentation "comes with a price", but proponents promise "you won't be disappointed."

Nauset Beach Club [S] [M] | 20 | 16 | 17 | $34

222 Main St. (Beach Rd.), East Orleans, 508-255-8547

◪ There's "always an interesting crowd" at this Italian "beach joint" in East Orleans, a "reliably good" year-rounder for "garlicky shrimp" and "great risotto"; even if some say it's "gone downhill" and "they try to rush you", the majority contends it's "well worth the wait in season."

Orleans Inn [S] [M] | – | – | – | M

3 Old Country Rd. (Rte. 6), Orleans, 508-255-2222

The prime waterfront location and historical setting (dating to 1875) make this inn on Town Cove a magnet for both tourists and locals; Victorian details like a grandfather clock and antique dolls set the period mood, and the American fare (including plenty of fresh seafood) tends toward the traditional as well.

Paddock [S] [M] | 22 | 20 | 21 | $33

W. End Rotary, 20 Scudder Ave., Hyannis, 508-775-7677

◪ This "informal", "always-crowded" regional American features "consistently good" Cape Cod food, "wonderful wine selections" and a "convenient location" that's "perfect before the Melody Tent show"; "family-run" and "great for a nice family meal", it's especially popular with the seniors; N.B. a full renovation has freshened the face of the dining room, possibly outdating the above decor score.

Painter's S M ▽ 20 | 18 | 20 | $33
50 Main St. (Rte. 6), Wellfleet, 508-349-3003
■ For a "slice of Boston without the prices", try this
"imaginative" New American on the water in Wellfleet
touting a seafood-heavy menu that's "refreshingly free of
tourist food" (read: fried); the "professional service" and
"laid-back style" also earn accolades, but even aficionados
admit the fare can be "uneven" from visit to visit.

Penguins Sea Grill S M 23 | 19 | 20 | $34
331 Main St. (Ocean St.), Hyannis, 508-775-2023
■ "After a day of combing the beach" in Hyannis, reviewers
"return to civilization" at this chef-owned contemporary
seafooder for an evening of "sophisticated dining"; expect
"marvelous food", "lovely plate presentations" and live jazz
guitar; regulars recommend "going in spring and winter"
when the crowds have subsided.

Playhouse Bistro ◗ S M – | – | – | M
36 Hope Ln. (Rte. 6A), Dennis, 508-385-7800
For a pre- or post-theater bite, Dennis denizens hit this
American in an old Cape house with an informal lounge feel
snazzed up with candlelit tables; Asian and Mediterranean
touches enhance the bistro fare, and being under the
management of top-scorer Chillingsworth doesn't hurt.

Red Pheasant S M 23 | 23 | 23 | $42
905 Rte. 6A (Elm St.), Dennis, 508-385-2133
■ Locals "love" the "original" and "excellent" food served
at this "delightful" Dennis American with Mediterranean
touches and "a variety of game dishes" on the menu;
coupled with "very accommodating" service and a "warm,
romantic atmosphere" in a "historic Cape property", it's
"a very pleasant surprise."

Regatta of Cotuit at the Crocker 25 | 24 | 23 | $48
House S M
4631 Falmouth Rd./Rte. 28 (Rte. 130), Cotuit, 508-428-5715
■ "Outstanding food and service" solidify the reputation of
this "landmark old house" in Cotuit serving "consistently"
"excellent", if "pricey", New American meals with an
emphasis on seafood; the warren of intimate dining rooms
is "quite lovely", as is the garden that grows herbs for the
kitchen, but "why must they be so pretentious?"

Regatta of Falmouth 24 | 24 | 23 | $47
by the Sea S M
217 Clinton Ave. (mouth of Falmouth Harbor), Falmouth,
508-548-5400
■ "Sexy waterfront dining" is the signature of this Falmouth
sibling of the Cotuit Regatta, a "special place for special
occasions" with "wonderful food" "worthy of the price",
"fabulous presentation" and "great views"; but some sour
on the "pretension" and say "lighten up – it's the Cape."

Sal's Place [S] [M] 18 | 16 | 17 | $33

99 Commercial St. (bet. Cottage & Mechanic Sts.), Provincetown, 508-487-1279

◪ "Sit overlooking the water and eat like a king" at this P-town old-timer (1962) where "true Southern Italian" and "true Cape Cod" combine to deliver "good portions" of "basic" fare with a focus on local seafood; just be sure to "eat on the deck" since some surveyors find the interior "cramped" and "dingy."

Wequassett Inn [S] [M] – | – | – | E

Pleasant Bay, Chatham, 508-432-5400

The dining room of this 18th-century ship captain's home on the shore of Cape Cod's Pleasant Bay offers a New England spread featuring regional seafood; the marine flavors are enhanced by a chandeliered setting with a pleasing waterfront view.

MARTHA'S VINEYARD

Alchemy [S] [M] – | – | – | E

71 Main St. (South St.), Edgartown, 508-627-9999

The good chemistry of Savoir Faire has spilled over to its new Edgartown sib, a seafooder that nets specialties like island lobster and monkfish; the room is made light and airy by an open cutout to the second floor, where there's a lounge for aficionados of martinis, cigars and billiards.

Amity, The [S] [M] – | – | – | M

1 Park Ave., Oak Bluffs, 508-696-9922

Named after the fictional island in *Jaws* (which was filmed on the Vineyard), this casual Oak Bluffs cafe now satisfies serious appetites with dinner as well as its renowned breakfasts; the International menu ranges widely from salmon spring rolls to gaucho steak, all served in a charming room with copper-topped tables.

Atria [S] [M] – | – | – | E

137 Main St. (Pine St.), Edgartown, 508-627-5850

Named for one of the navigational stars, this new Edgartown entry steers diners to International cuisine with Thai, Creole and Indonesian influences (among others); jambalaya risotto with spiced prawns and homemade Irish soda bread figure among the stars on the menu.

Balance [S] [M] – | – | – | E

57 Circuit Ave. (Narragansett St.), Oak Bluffs, 508-696-3000

This brasserie on Oak Bluffs' main drag showcases an open, airy room with a long wooden bar and a semi-dressy ambiance defined by white tablecloths, high ceilings and large paintings; chef Benjamin deForest's New American menu delivers game and seafood from an exposed kitchen, as well as a six-course tasting menu for $85.

Beach Plum Inn [S][M] | 22 | 23 | 23 | $45 |
50 Beach Plum Ln. (North Rd.), Menemsha, 508-645-9454
◪ "Truly beautiful views" through three oceanfront windows command the attention of customers at this "elegant" Menemsha farmhouse; "personal service" and "excellent" New American fare with a seafood focus add to the "special occasion" experience and outweigh the comments of a few critics who call it a "dining disappointment"; N.B. restored after a recent fire, it now offers expanded seating.

Black Dog Tavern [S][M] | 18 | 17 | 16 | $26 |
Beach St. ext. (Vineyard Haven Harbor), Vineyard Haven, 508-693-9223
◪ Naysayers love to hate this "popular" BYO American on Vineyard Haven Harbor, the most trafficked spot on the island, barking "tourist trap", "massive hype about nothing", "get the T-shirt and eat elsewhere"; but this "wild" dog has a pack of admirers who call it "a classic" with "awesome breakfasts" ("get there early"), "fresh fish" and lots of "local color"; "you must go once just to say you've been."

Café Moxie [S][M] ▽ | 22 | 18 | 21 | $30 |
48 Main St. (Center St.), Vineyard Haven, 508-693-1484
■ "Eclectic comes to the Vineyard" at this verve-filled BYO boasting a "great" location on Vineyard Haven's main drag; count on a "small" but "tasty" selection of "inventive" seasonal bistro fare served in a "cozy" storefront room with rotating art exhibits on the walls.

Cafe Tsunami [S][M] | – | – | – | E |
8 Circuit Ave. ext., Oak Bluffs, 508-696-8900
Wide-open water views make this new Oak Bluffs Pan-Asian a hip harborside stop-off for admirers who appreciate seafood offerings and French flair; a buzzing lounge with velvet drapes and couches fills the first floor, while a more subdued upstairs dining room offers a sunset panorama.

Daggett House [S][M] | – | – | – | E |
59 N. Water St. (Daggett St.), Edgartown, 508-627-4600
Founded in 1660, this historic inn perched on Edgartown Harbor specializes in New England–style dishes updated with contemporary touches; linger over breakfast or lunch amid an ambiance of casual country elegance while enjoying the view of the waterfront gardens.

David Ryan's [S][M] | 16 | 14 | 16 | $25 |
11 N. Water St. (Main St.), Edgartown, 508-627-4100
■ Visitors have two options at this "fun place" in Edgartown that's an "easy walk from the hotels" – grab a beer while watching the game on TV in the "friendly" street-level bar or head upstairs for "fair" American fare with a seafood emphasis; a recent dining room renovation pays off with "beautiful light wood" and a spruced-up bar, but downstairs is still best for "nightlife" and "basic food before a party."

Homeport 🇸🇲 | 19 | 16 | 18 | $31 |
512 North Rd. (Basin Rd.), Menemsha, 508-645-2679
◪ "Location, location, location" must be what makes this seafooder "so popular" conclude head-scratchers about this "casual" Menemsha institution (1931) offering "perfect" harborside views plus "classic fried food"; do as the locals do – get a "mammoth portion" of the "finest stuffed quahogs" to go and watch the "best sunset" outside.

La Cucina 🇸🇲 | 26 | 25 | 23 | $51 |
Tuscany Inn, 22 N. Water St., Edgartown, 508-627-5999
■ "Eat in the garden for a romantic meal" advise admirers of the "lovely" patio at this "idyllic" New American with Tuscan influences secluded from the bustle of central Edgartown; the "fabulous food" also earns praise – "every dish is superb" – prompting partisans to cheer "excellent in every way!"

Le Grenier 🇸🇲 | ▽ 22 | 18 | 21 | $41 |
96 Main St. (north of ferry dock), Vineyard Haven, 508-693-4906
◪ Some consider this French BYO veteran above a bagel shop on the edge of Vineyard Haven "a nice surprise" for "rich, delicious" Gallic standards like sweetbreads, shrimp Pernod and frog legs Provençal in a "lovely" peaked space (*grenier* means 'attic'); "disappointed" diners, on the other hand, opine "overrated" and "overpriced"; your call.

L'Etoile 🇸🇲 | 27 | 27 | 26 | $61 |
Charlotte Inn, 27 S. Summer St. (Davis Ln.), Edgartown, 508-627-5187
■ Expect a "magical evening" at "without a doubt the best restaurant on the island", a "formal" (aka "stuffy") New French in the Charlotte Inn in Edgartown where "wonderful food", "outstanding service" and a "gorgeous", "romantic" setting (including "beautiful outdoor tables") add up to an "unsurpassed" culinary experience; it's "expensive", but Francophiles feel it's "worth every penny."

Lola's 🇸🇲 | – | – | – | M |
Beach Rd. (near State Beach), Oak Bluffs, 508-693-5007
Anything goes at this casual Southern specialist in Oak Bluffs adorned with colorful murals that depict the eponymous owner and her local patrons; adding to the party atmosphere is an active bar, dance floor and live rock, jazz and blues.

Martha's Vineyard Seafood Authority 🇸🇲 | – | – | – | E |
266-268 Upper Main St., Edgartown, 508-627-8883
This new Edgartown seafooder is the latest port of call for chef Ray Schiltzer (ex Water, The Oyster Bar), who offers an extensive menu and a raw bar for good measure; expect a bistro atmo right down to the paper-covered tablecloths.

Navigator, The [S][M] 16 | 18 | 16 | $27

2 Main St. (Dock St.), Edgartown, 508-627-4320

◪ A "yacht-watchers paradise", this seafooder on the harbor in Edgartown is a "fun hangout" serving "fresh" fin fare in "nothing-fancy" surroundings; so "kick back and relax" at a "table overlooking the water" – "otherwise you could be dining at any family restaurant."

Offshore Brewing Co. [S][M] ▽ 16 | 18 | 15 | $25

30 Kennebec Ave., Oak Bluffs, 508-693-2626

■ Where "casual" types "want to be in the summer", this mill-style brewery in Oak Bluffs offers an American menu of "always fresh" seafood and "pub-type" fare that's a "great value"; fans of the wood-booth ambiance say "it's impossible not to feel at home" and wonder where else "you can throw peanuts on the floor."

Savoir Fare [S][M] 27 | 23 | 24 | $49

Old Post Office Sq. (opp. Town Hall), Edgartown, 508-627-9864

■ You can always count on a "memorable meal" at this Edgartown New American, especially if you're sitting on the "wonderful outdoor porch" sampling the "best oysters" or Italian-tinged pastas, seafood and game; the "elegant" atmosphere is somewhat "pretentious" – you "always meet a celebrity here" – so "be prepared to pay for it."

South Beach Cafe [S][M] – | – | – | M

25 Dunes Rd. (S. Beach Rd.), Edgartown, 508-627-4908

A clamshell's throw from Edgartown's South Beach, this New American grill showcases Mediterranean-influenced fare from chef Perry Ambulos (ex Water, Brasserie 162); standouts like the crab spring roll and grilled rack of lamb are served in a dining room where oil paintings compete with a view of the dunes.

Stripers [S][M] ▽ 18 | 17 | 19 | $33

52 Beach Rd. (Oak Bluff), Vineyard Haven, 508-693-8383

■ "Can't beat the view from their upper deck" claim customers of this simple Vineyard Haven New American seafooder with a Latin accent, courtesy of new chef Miriam Cordova (the change may outdate the above food score); batik tablecloths and painted platters brighten otherwise simple rooms, with three decks as the favorites for seating.

Sweet Life Cafe, The [S][M] – | – | – | M

63 Circuit Ave. (Pequot St.), Oak Bluffs, 508-696-0200

A demure house sets the stage for a graceful dining experience in the heart of Oak Bluffs' hubbub, where the Cal-American cuisine focuses on light salads and lavish seafood; the 130-year-old Victorian house is covered with flowers, and the service is as genteel as the setting.

Zapotec ◐ⓈⓂ
▽ 21 · 16 · 19 · $26

14 Kennebec Ave. (Atlantic Ave.), Oak Bluffs, 508-693-6800
■ For "great Mexican food", this Oak Bluffs amigo is "a must", dishing out solid South of the Border selections like chimichangas, fish tacos and paella in a "fun" colorful house that gets a crowd lining up for dinner and cervezas; it's "reasonably priced compared to other island food" too.

Zephrus ⓈⓂ
– · – · – · M

9 Main St. (Beach Rd.), Vineyard Haven, 508-693-3416
This casual streetfront cafe brings New American dining with International inflections to the bustle of the Vineyard Haven ferry environs; steak, salmon and entrees with Asian and Portuguese accents are served in a bright bistro setting bedecked with island artwork.

NANTUCKET

American Seasons ⓈⓂ
25 · 21 · 22 · $48

80 Centre St. (W. Chester St.), 508-228-7111
■ Just outside bustling Downtown, this "romantic" regional American offers an "imaginative menu", resulting in the "most creative food on the island" with an "unbeatable combination of flavors"; the "interesting wine list", "helpful staff" and "incredible ambiance" are more reasons to "love this place."

Black Eyed Susan's ⓈⓂ⊜
24 · 15 · 20 · $29

10 India St. (Centre St.), 508-325-0308
■ "Don't let appearances fool you" – namely, the "small", "unpretentious" room – at this "funky BYO diner" because the "imaginative, changing menu" ("wonderful breakfasts"), "relaxing atmosphere" and "fair prices" make it "worth the hassle of getting a table"; N.B. closed for lunch.

Boarding House Ⓢ
25 · 21 · 22 · $44

12 Federal St. (India St.), 508-228-9622
■ In the heart of town, New American fare takes on an Asian accent at this "lovely restaurant" offering "original ideas that take you by surprise", complemented by a 350-bottle wine list, "upscale" ambiance, "nice bar" and "pleasant" patio; it's "hard to get into", but if you do, it's a "great place to splurge."

Brant Point Grill ⓈⓂ
– · – · – · VE

White Elephant Inn, 50 Easton St. (Harbor View Way), 508-228-2500
The seasonal reopening of the White Elephant brings with it the yearly return of the inn's standout American seafooder to the island's fine dining scene; trendy preparations of surf 'n' turf classics top the menu, and the elegant, light-filled room with a harborfront terrace supplies New England atmosphere to spare; N.B. open May–October.

Cambridge Street 🅂🅜

– – – M

14 Cambridge St., 508-228-7109

The newly expanded space at this dinner-only Downtown American means there's extra breathing room for patrons bulking up on BBQ ribs and chicken; the relaxed setting features eclectic art, and though the kitchen closes at 10 PM, the bar carries on into the wee hours.

Centre Street Bistro 🅂🅜🔶

▽ 21 14 17 $31

Meeting House, 29 Centre St. (E. Chestnut St.), 508-228-8470

◪ "Imaginative" food makes this tiny Downtown New American tucked inside a shopping arcade "worth the wait", particularly for the weekend breakfast; a less-than-stellar decor score suggests the "very simple setting" "needs sprucing up", but if you "try the seats outside" you won't notice.

Chanticleer, The 🅂

26 26 24 $62

9 New St. (King St.), Siasconset, 508-257-6231

■ "One of the most romantic spots in the world" is this "idyllic" Classic French serving "the most delicious food in a setting of comfort and elegance"; it's "a bit too stuffy" for some surveyors, but "outside dining in the courtyard is glorious" – where "roses in bloom" take the blush off the "obscenely expensive" tab.

Club Car, The 🅂🅜

23 21 22 $49

1 Main St. (Easy St.), 508-228-1101

◪ The "unassuming exterior" gives a weathered look to this "convenient" Main Streeter that's "a real surprise" for "fabulous" Continental classics like beef Wellington and rack of lamb; the interior decor is "elegant" to some, while others suggest a "makeover" is in order and warn claustrophobes it "can get crowded."

Company of the Cauldron ◑🅂

25 24 23 $52

5 India St. (bet. Centre & Federal Sts.), 508-228-4016

■ Two seatings (7 and 9 PM) and a fixed menu that changes nightly make this Downtown American "unique" and a "special treat" – just don't forget to "call ahead" to "make sure you like the menu" (available to inquirers one week in advance); seating in the "old tavern" setting is "slightly cramped" but made even more "warm" and "romantic" by a "wonderful harpist."

56 Union 🅂🅜

– – – E

56 Union St. (E. York St.), 508-228-6135

Global cuisine goes accessibly local at this Downtowner, which brings together an eclectic mix of International dishes; globetrotters will find the Nantucket setting firmly established with black-and-white photos of island scenery; N.B. dinner only.

Jared Coffin House [S] [M] — 22 | 23 | 22 | $40

29 Broad St. (Centre St.), 508-228-2400

◪ This "island institution" draws an "older crowd" with its "plentiful" portions of "good, simple" American food "conscientiously" served in a "beautiful" "historic mansion"; the "quiet and relaxing" "formal room" upstairs is offset by a "fun" (and "less expensive") downstairs taproom and patio dining that's a "must"; less-impressed patrons, however, nail this coffin as "dull" and "dated."

Kendrick's at Quaker House [S] [M] ▽ 22 | 20 | 22 | $44

5 Chestnut St. (Centre St.), 508-228-9156

■ "Loved it" cheer the few surveyors who've happened upon this "wonderful small gem" Downtown, noted for its "incredibly fresh, innovative" American cooking; some observe the decor is "sparse", but "what do you expect at a Quaker house?"

Le Languedoc [M] — 25 | 22 | 23 | $50

24 Broad St. (bet. Centre & Federal Sts.), 508-228-2552

■ "Great seafood", "beautiful decor" and "professional service" attract admirers to this "elegant", "romantic" French-American enclave offering two dining options: a main room upstairs and an "intimate cafe" with a "lovely outdoor garden" that's "great" for "people-watching"; most voters feel the latter is the "best bet."

Nantucket Tapas [S] [M] ▽ 23 | 14 | 18 | $29

15 S. Beach St. (Steamboat Wharf), 508-228-2033

◪ Spanish nibbles are the headliner at this "yummy" nook disguised as a flower-covered home just outside Downtown; diners applaud the "great concept" but warn that the "tapas are better than the entrees" and the "bill adds up quickly."

Oran Mor [S] [M] ▽ 27 | 21 | 23 | $58

2 S. Beach St. (Broad St.), 508-228-8655

◪ Fans feel this "small", "friendly" International Downtown near the steamship gets "better each time [they] eat there"; service is "top-notch" and the "unpretentious" atmosphere is "relaxing", though some are put off by "outrageous prices" for a "plain room" with undersized servings.

Pearl, The [S] [M] — – | – | – | E

12 Federal St. (India St.), 508-228-9701

From the owners of the Boarding House comes this gem with a luminescent room designed by Chris Smith to resemble an underwater seascape, replete with a 300-gallon fish tank, pearlescent banquettes and diaphanous curtains set off by the pale blue lights from below; it's a truly spectacular setting in which to savor chef Seth Raynor's coastal cuisine prepared with a Franco-Asian flair; N.B. closed January–April.

Ropewalk [S] [M] 16 | 20 | 16 | $34

1 Straight Wharf (end of Straight Wharf), 508-228-8886

◪ There's "good" food and drink (including a raw bar) to be had at this "casual" New American seafooder on the wharf, but it's "the view" and "great nautical setting" that make it "special" and "every local's favorite"; so "sit on the terrace overlooking the harbor" as "the sun goes down."

Straight Wharf [S] 24 | 23 | 21 | $48

6 Harbor Sq. (Straight Wharf), 508-228-4499

■ A "super location" on the harbor makes this "out-of-this-world" seafooder a "favorite" among afishionados seeking "fabulous views" with their "delicious" fin fare; "beautiful decor" and a "really hopping" bar scene add value to the "NYC prices."

Summer House ◐ [S] [M] 25 | 27 | 24 | $54

17 Ocean Ave. (Magnolia Rd.), Siasconset, 508-257-9976

◪ Walk past quaint flower box–filled cottages to reach the "intimate" dining room at this "paradise" in 'Sconset where the "outstanding" Eclectic menu emphasizes pristine seafood and the "beautiful" decor is designed for "romance"; it's "what a Nantucket dining experience should be"; N.B. try to snag a seat on the casual porch.

Topper's [S] [M] 28 | 27 | 26 | $65

Wauwinet Inn, 120 Wauwinet Rd. (Polpis Rd.), 508-228-8768

■ The Wauwinet Inn is home to the highest-rated restaurant on the island, a "romantic" New American that pleases patrons with "exceptional food", an "outstanding" wine list, "warm service" and a "magical setting" filled with flowers, classic art and "Waspy blue-blazers" who aren't daunted by the "breathtaking prices"; admirers promise it's "worth the trip to this side of the island" near the Great Point Lighthouse.

21 Federal [S] [M] 26 | 24 | 24 | $50

21 Federal St. (bet. Chestnut & India Sts.), 508-228-2121

■ "Make reservations early" urge islanders who call this "wonderful" American in a tastefully restored mansion "always a favorite" for a "classy" (read: "pricey") dinner or a casual night out at the "best bar on Nantucket"; the food is "consistently good", the service "attentive" and the "soothing surroundings" "elegant" yet "comfortable" – in all, a "classic" that's "not to be missed."

West Creek Cafe [S] [M] ▽ 27 | 21 | 25 | $47

11 W. Creek Rd. (bet. Orange & Pleasant Sts.), 508-228-4943

◪ Satisfied surveyors say this "small", "out-of-town" New American is worth the slight hike for its "luscious" fare (including "superb fish") brought to table by a "super staff"; there's debate about the bold decor – "sleek, sophisticated" vs. "a bit much" – but there's no disagreement about the "marvelous", frequently changing menu.

Indexes

CUISINES*

Afghan
Helmand

American (New)
Aesop's Tables/C
American Seasons/N
Anago
Aspasia
Audubon Circle
Aujourd'hui
Aura
Baker's Best
Balance/M
Beach Plum Inn/M
Biba
Blackstone on Square
Blue Cat Cafe
Boarding House/N
Boathouse Grille
Brant Point Grill/N
Brew Moon
Bristol Lounge
B-Side Lounge
Butterfish American
Cafe Edwige/C
Cape Sea Grille/C
Centre St. Bistro/N
Club Cafe
Company of Cauldron/N
Daddy-O's
Fava
Flashes
Flora
Franklin Cafe
Full Moon
Gallerani's/C
Gargoyles
Glenn's
Glory
Grapevine
Hamersley's Bistro
Harry's Too
Harvard Gardens
Harvest
Icarus
Intrigue Café
Isabella
La Cucina/M
Landing
Laurel

Le Languedoc/N
Library Grill
Lyceum B&G
Marketplace Cafe & Grill
Metropolis Cafe
Milk St. Café
Miracle of Science
Museum of Fine Arts Rest.
No. 9 Park
Oskar's
Other Side Cosmic
Painter's/C
Pillar House
Playhouse Bistro/C
Pravda 116
Prose
Red Pheasant/C
Red Raven's Love
Regatta of Cotuit/C
Regatta of Falmouth/C
Ritz-Carlton Cafe
Ropewalk/N
R Place
Sage
Salts
Sam's
Savoir Fare/M
Seasons
75 Chestnut
Sidney's Grille
6 Burner Urban Diner
South Beach Cafe/M
Stephanie's
Stripers/M
Sweet Life Café/M
Temple Bar
Ten Center St.
Tiernan's
Top Kat Lounge
Top of Hub
Topper's/N
Tremont 647
21 Federal/N
224 Boston St.
Up Stairs at the Pudding
Vault Bistro/Wine Bar
Veronique
Vicki Lee Boyajian
Vox Populi
Walden Grille

* All restaurants are in the greater Boston area unless otherwise
noted (C=Cape Cod; M=Martha's Vineyard; N=Nantucket).

Water Club
West Creek Cafe/N
West St. Grille
White Star Tav.
Zephrus/M

American (Regional)

Amrheins
Anthony's Pier 4
Barker Tavern
Barley Neck Inn/C
Blue Ribbon BBQ
Christian's/C
Daggett House/M
Dodge St. B&G
Flume/C
Henrietta's Table
House of Blues
Martin House/C
North East Brewing
Paddock/C
Parker's
Rowes Wharf
Scandia
Sherborn Inn
Tom Shea's
29 Newbury
Warren Tavern
Wayside Inn
Wequassett Inn/C

American (Traditional)

Amelia's
Anchovies
Andover Inn
Atlas B&G
B.B. Wolf
Black Dog Tavern/M
Black Rose
Blue Cat Cafe
Blue Diner
Boodle's
Boston Beer Garden
Boston Beer Works
Boston Sail Loft
Brandy Pete's
Bull & Finch Pub
Burren
Cafe 300
Cambridge Brewing
Cambridge Common
Cambridge St./N
Charley's Saloon
Charlie's Sandwich
Chart House

Christopher's American Rib/C
Cityside B&G
Clarke's
Clery's
Colonial Inn
Commonwealth Fish
Coolidge Corner Clubhse.
Copley's
Cranebrook
Daddy-O's
Dakota's
David Ryan's/M
Desmond O'Malley's
Dick's Last Resort
Dockside
Doyle's Cafe
Durgin Park
Federalist
Geoffrey's
Good Life
Grafton St. Pub
Grand Canal
Green Dragon
Grille at Hobbs Brook
Grill 23
Halfway Cafe
Hard Rock Cafe
Harry's
Hartwell House
Harvest
High Brewster Inn/C
Hill Tavern
Ironside Grill
Jacob Wirth
Jared Coffin Hse./N
Joe's American
John Harvard's
Johnny's Luncheonette
Joseph's on High
Kendrick's/N
Last Hurrah
L Street Diner
Maddie's Sail
Ma Glockner's
Matt Murphy's Pub
Medieval Manor
Mr. & Mrs. Bartley's
New Bridge Cafe
Not Your Average Joe's
Oak Room
Offshore Brewing/M
Original Sports Saloon
Orleans Inn/C

Palm
Parrish Cafe
Porters Bar & Grill
Roggie's
Rosebud Diner
Ruggieri's
Salty Dog
Samuel Adams Brewhse.
S&S Rest.
Silvertone Bar & Grill
Sorella's
Sound Bites
Sports Depot
Stars
Stockyard
Sunset Grill
Ten Center St.
Tim's Tavern
Union Street
Vidalia's Truck Stop
Watch City

Armenian
Karoun

Asian
Ambrosia on Huntington
BARCODE
Bernard's
Betty's Wok & Noodle Diner
Billy Tse
Blue Ginger
Boarding House/N
Cafe Tsunami/M
Fire & Ice
Grasshopper
Jae's Cafe
J.T.K. Grill & Sushi
Ma Soba
Ming Garden
Moon Villa
Poppa & Goose
Red Pheasant/C
Salamander
Sapporo
Tiger Lily

Bakery
Hi-Rise Bread
Vicki Lee Boyajian

Barbecue
B.B. Wolf
Bison County BBQ
Blue Ribbon BBQ
East Coast Grill

Jake's Boss BBQ
Linwood Grill & BBQ
Original Sports Saloon
Pit Stop BBQ
Redbones BBQ
Rudy's Cafe
Uncle Pete's Hickory Ribs
Village Smokehse.
Whiskey's

Brazilian
Bomboa
Buteco
Cafe Brazil
Midwest Grill

Cajun/Creole
Dixie Kitchen
House of Blues
Jumbalaya
Magnolia's Southern

Californian
Blossoms Cafe
Bluestone Bistro
California Pizza Kit.
Sage
Sweet Life Café/M

Cambodian
Carambola
Elephant Walk

Caribbean
Chez Henri
Green St. Grill
Rhythm & Spice

Chinese
Bernard's
Billy Tse
Buddha's Delight
Cafe China
Changsho
Chau Chow City
Chef Chang's
Chef Chow's
China Pearl
Ducky Wok
Eastern Pier Seafood
East Ocean City
Golden Palace
Golden Temple
Grand Chau Chow
Imperial Seafood
Joy Luck Café

Kong Luh
Kowloon
Lotus Blossom
Lucky Garden
Mary Chung
Moon Villa
New Asia
New Shanghai
Noble House
Ocean Wealth
Peach Farm
Peking Cuisine
P. F. Chang's
Royal East
Shalom Hunan
Sichuan Garden
Yangtze River
Yenching Palace

Coffeehouse/Dessert

Ambrosia on Huntington
Anago
Caffe Vittoria
Finale
Radius
Rauxa
Rave
1369 Coffee Hse.

Coffee Shop/Diner

Black Eyed Susan's/N
Cafe Pamplona
Caffe Paradiso
Charlie's Sandwich
Harry's
Johnny's Luncheonette
L Street Diner
Mike's City Diner
New Yorker Diner
Rosebud Diner
Ruby's
S&S Rest.
6 Burner Urban Diner
Victoria
Vidalia's Truck Stop

Colombian

El Cafetal

Continental

Andover Inn
Cafe Budapest
Cafe Escadrille
Cafe Suisse
Club Car/N
57 Rest.

Hartwell House
Locke-Ober Cafe
Raffael's
Sophia's
White Rainbow

Cuban

Chez Henri

Deli/Sandwich Shop

Baker's Best
B & D Deli
Cafe de Paris
Hi-Rise Bread
Manhattan Sammy's Deli
Milk St. Café
Other Side Cosmic
Rubin's
S&S Rest.
Wrap
Zaftigs Deli

Dim Sum

Bernard's
Chau Chow City
China Pearl
Dynasty
Golden Palace
Imperial Seafood
Mary Chung
Ma Soba
Ming Garden

Eclectic/International

Ambrosia on Huntington
Amity, The/M
Atria/M
Biba
Blue Ginger
Blue Room
Café Moxie/M
Centre St. Café
Cheesecake Factory
Christopher's
Claremont Café
Contrast/C
Delux Cafe
Dish
Duckworth Lane
eat
83 Main
Evoo
56 Union/N
Fire & Ice
Fire King
Gardner Museum Cafe

Glenn's
Glory
Grendel's Bar
Il Bacio
Jasmine Bistro
Johnny D's Uptown
Metropolis Cafe
Mistral
On The Park
Oran Mor/N
Playhouse Bistro/C
Prose
Red Raven's Love
R. Wesley's
Salamander
Sonsie
Summer House/N
Temple Bar
Ten Center St.
224 Boston St.
Wonder Bar
Wrap

English
Cornwall's

Ethiopian
Addis Red Sea

French (Bistro)
Aquitaine
Brasserie Jo
Cassis
Chanterelle
Chez Henri
Contrast/C
Hamersley's Bistro
Le Gamin
Le Languedoc/N
Les Zygomates
Sandrine's
Sel de la Terre
Truc

French (Classic)
Cafe Fleuri
Caprice
Chanticleer/N
Garden of Eden
Le Bocage
Le Grenier/M
Le Lyonnais
Maison Robert
Mistral
Ritz-Carlton Din. Rm.
Torch

French (New)
Ambrosia on Huntington
Bay Tower
Bomboa
Caprice
Chillingsworth/C
Clio
Elephant Walk
Exchange
Hungry I
Jasmine Bistro
Julien
L'Espalier
L'Etoile/M
Lumière
No. 9 Park
Radius
Silks
Torch
Veronique

German
Jacob Wirth

Greek
Demo's
Omonia

Hamburger
Audubon Circle
Charley's Saloon
Good Life
Hard Rock Cafe
Joe's American
Johnny's Luncheonette
Manhattan Sammy's Deli
Miracle of Science
Mr. & Mrs. Bartley's
Sunset Grill
Tim's Tavern
Warren Tavern

Health Food
Country Life
Five Seasons
Grasshopper

Hungarian
Cafe Budapest
Jasmine Bistro

Indian
Ajanta
Akbar India
Bawarchi
Bombay Bistro

Bombay Cafe
Bombay Club
Bukhara
Cafe of India
Diva Indian Bistro
Himalaya
India House
Indian Cafe
Indian Club
India Pavilion
India Quality
India Samraat
Kashmir
Kebab-N-Kurry
Maharaja's
New Mother India
Passage to India
Rangoli
Rasol
Saffron
Shalimar of India
Tandoor House
Tanjore
Taste of India

Irish

Burren
Desmond O'Malley's
Doyle's Cafe
Grafton St. Pub
Grand Canal
Green Dragon
Matt Murphy's Pub
Tiernan's

Italian

(N=Northern; S=Southern;
N&S=Includes both)
Abbicci/C (N&S)
Abbondanza Ristorante (N&S)
Adrian's/C (N&S)
Al Dente (S)
Alloro (N&S)
Amelia's (N&S)
Anchovies (N&S)
Angelo & Son's Seafood (S)
Angelo's (N&S)
Antico Forno (S)
Antonio's (N&S)
Appetito (N&S)
Armani Cafe (N&S)
Armida's (S)
Artu (N&S)
Assaggio (N&S)
Bella's (S)

Bertucci's (N)
Bistro 5 (N)
Black Goose (N&S)
Café Louis (N)
Cafe Marliave (N&S)
Caffe Luna (N)
Caffe Paradiso (N&S)
Caffe Vittoria (N&S)
Cantina Italiana (S)
Carla's (N)
Carlo's Cucina (N&S)
Ciao Bella (N&S)
Daily Catch (S)
Dancing Lobster/C (N&S)
Davide Rist. (N&S)
Davio's (N&S)
De Pasquale's (N&S)
Dom's (N&S)
Donatello Rist. (N&S)
Euno (N&S)
Figs (N&S)
Filippo Rist. (N&S)
Five North Sq. (N&S)
Florentina (N&S)
Florentine Cafe (N&S)
Gallerani's/C (N&S)
Galleria Italiana (N&S)
Galleria Umberto (S)
Giacomo's (S)
Giannino's (N)
Greg's (N&S)
G'Vanni's (N&S)
Il Bacio (N&S)
Il Capriccio (N)
Il Giardino (N&S)
Il Moro (N)
Joe Tecce's (N&S)
La Campania (N&S)
La Famiglia Giorgio (N&S)
La Groceria (N&S)
La Summa (S)
L'Osteria (N&S)
Lucia's Rist. (N&S)
Maggiano's Little Italy (S)
Mamma Maria (N)
Marcellino (N&S)
Marcuccio's (N)
Marino Rist. (N&S)
Massimino's Cucina (N&S)
Matteo's (N&S)
Maurizio's (N&S)
Milano's Italian Kit. (N&S)
Mother Anna's (N&S)
Nauset Beach Club/C (N&S)
Nicole Rist. (N&S)

No. 9 Park (N&S)
Pagliuca's (S)
Papa Razzi (N)
Papa Razzi (N&S)
Pat's Pushcart (N&S)
Pellino's (N)
Piccola Luna (N)
Piccola Venezia (N&S)
Piccolo Nido (N&S)
Pignoli (N&S)
Polcari's (N&S)
Pomodoro (N&S)
Ponte Vecchio (N&S)
Rest. Bricco (N&S)
Rist. Toscano (N)
Rita's Place (N&S)
Ruggieri's (N&S)
Sablone's (N&S)
Sage (N&S)
Sal's Place/C (S)
Saporito's (N)
Saraceno (N&S)
Siros (N)
Sorento's (N)
South End Galleria (N&S)
Spinnaker Italia (N)
Stellina (N&S)
Sweet Basil (N&S)
Terramia (N&S)
Tosca (N)
Tratt. A Scalinatella (S)
Tratt. Il Panino (N&S)
Tratt. Pulcinella (N&S)
Tullio's (N&S)
Tuscan Grill (N)
Verona (N&S)
Villa Francesca (N&S)
Village Fish (N&S)
Vin & Eddie's (N)
Vinny's at Night (S)
Vinny Testa's (S)
West Side Lounge (S)
Yerardi's (N&S)

Japanese
Apollo Grill
Bisuteki
Cafe Sushi
Fugakyu
Ginza
Goemon
Gyuhama
Inaho/C
Jae's Cafe

JP Seafood
Kaya
Nara
Narita
Roka
Sakurabana
Shilla
Shogun
Suishaya
Takeshima
Tatsukichi
Tokyo
Yama
Yokohama

Jewish
B & D Deli
Manhattan Sammy's Deli
Milk St. Café*
Rubin's*
S&S Rest.
Shalom Hunan*
Zaftigs Deli

Korean
Apollo Grill
Arirang House
JP Seafood
Kaya
Koreana
Shilla
Suishaya
Woo Chun
Yokohama

Malaysian
Pandan Leaf
Penang

Mediterranean
Abbicci/C
Ardeo/C
Atara Bistro/Wine Bar
Bar 10
Caffe Bella
Caprice
Casablanca
Dalya's
Front Street/C
Gala Rist.
Il Bacio
Il Moro
Karoun
Maurizio's
Olives
Red Clay

Red Pheasant/C
Rest. Bricco
Rialto
Siros
West Side Lounge

Mexican/Tex-Mex
Andale! Taqueria
Anna's Taqueria
Baja Betty's
Baja Mexican
Boca Grande
Border Cafe
Cactus Club
Casa Mexico
Casa Romero
El Pelon Taqueria
Fajitas & 'Ritas
Forest Cafe
Iguana Cantina
Jose's
Jumbalaya
La Paloma
Olé, Mexican Grille
Palenque
Purple Cactus
Rattlesnake B&G
Rudy's Cafe
Sol Azteca
Tacos El Charro
Taqueria la Mexicana
Taqueria Mexico
Zapotec/M
Zuma Tex-Mex

Middle Eastern
Bishop's
Cafe Barada
Cafe Jaffa
Kareem's
Karoun
Lala Rokh
Middle East
Phoenicia
Sabra
Skewers
Sultan's Kitchen
Zaatar's Oven

Moroccan
Marrakesh

Persian
Lala Rokh

Pizza
Adrian's/C
Bertucci's
Bluestone Bistro
Café Louis
California Pizza Kit.
De Pasquale's
Figs
Galleria Umberto
L Street Diner
Not Your Average Joe's
Papa Razzi
Pizzeria Regina
Pizzeria Uno
Santarpio's Pizza
Woody's

Portuguese
Atasca
Casa Portugal
Neighborhood Rest.
O'Fado
Sunset Cafe

Russian
Cafe St. Petersburg

Seafood
Aesop's Tables/C
Alchemy/M
Angelo & Son's Seafood
Anthony's Pier 4
Atlantic Fish Co.
Atlantic 101
Back Eddy
Barking Crab
Boston Sail Loft
Brant Point Grill/N
Bubala's by the Bay/C
Captain's Wharf
Court Hse. Seafood
Daggett House/M
Daily Catch
Dancing Lobster/C
David Ryan's/M
Dino's Sea Grille
Dockside
Dolphin
East Coast Grill
Eastern Pier Seafood
East Ocean City
Fish Landing B&G/C
Five Seasons
Flume/C
Giacomo's
Grand Chau Chow

Grillfish
Grill 23
Homeport/M
Imperial Seafood
Jasper White's
Jimbo's Fish Shanty
Jimmy's Harborside
JP Seafood
Jumbo Seafood
KingFish Hall
Landing
Legal Sea Foods
Maddie's Sail
Martha's Vineyard Seafood/M
Naked Fish
Navigator/M
No Name
Ocean Wealth
Peach Farm
Pearl/N
Penguins/C
Ropewalk/N
Ruggieri's
Salty Dog
Scandia
Skipjack's
Straight Wharf/N
Stripers/M
Summer House/N
Tavern on Water
Tom Shea's
Turner Fisheries
Union Oyster Hse.
Village Fish
Wequassett Inn/C
White Rainbow
Woodman's

South American
Pandorga's

Southern/Soul
Blue Ribbon BBQ
Bob the Chef
House of Blues
Linwood Grill & BBQ
Lola's/M
Magnolia's Southern

Southwestern
Cottonwood Cafe
Kokopelli Chili
Masa
R Place

Spanish
Dali
Iruna
Rauxa
Sophia's
Taberna de Haro
Tapeo
Tasca

Steakhouse
Abe & Louie's
Bisuteki
Bugaboo Creek Steak
Capital Grille
Fleming's
Frank's Steak
Grill 23
Hilltop Steak
Jimmy's Steer Hse.
Ken's Steak
Morton's of Chicago
Oak Room
Palm
Plaza III
Stockyard

Swiss
Marché Boston

Tapas
Dali
Nantucket Tapas/N
Taberna de Haro
Tapeo

Thai
Amarin of Thailand
Bangkok Basil
Bangkok Bistro
Bangkok Blue
Bangkok Cuisine
Bangkok House
Billy Tse
Brown Sugar Cafe
Brown Sugar Cafe
Erawan of Siam
Green Papaya
House of Siam
Jae's Cafe
King & I
Kowloon
Montien
Rod Dee
Sawasdee
Siam Cuisine

Siam Garden
Thai Basil
Thai's

Tibetan
House of Tibet

Turkish
Sultan's Kitchen

Vegetarian
(Most Chinese, Indian and
Thai restaurants)
Buddha's Delight
Centre St. Café
Country Life

Five Seasons
Grapevine
Grasshopper
Helmand
Milk St. Café

Vietnamese
Billy Tse
Dong Khanh
Ducky Wok
Pho Pasteur
Pho République
Saigon
Viet Hong
V. Majestic

LOCATIONS

BOSTON

Allston/Brighton
Atara Bistro/Wine Bar
Bangkok Bistro
Bluestone Bistro
Boathouse Grille
Brown Sugar Cafe
Cafe Brazil
Carlo's Cucina
Chef Chow's
Cityside B&G
Ducky Wok
El Cafetal
Grasshopper
Jasmine Bistro
North East Brewing
Pho Pasteur
Pizzeria Uno
Rangoli
Roggie's
Saigon
Siam Cuisine
6 Burner Urban Diner
Sports Depot
Stockyard
Sunset Grill
Tasca
Viet Hong
V. Majestic
Wonder Bar
Wrap

Back Bay
Abe & Louie's
Ambrosia on Huntington
Anago
Angelo's
Armani Cafe
Atlantic Fish Co.
Baja Mexican
Bangkok Blue
BARCODE
Bar 10
Biba
Blue Cat Cafe
Bomboa
Boodle's
Bristol Lounge
Cactus Club
Cafe Budapest
Cafe de Paris
Cafe Jaffa

Café Louis
California Pizza Kit.
Capital Grille
Casa Romero
Chanterelle
Charley's Saloon
Ciao Bella
Clio
Copley's
Cottonwood Cafe
Davio's
Dick's Last Resort
Fire & Ice
Grill 23
Gyuhama
Hard Rock Cafe
Himalaya
India Samraat
Joe's American
Kashmir
Kaya
Kebab-N-Kurry
La Famiglia Giorgio
Legal Sea Foods
L'Espalier
Marché Boston
Milano's Italian Kit.
Morton's of Chicago
Oak Room
Original Sports Saloon
Palm
Papa Razzi
Parrish Cafe
Pho Pasteur
Pignoli
Pizzeria Uno
Rattlesnake B&G
Ritz-Carlton Cafe
Ritz-Carlton Din. Rm.
Saffron
Salamander
Samuel Adams Brewhse.
Skipjack's
Sonsie
Stephanie's
Tapeo
Thai Basil
Top of Hub
Turner Fisheries
29 Newbury
Vinny Testa's

Vox Populi
Whiskey's
White Star Tav.
Wrap
Yenching Palace

Beacon Hill

Antonio's
Artu
Black Goose
Bull & Finch Pub
Federalist
Figs
Harvard Gardens
Hill Tavern
Hungry I
King & I
Lala Rokh
Library Grill
Ma Soba
No. 9 Park
Phoenicia
Rist. Toscano
Ruby's
75 Chestnut
Torch

Charlestown

83 Main
Figs
Ironside Grill
Olives
R. Wesley's
Tavern on Water
Warren Tavern

Chelsea/East Boston/Revere

Angelo & Son's Seafood
Billy Tse
Bisuteki
New Bridge Cafe
Rita's Place
Sablone's
Santarpio's Pizza
Uncle Pete's Hickory Ribs

Chinatown/Leather Dist.

Apollo Grill
Buddha's Delight
Chau Chow City
China Pearl
Dong Khanh
Dynasty
East Ocean City
Ginza

Golden Palace
Grand Chau Chow
Imperial Seafood
Jumbo Seafood
Les Zygomates
Moon Villa
New Shanghai
Ocean Wealth
Oskar's
Peach Farm
Peking Cuisine
Penang
Pho Pasteur
Suishaya

Downtown Boston/ Financial District

Aujourd'hui
Blossoms Cafe
Blue Diner
Brandy Pete's
Cafe Fleuri
Cafe Marliave
Cafe Suisse
Cafe 300
California Pizza Kit.
Country Life
Dakota's
Exchange
Fajitas & 'Ritas
Goemon
Good Life
Intrigue Café
Joseph's on High
Julien
Last Hurrah
Legal Sea Foods
Locke-Ober Cafe
Maison Robert
Milk St. Café
Nara
Parker's
Pho Pasteur
Radius
Sakurabana
Sam's
Sel de la Terre
Silvertone Bar & Grill
Sultan's Kitchen
Tatsukichi
Tiernan's
Vault Bistro/Wine Bar
West St. Grille
Wrap

Faneuil Hall

Bay Tower
Bertucci's
Black Rose
Clarke's
Durgin Park
Green Dragon
KingFish Hall
Marketplace Cafe & Grill
Pizzeria Regina
Pizzeria Uno
Plaza III
Salty Dog
Seasons
Tratt. Il Panino
Union Oyster Hse.
Zuma Tex-Mex

Jamaica Plain/ West Roxbury

Bukhara
Centre St. Café
Doyle's Cafe
Jake's Boss BBQ
JP Seafood
Purple Cactus
Sorella's
Tacos El Charro

Kenmore Square/Fenway

Atlas B&G
Audubon Circle
Bawarchi
Boston Beer Works
Brown Sugar Cafe
Buteco
Cornwall's
Elephant Walk
El Pelon Taqueria
Gardner Museum Cafe
Il Giardino
India Quality
Linwood Grill & BBQ
Museum of Fine Arts Rest.
Other Side Cosmic
Pizzeria Uno
Sophia's
Sorento's
Woody's

North End/North Station

Al Dente
Alloro
Antico Forno
Armida's
Artu

Assaggio
Atlantic 101
Billy Tse
Caffe Paradiso
Caffe Vittoria
Cantina Italiana
Commonwealth Fish
Daily Catch
Davide Rist.
Dom's
Euno
Filippo Rist.
Five North Sq.
Florentine Cafe
Galleria Umberto
Giacomo's
Grand Canal
G'Vanni's
Il Bacio
Joe's American
Joe Tecce's
La Famiglia Giorgio
La Summa
L'Osteria
Lucia's Rist.
Mamma Maria
Marcuccio's
Massimino's Cucina
Maurizio's
Mother Anna's
Naked Fish
Nicole Rist.
Pagliuca's
Pat's Pushcart
Piccola Venezia
Piccolo Nido
Pizzeria Regina
Pomodoro
Porters Bar & Grill
Rest. Bricco
Sage
Saraceno
Terramia
Top Kat Lounge
Tratt. A Scalinatella
Villa Francesca

South End/Roxbury/ Dorchester/Mattapan

Addis Red Sea
Anchovies
Appetito
Aquitaine
Blackstone on Square
Bob the Chef

Charlie's Sandwich
Claremont Café
Clery's
Club Cafe
Delux Cafe
Dish
Franklin Cafe
Garden of Eden
Geoffrey's
Giacomo's
Grillfish
Hamersley's Bistro
House of Siam
Icarus
Jae's Cafe
Laurel
Le Gamin
Masa
Medieval Manor
Metropolis Cafe
Mike's City Diner
Mistral
On The Park
Pho République
Pit Stop BBQ
Rave
South End Galleria
Tim's Tavern
Tremont 647
Truc
224 Boston St.
Victoria

Symphony

Arirang House
Bangkok Cuisine
Betty's Wok & Noodle Diner

Bombay Cafe
Brasserie Jo
Dixie Kitchen
Tiger Lily

Theater District

Brew Moon
Caprice
57 Rest.
Finale
Flashes
Fleming's
Galleria Italiana
Jacob Wirth
Maggiano's Little Italy
Montien
Omonia
P. F. Chang's
Pravda 116

Waterfront/South Boston

Amrheins
Anthony's Pier 4
Aura
Barking Crab
Boston Beer Garden
Boston Sail Loft
Chart House
Daily Catch
Eastern Pier Seafood
Jimbo's Fish Shanty
Jimmy's Harborside
Joe's American
L Street Diner
No Name
Rowes Wharf

CAMBRIDGE

Central Square

Atasca
Bisuteki
Good Life
Green St. Grill
India Pavilion
Koreana
La Groceria
Mary Chung
Middle East
Midwest Grill
Miracle of Science
Rhythm & Spice
Roka
Royal East
Salts

Shalimar of India
Sidney's Grille
Spinnaker Italia
Tandoor House

Fresh Pond

Aspasia
Full Moon
Hi-Rise Bread
Jasper White's
Tokyo

Harvard Square

Bangkok House
Bertucci's
Boca Grande
Bombay Club

Border Cafe
Brew Moon
Butterfish American
Cafe of India
Cafe Pamplona
Cafe Sushi
Caffe Paradiso
Cambridge Common
Casablanca
Casa Mexico
Chez Henri
Dolphin
Fire & Ice
Forest Cafe
Giannino's
Grafton St. Pub
Grendel's Bar
Harvest
Henrietta's Table
Hi-Rise Bread
House of Blues
Iruna
John Harvard's
Johnny's Luncheonette
Jose's
Lucky Garden
Mr. & Mrs. Bartley's
Narita
Pho Pasteur
Pizzeria Uno
Rialto
Sandrine's
Shilla
Siam Garden
Skewers
Tanjore
Tratt. Il Panino
Tratt. Pulcinella
Up Stairs at the Pudding
Wrap
Yenching Palace

Inman Square
Akbar India
Cafe China

Casa Portugal
Court Hse. Seafood
Daddy-O's
East Coast Grill
Jae's Cafe
Magnolia's Southern
Olé, Mexican Grille
S&S Rest.
Sunset Cafe
1369 Coffee Hse.

Kendall Square
Ajanta
Blue Room
Boca Grande
Boston Sail Loft
B-Side Lounge
Cambridge Brewing
Cheesecake Factory
Davio's
Florentina
Helmand
Legal Sea Foods
Manhattan Sammy's Deli
Marrakesh
Papa Razzi
Poppa & Goose
Thai's

Porter Square
Anna's Taqueria
Changsho
Christopher's
Cottonwood Cafe
Elephant Walk
Frank's Steak
Indian Club
Kaya
Maharaja's
Marino Rist.
Passage to India
Pizzeria Uno
Temple Bar
West Side Lounge

NEARBY SUBURBS

Arlington/Winchester/ Belmont
Blue Ribbon BBQ
Cafe Barada
Flora
Gala Rist.
Jimmy's Steer Hse.
Kong Luh
Lucia's Rist.
New Asia

Olé, Mexican Grille
Prose

Brookline/Chestnut Hill
Anna's Taqueria
Baja Betty's
B & D Deli
Bangkok Basil
B.B. Wolf
Bernard's

Bertucci's
Boca Grande
Bombay Bistro
Buddha's Delight
Cafe St. Petersburg
Caffe Luna
Capital Grille
Captain's Wharf
Charley's Saloon
Cheesecake Factory
Chef Chang's
Chef Chow's
Coolidge Corner Clubhse.
Daily Catch
Duckworth Lane
Fajitas & 'Ritas
Figs
Five Seasons
Fugakyu
Ginza
Golden Temple
India House
Indian Cafe
Jae's Cafe
Kaya
Kokopelli Chili
Legal Sea Foods
Matt Murphy's Pub
Ming Garden
Noble House
Pandan Leaf
Papa Razzi
Red Clay
Rod Dee
Rubin's
Sawasdee
Shalom Hunan
Sichuan Garden
Skipjack's
Sol Azteca
Taberna de Haro
Takeshima
Veronique
Village Fish
Village Smokehse.
Vinny Testa's
Wrap
Yokohama
Zaatar's Oven
Zaftigs Deli

Lexington
Yangtze River

Newton/Needham
Amarin of Thailand
Appetito
Baker's Best
Blue Ribbon BBQ
Duckworth Lane
Fava
Johnny's Luncheonette
Joy Luck Café
Karoun
Lumière
Matteo's
Naked Fish
Not Your Average Joe's
Peking Cuisine
Piccola Luna
Pillar House
Pizzeria Uno
Sabra
Sapporo
Shogun
Skipjack's
Sol Azteca
Sweet Basil
Union Street
Vicki Lee Boyajian
Yerardi's

Quincy/Dedham
Bertucci's
Halfway Cafe
Isabella
Joe's American
La Paloma
Naked Fish
Pizzeria Regina
Raffael's
Siros
Tullio's
Vinny Testa's
Water Club

Somerville/Medford
Andale! Taqueria
Bertucci's
Bistro 5
Burren
Dali
De Pasquale's
Diva Indian Bistro
eat
Evoo
Gargoyles
House of Tibet
Johnny D's Uptown

Neighborhood Rest.
New Asia
Palenque
Rauxa
Redbones BBQ
Rosebud Diner
Rudy's Cafe
Sound Bites
Taqueria la Mexicana
Vinny's at Night
Woo Chun

Watertown/Waltham

Bertucci's
Bison County BBQ
Bugaboo Creek Steak
Carambola
Demo's
Dino's Sea Grille
Erawan of Siam
Green Papaya
Greg's

Grille at Hobbs Brook
Halfway Cafe
Iguana Cantina
Il Capriccio
Joe's American
J.T.K. Grill & Sushi
Kareem's
La Campania
Le Bocage
Marcellino
Naked Fish
New Mother India
New Yorker Diner
Not Your Average Joe's
Pandorga's
Stellina
Taqueria Mexico
Taste of India
Tuscan Grill
Verona
Watch City

OUTLYING SUBURBS

North of Boston

Abbondanza Ristorante
Andover Inn
Angelo's
Bertucci's
Bishop's
Border Cafe
Bugaboo Creek Steak
Cassis
Dockside
Dodge St. B&G
Donatello Rist.
Glenn's
Glory
Grapevine
Hilltop Steak
Il Moro
Joe's American
Jumbalaya
Kowloon
Landing
Legal Sea Foods
Lyceum B&G
Maddie's Sail
Naked Fish
New Asia
O'Fado
Papa Razzi

Pellino's
Pizzeria Uno
Polcari's
Ponte Vecchio
Rasol
Red Raven's Love
Ruggieri's
Scandia
Ten Center St.
Tom Shea's
Tratt. Il Panino
Vinny Testa's
White Rainbow
Woodman's

South of Boston

Amelia's
Back Eddy
Barker Tavern
Bella's
Bertucci's
Brew Moon
Bugaboo Creek Steak
Caffe Bella
Carla's
Cranebrook
Dockside
Fire King

Hilltop Steak
Legal Sea Foods
Naked Fish
Not Your Average Joe's
Pizzeria Regina
Pizzeria Uno
Saporito's
Siros
Stars
Tosca
Vin & Eddie's
Vinny Testa's

West of Boston
Amarin of Thailand
Bertucci's
Blue Ginger
Bugaboo Creek Steak
Cafe Escadrille
California Pizza Kit.
Colonial Inn
Dalya's
Desmond O'Malley's
Dolphin
Figs

Halfway Cafe
Harry's
Harry's Too
Hartwell House
Iguana Cantina
John Harvard's
Ken's Steak
Legal Sea Foods
Le Lyonnais
Lotus Blossom
Ma Glockner's
Naked Fish
New Asia
Not Your Average Joe's
Papa Razzi
Pizzeria Regina
R Place
Sherborn Inn
Silks
Vidalia's Truck Stop
Vinny Testa's
Walden Grille
Wayside Inn
Yama

FAR OUTLYING AREAS

Cape Cod
Abbicci
Adrian's
Aesop's Tables
Ardeo
Barley Neck Inn
Bubala's by the Bay
Cafe Edwige
Cape Sea Grille
Chillingsworth
Christian's
Christopher's American Rib
Contrast
Dancing Lobster
Fish Landing B&G
Flume
Front Street
Gallerani's
High Brewster Inn
Inaho
Martin House
Nauset Beach Club
Orleans Inn
Paddock

Painter's
Penguins
Playhouse Bistro
Red Pheasant
Regatta of Cotuit
Regatta of Falmouth
Sal's Place
Wequassett Inn

Martha's Vineyard
Alchemy
Amity, The
Atria
Balance
Beach Plum Inn
Black Dog Tavern
Café Moxie
Cafe Tsunami
Daggett House
David Ryan's
Homeport
La Cucina
Le Grenier
L'Etoile
Lola's

Martha's Vineyard Seafood
Navigator
Offshore Brewing
Savoir Fare
South Beach Cafe
Stripers
Sweet Life Café
Zapotec
Zephrus

Nantucket

American Seasons
Black Eyed Susan's
Boarding House
Brant Point Grill
Cambridge St.
Centre St. Bistro

Chanticleer
Club Car
Company of Cauldron
56 Union
Jared Coffin Hse.
Kendrick's
Le Languedoc
Nantucket Tapas
Oran Mor
Pearl
Ropewalk
Straight Wharf
Summer House
Topper's
21 Federal
West Creek Cafe

SPECIAL FEATURES AND APPEALS

Additions

Alchemy/M
Amity, The/M
Ardeo/C
Aspasia
Atara Bistro/Wine Bar
Atria/M
BARCODE
Bar 10
Betty's Wok & Noodle Diner
Bistro 5
Bomboa
Brant Point Grill/N
Butterfish American
Cafe Pamplona
Cafe Tsunami/M
Cambridge St./N
Caprice
Christopher's American Rib/C
Dish
Diva Indian Bistro
83 Main
56 Union/N
Fish Landing B&G/C
Flashes
Fleming's
Garden of Eden
Jasper White's
J.T.K. Grill & Sushi
KingFish Hall
Last Hurrah
Maggiano's Little Italy
Martha's Vineyard Seafood/M
Masa
Ma Soba
Matteo's
Orleans Inn/C
Porters Bar & Grill
Pravda 116
Raffael's
Rave
Saffron
Sam's
Sapporo
Sel de la Terre
Silvertone Bar & Grill
South Beach Cafe/M
South End Galleria
Top Kat Lounge
Vox Populi
Water Club
Wequassett Inn/C
White Star Tav.
Zephrus/M

Breakfast

(All hotels and the
following standouts)
B & D Deli
Black Dog Tavern/M
Black Eyed Susan's/N
Cafe Edwige/C
Charlie's Sandwich
Claremont Café
Daggett House/M
Geoffrey's
Harry's
Hi-Rise Bread
Jared Coffin Hse./N
Johnny's Luncheonette
Le Gamin
Mike's City Diner
Rosebud Diner
S&S Rest.
Sorella's
Sound Bites
Tiernan's
Zaftigs Deli

Brunch

(Best of many)
Aquitaine
Aujourd'hui
Aura
Biba
Blue Diner
Blue Room
Bluestone Bistro
Bob the Chef
Brasserie Jo
Brew Moon
Bristol Lounge
Cafe Fleuri
Cafe 300
Charley's Saloon
Cheesecake Factory
Ciao Bella
Cityside B&G
Claremont Café
Clery's
Club Cafe
Cottonwood Cafe

Cranebrook
Davio's
East Coast Grill
Franklin Cafe
Gardner Museum Cafe
Geoffrey's
Golden Palace
Harvest
Henrietta's Table
Hill Tavern
Hi-Rise Bread
Hungry I
Joe's American
Johnny D's Uptown
Landing
Laurel
Le Gamin
Library Grill
Lyceum B&G
Maddie's Sail
Matt Murphy's Pub
Metropolis Cafe
North East Brewing
On The Park
Plaza III
Ritz-Carlton Cafe
Rosebud Diner
Rowes Wharf
S&S Rest.
Sherborn Inn
Sidney's Grille
Silks
6 Burner Urban Diner
Temple Bar
Tom Shea's
Top of Hub
Tremont 647
Turner Fisheries

Buffet Served

(Check prices, days
and times)
Akbar India
Amrheins
Anago
Andover Inn
Appetito
Aujourd'hui
Bawarchi
Blue Room
Bob the Chef
Bombay Bistro
Bombay Cafe
Bombay Club

Bristol Lounge
Cafe of India
Cafe Suisse
Cantina Italiana
Colonial Inn
Court Hse. Seafood
Dali
Diva Indian Bistro
Grendel's Bar
Grille at Hobbs Brook
House of Blues
India House
Indian Club
India Pavilion
Intrigue Café
Landing
Library Grill
Magnolia's Southern
Midwest Grill
New Mother India
Parker's
Passage to India
Penguins/C
Poppa & Goose
Redbones BBQ
Ritz-Carlton Din. Rm.
Roggie's
Rowes Wharf
Sablone's
Shalimar of India
Sidney's Grille
Spinnaker Italia
Stephanie's
Tanjore
Turner Fisheries
Verona
Yangtze River

Business Dining

Ambrosia on Huntington
Aquitaine
Aujourd'hui
Bay Tower
Biba
Bristol Lounge
Cafe Fleuri
Café Louis
Capital Grille
Chanticleer/N
Chillingsworth/C
Cottonwood Cafe
Davio's
Donatello Rist.
Exchange
Federalist

Filippo Rist.
Grapevine
Grille at Hobbs Brook
Grill 23
Hamersley's Bistro
House of Blues
Il Capriccio
Legal Sea Foods
L'Espalier
Library Grill
Locke-Ober Cafe
Maison Robert
Mamma Maria
Mistral
Morton's of Chicago
No. 9 Park
Palm
Plaza III
Ponte Vecchio
Radius
Rialto
Salamander
Sandrine's
Seasons

BYO

Angelo's
Anna's Taqueria
Bawarchi
Beach Plum Inn/M
Bistro 5
Black Dog Tavern/M
Black Eyed Susan's/N
Café Moxie/M
Dong Khanh
Homeport/M
Jake's Boss BBQ
6 Burner Urban Diner
Skewers
Stripers/M
Sweet Basil
Yama

Caters

(Best of many)
Addis Red Sea
Akbar India
Al Dente
Amelia's
American Seasons/N
Anago
Angelo's
Anthony's Pier 4
Antico Forno
Antonio's
Appetito
Ardeo/C
Artu

Aspasia
Atlas B&G
Baja Betty's
Baker's Best
B & D Deli
Bangkok Basil
Bangkok Cuisine
Barley Neck Inn/C
Bar 10
Beach Plum Inn/M
Bernard's
Billy Tse
Bistro 5
Black Dog Tavern/M
Blue Ribbon BBQ
Bob the Chef
Boca Grande
Bombay Club
Bomboa
Boston Beer Garden
Boston Beer Works
Boston Sail Loft
Brown Sugar Cafe
Cactus Club
Cafe Edwige/C
Cafe Jaffa
Cafe of India
Caffe Luna
California Pizza Kit.
Cantina Italiana
Carla's
Carlo's Cucina
Casablanca
Casa Mexico
Casa Portugal
Chanticleer/N
Chart House
Chef Chow's
Chez Henri
Chillingsworth/C
Cityside B&G
Claremont Café
Club Cafe
Colonial Inn
Contrast/C
Cottonwood Cafe
Demo's
Dish
Dockside
Donatello Rist.
Dong Khanh
Ducky Wok
East Coast Grill
El Pelon Taqueria
Fajitas & 'Ritas
Fava
Filippo Rist.

Finale
Fire King
Florentina
Florentine Cafe
Forest Cafe
Fugakyu
Full Moon
Gargoyles
Goemon
Golden Temple
Gyuhama
Harry's
Harry's Too
Hilltop Steak
House of Blues
Iguana Cantina
Il Moro
Indian Club
India Quality
Isabella
Jae's Cafe
Jake's Boss BBQ
Joe's American
Kaya
Kebab-N-Kurry
Kowloon
La Paloma
Last Hurrah
Laurel
Le Bocage
Legal Sea Foods
Le Lyonnais
Les Zygomates
Linwood Grill & BBQ
Lola's/M
L Street Diner
Maison Robert
Manhattan Sammy's Deli
Marrakesh
Martin House/C
Matteo's
Middle East
Midwest Grill
Milk St. Café
Nicole Rist.
North East Brewing
Olé, Mexican Grille
On The Park
Pagliuca's
Palenque
Papa Razzi
Passage to India
Pat's Pushcart
Pellino's
Penguins/C
Pho République
Pit Stop BBQ
Playhouse Bistro/C

Poppa & Goose
Prose
Rangoli
Rasol
Redbones BBQ
Rhythm & Spice
Rita's Place
Rubin's
Ruggieri's
Sabra
Salamander
Sam's
Sandrine's
S&S Rest.
Sawasdee
Seasons
Sel de la Terre
Sherborn Inn
Siam Garden
Sichuan Garden
Siros
Skewers
Skipjack's
Straight Wharf/N
Stripers/M
Sultan's Kitchen
Summer House/N
Sweet Basil
Sweet Life Café/M
Taqueria la Mexicana
Tasca
Tatsukichi
Ten Center St.
Tiernan's
Tosca
Tratt. Il Panino
29 Newbury
Uncle Pete's Hickory Ribs
Vicki Lee Boyajian
Village Smokehse.
Vin & Eddie's
Walden Grille
West Side Lounge
White Star Tav.
Woodman's
Wrap
Yama
Yerardi's
Zaatar's Oven
Zaftigs Deli

Cigar Friendly

Ambrosia on Huntington
Amelia's
Angelo's
Anthony's Pier 4
Assaggio
Atlas B&G

Barking Crab
Bar 10
B.B. Wolf
Biba
Billy Tse
Bomboa
Boston Beer Garden
Boston Beer Works
Bristol Lounge
Caprice
Casablanca
Chanticleer/N
Chez Henri
Colonial Inn
Donatello Rist.
Doyle's Cafe
Exchange
Federalist
57 Rest.
Florentine Cafe
Forest Cafe
Good Life
Green Dragon
Grill 23
Il Giardino
Il Moro
Jacob Wirth
Jimmy's Harborside
Joe's American
Joe Tecce's
Julien
Ken's Steak
Les Zygomates
Locke-Ober Cafe
Maggiano's Little Italy
Marcuccio's
Paddock/C
Palm
Plaza III
Sablone's
Seasons
Sel de la Terre
Silks
Sophia's
Sports Depot
Tratt. Il Panino
Turner Fisheries

Dancing/Entertainment

(Check days, times and
performers for entertainment;
D=dancing; best of many)
Aesop's Tables/C (varies)
Andover Inn (piano)
Atlantic 101 (piano/vocals)

Barley Neck Inn/C (piano)
Bay Tower (D/piano)
Black Rose (Irish)
Blue Room (jazz/piano)
Bob the Chef (jazz)
Brew Moon (blues/jazz)
Bristol Lounge (jazz)
Bubala's by the Bay/C (jazz)
Bull & Finch Pub (varies)
Cafe Brazil (Brazilian)
Cafe Budapest (piano/violin)
Cafe St. Petersburg (piano)
Cafe Suisse (piano)
Cambridge Common (bands)
Caprice (Cuban band)
Chillingsworth/C (piano)
Christian's/C (piano)
Clarke's (band)
Club Cafe (piano/vocals)
Club Car/N (piano/vocals)
Colonial Inn (folk/jazz)
Commonwealth Fish (bands)
Company of Cauldron/N (harp)
Desmond O'Malley's (Irish)
Dockside (bands/karaoke)
Dodge St. B&G (bands)
Donatello Rist. (D)
Exchange (jazz)
57 Rest. (piano)
Frank's Steak (piano)
Gargoyles (jazz)
Glenn's (blues/jazz)
Good Life (jazz)
Grand Canal (D/bands)
Green Dragon (varies)
Green St. Grill (D/bands)
Grille at Hobbs Brook (piano)
Hard Rock Cafe (bands)
Hartwell House (piano)
House of Blues (D/blues)
Icarus (jazz)
Jacob Wirth (jazz/piano)
Jared Coffin Hse./N (jazz)
Jimbo's Fish Shanty (bands)
Jimmy's Harborside (piano)
Joe's American (D)
John Harvard's (bands)
Johnny D's Uptown (D/varies)
Julien (D/jazz/piano)
Karoun (D/belly dancer)
Ken's Steak (vocals)
Kowloon (D/bands/comedy)
La Famiglia Giorgio (jazz)
Library Grill (D)

Lola's/M (D/blues/jazz/soul)
Lyceum B&G (piano)
Marino Rist. (piano)
Matt Murphy's Pub (Irish)
Medieval Manor (Theatre show)
Middle East (D/belly dancer)
Midwest Grill (Brazilian)
North East Brewing (D/bands)
Offshore Brewing/M (D/Irish)
Olé, Mexican Grille (Latin)
Paddock/C (D/piano)
Parker's (piano)
Penguins/C (guitar/jazz)
Polcari's (D/bands)
Porters Bar & Grill (bands)
Pravda 116 (D)
Rhythm & Spice (D/Caribbean)
Ritz-Carlton Cafe (harp)
Sandrine's (guitarist)
Seasons (jazz)
Sherborn Inn (D/jazz)
Silks (piano)
Siros (piano)
Skipjack's (jazz)
Sophia's (D/Latin)
Spinnaker Italia (D)
Summer House/N (piano)
Tacos El Charro (mariachi)
Tasca (guitar)
Tiernan's (D)
Top Kat Lounge (D/bands)
Top of Hub (D/jazz)
Tosca (jazz)
Tratt. Il Panino (D/jazz)
Turner Fisheries (D)
Vin & Eddie's (piano)
Watch City (blues/jazz)
Water Club (D)
Yerardi's (blues)

Delivers*/Takeout

(Nearly all Asians, coffee
shops, delis, diners and
pasta/pizzerias deliver or do
takeout; here are some
interesting possibilities;
D=delivery, T=takeout; *call
to check range and charges,
if any)
Abbondanza Ristorante (T)
Addis Red Sea (T)
Akbar India (D,T)
Amelia's (T)
Amrheins (T)
Anago (T)

Andale! Taqueria (T)
Angelo & Son's Seafood (T)
Angelo's (D,T)
Anna's Taqueria (T)
Antico Forno (T)
Antonio's (T)
Ardeo/C (T)
Armani Cafe (D,T)
Artu (D,T)
Aspasia (T)
Assaggio (D,T)
Atara Bistro/Wine Bar (T)
Atasca (T)
Atlantic 101 (T)
Atlas B&G (T)
Baja Betty's (T)
Baja Mexican (D,T)
Baker's Best (D,T)
Barker Tavern (T)
Barley Neck Inn/C (T)
Bawarchi (T)
B.B. Wolf (T)
Bella's (T)
Black Goose (D,T)
Black Rose (T)
Blue Diner (T)
Blue Ribbon BBQ (T)
Blue Room (T)
Bob the Chef (D,T)
Boca Grande (D,T)
Bombay Bistro (T)
Bombay Cafe (D,T)
Boodle's (T)
Bristol Lounge (T)
Bubala's by the Bay/C (T)
Buteco (T)
Butterfish American (T)
Cafe Brazil (T)
Cafe Edwige/C (T)
Cafe Jaffa (T)
Café Moxie/M (T)
Cafe of India (D,T)
Cafe St. Petersburg (T)
Caffe Luna (T)
Cantina Italiana (T)
Carambola (D,T)
Carla's (T)
Carlo's Cucina (T)
Casablanca (T)
Casa Mexico (D,T)
Casa Portugal (D,T)
Centre St. Café (T)
Chanterelle (T)
Claremont Café (T)
Club Cafe (T)

Colonial Inn (D,T)
Commonwealth Fish (T)
Contrast/C (T)
Cottonwood Cafe (D,T)
Court Hse. Seafood (T)
Daddy-O's (T)
Daily Catch (T)
Dalya's (T)
Demo's (T)
Dish (T)
Dodge St. B&G (T)
Dolphin (T)
Donatello Rist. (T)
Doyle's Cafe (T)
East Coast Grill (T)
El Cafetal (D,T)
Elephant Walk (D,T)
El Pelon Taqueria (T)
Fava (T)
Filippo Rist. (T)
Finale (D,T)
Fire King (T)
Five North Sq. (T)
Florentine Cafe (D,T)
Flume/C (T)
Forest Cafe (D,T)
Franklin Cafe (T)
Frank's Steak (T)
Full Moon (T)
Gala Rist. (T)
Gallerani's/C (D,T)
Galleria Italiana (T)
Gargoyles (D,T)
Geoffrey's (T)
Giacomo's (T)
Grapevine (T)
Green St. Grill (T)
Greg's (T)
Grillfish (D,T)
G'Vanni's (T)
Hamersley's Bistro (T)
Hartwell House (T)
Harvard Gardens (T)
Henrietta's Table (T)
Hilltop Steak (T)
Homeport/M (T)
Iguana Cantina (D,T)
Il Bacio (T)
Il Giardino (T)
Il Moro (T)
India House (T)
Indian Cafe (T)
India Pavilion (D,T)
India Quality (D,T)
India Samraat (D,T)

Isabella (D,T)
Jake's Boss BBQ (T)
Jasmine Bistro (D,T)
Jimbo's Fish Shanty (T)
Jimmy's Harborside (T)
Joe's American (D,T)
Joe Tecce's (D,T)
John Harvard's (T)
Johnny D's Uptown (T)
Jose's (D,T)
Julien (T)
Karoun (T)
Kebab-N-Kurry (D,T)
Ken's Steak (T)
Kokopelli Chili (T)
La Groceria (D,T)
Lala Rokh (T)
La Paloma (T)
Last Hurrah (T)
Laurel (T)
Legal Sea Foods (D,T)
Le Gamin (T)
Le Languedoc/N (D)
Le Lyonnais (T)
Lyceum B&G (T)
Maddie's Sail (T)
Ma Glockner's (T)
Magnolia's Southern (T)
Maison Robert (T)
Marcuccio's (T)
Marino Rist. (T)
Marrakesh (T)
Maurizio's (T)
Metropolis Cafe (T)
Middle East (T)
Midwest Grill (T)
Mother Anna's (T)
New Mother India (T)
No Name (T)
North East Brewing (T)
Offshore Brewing/M (T)
Olé, Mexican Grille (T)
On The Park (T)
Paddock/C (T)
Pagliuca's (T)
Palenque (D,T)
Pandorga's (T)
Passage to India (D,T)
Pat's Pushcart (T)
Pellino's (T)
Penang (T)
Penguins/C (D,T)
Phoenicia (D)
Piccolo Nido (T)
Pit Stop BBQ (T)

Plaza III (T)
Ponte Vecchio (T)
Porters Bar & Grill (T)
Purple Cactus (D,T)
Rangoli (D,T)
Rasol (D,T)
Redbones BBQ (D,T)
Red Raven's Love (T)
Ruggieri's (D,T)
Sablone's (T)
Salty Dog (T)
Sam's (D,T)
Samuel Adams Brewhse. (T)
Sandrine's (T)
Sel de la Terre (T)
Shalimar of India (D,T)
Sidney's Grille (T)
Siros (T)
Skewers (D,T)
Skipjack's (D,T)
Sol Azteca (T)
Sonsie (T)
Sorella's (T)
Sound Bites (T)
Sports Depot (T)
Stellina (T)
Stockyard (T)
Stripers/M (T)
Sultan's Kitchen (D,T)
Sweet Basil (T)
Taberna de Haro (T)
Tacos El Charro (T)
Tanjore (T)
Taqueria la Mexicana (T)
Tasca (T)
Ten Center St. (T)
Tiernan's (D,T)
Tom Shea's (T)
Tosca (T)
Tratt. Il Panino (T)
Tratt. Pulcinella (T)
Tremont 647 (T)
Turner Fisheries (T)
29 Newbury (T)
Uncle Pete's Hickory Ribs (D,T)
Union Oyster Hse. (T)
Verona (T)
Vicki Lee Boyajian (D,T)
Village Smokehse. (D,T)
Vin & Eddie's (T)
Vinny Testa's (D,T)
Walden Grille (T)
Warren Tavern (T)
Watch City (T)
Wayside Inn (T)

West St. Grille (T)
White Star Tav. (D,T)
Woodman's (T)
Wrap (D,T)
Yerardi's (T)
Zaatar's Oven (D,T)
Zuma Tex-Mex (D,T)

Dessert/Ice Cream

Cafe de Paris
Cafe Fleuri
Caffe Paradiso
Caffe Vittoria
Chanticleer/N
Cheesecake Factory
Finale
Hi-Rise Bread
Salamander
Vicki Lee Boyajian

Dining Alone

(Other than hotels, coffee
shops, sushi bars and places
with counter service)
Chanticleer/N
Claremont Café
Cottonwood Cafe
eat
Jae's Cafe
Le Gamin
Le Languedoc/N
Locke-Ober Cafe
Maison Robert
Salamander
Sandrine's
Stephanie's
Tatsukichi
Veronique

Expense Account

Ambrosia on Huntington
Anago
Aujourd'hui
Blue Ginger
Capital Grille
Clio
Exchange
Federalist
Grill 23
Hamersley's Bistro
Harvest
Il Bacio
Il Capriccio
L'Espalier
Locke-Ober Cafe
Lumière

Maison Robert
Mistral
Morton's of Chicago
No. 9 Park
Olives
Plaza III
Radius
Rialto
Ritz-Carlton Din. Rm.
Salamander
Seasons
29 Newbury

Fireplace

Amelia's
Andover Inn
Anthony's Pier 4
Barker Tavern
Barley Neck Inn/C
Bar 10
Black Dog Tavern/M
Bristol Lounge
Chanticleer/N
Chillingsworth/C
Clery's
Colonial Inn
Cranebrook
Dalya's
Desmond O'Malley's
Donatello Rist.
Good Life
Grand Canal
Helmand
High Brewster Inn/C
Hungry I
Jared Coffin Hse./N
Jimmy's Steer Hse.
Julien
Ken's Steak
L'Espalier
Library Grill
Martin House/C
Mistral
North East Brewing
Oran Mor/N
Orleans Inn/C
Piccolo Nido
Red Pheasant/C
Sherborn Inn
Silks
Stockyard
Summer House/N
Tapeo
Ten Center St.

Topper's/N
Up Stairs at the Pudding
Vault Bistro/Wine Bar
Warren Tavern
West St. Grille
White Rainbow
Yerardi's

Game in Season

Al Dente
American Seasons/N
Andover Inn
Atlantic 101
Aura
Barker Tavern
Caffe Paradiso
Cassis
Chanticleer/N
Chillingsworth/C
Colonial Inn
Cottonwood Cafe
Cranebrook
Daggett House/M
Dalya's
Dockside
Donatello Rist.
Fava
Glenn's
Grand Canal
Hamersley's Bistro
Hartwell House
Henrietta's Table
High Brewster Inn/C
Hungry I
Icarus
Il Capriccio
Iruna
Joe's American
Johnny D's Uptown
Julien
La Campania
Le Bocage
Le Languedoc/N
Le Lyonnais
L'Etoile/M
Lyceum B&G
Martin House/C
Papa Razzi
Penguins/C
Red Pheasant/C
Rist. Toscano
R Place
Salamander
Seasons

Straight Wharf/N
Top of Hub
Tratt. Pulcinella
Up Stairs at the Pudding

Historic Interest
(Year opened; *building)

1634 Barker Tavern
1702 Wayside Inn*
1745 Chillingsworth/C*
1758 Sherborn Inn*
1760 Chart House*
1760 Colonial Inn
1780 Warren Tavern*
1826 Union Oyster Hse.
1827 Durgin Park*
1833 Andover Inn*
1847 21 Federal/N
1855 Cranebrook*
1856 Parker's
1865 Café Louis*
1865 Maison Robert*
1868 Barley Neck Inn/C*
1868 Jacob Wirth*
1875 Locke-Ober Cafe
1876 L'Espalier*
1882 Cafe Marliave
1882 Doyle's Cafe*
1883 White Rainbow*
1887 Up Stairs at the Pudding*
1889 Casablanca*
1910 Library Grill
1912 Copley's
1914 Woodman's
1917 No Name
1918 Grill 23*
1922 Julien*
1927 Charlie's Sandwich
1930 Santarpio's Pizza
1931 Cantina Italiana
1938 Frank's Steak
1943 Joe Tecce's
1946 Harry's

Hotel Dining
Adrian's/C
Anago
Andover Inn
Aujourd'hui
Aura
Bar 10
Bisuteki
Boathouse Grille
Boodle's

Brant Point Grill/N
Brasserie Jo
Bristol Lounge
Cafe Budapest
Cafe Fleuri
Cafe Suisse
Caprice
Clio
Copley's
Davio's
Federalist
57 Rest.
Giannino's
Grille at Hobbs Brook
Henrietta's Table
High Brewster Inn/C
Intrigue Café
Julien
La Cucina/M
Last Hurrah
L'Etoile/M
Oak Room
Original Sports Saloon
Palm
Parker's
Rialto
Ritz-Carlton Cafe
Ritz-Carlton Din. Rm.
Rowes Wharf
Samuel Adams Brewhse.
Seasons
Sidney's Grille
Silks
Spinnaker Italia
Topper's/N
Turner Fisheries
Wayside Inn

"In" Places
Ambrosia on Huntington
Armani Cafe
Blue Ginger
Blue Room
Bristol Lounge
Casablanca
Chez Henri
Claremont Café
Dali
East Coast Grill
eat
Federalist
Flora
Franklin Cafe
Ginza
Grill 23

Hamersley's Bistro
Harvest
Il Bacio
Jae's Cafe
La Cucina/M
Lumière
Maison Robert
Matt Murphy's Pub
Mistral
No. 9 Park
Pomodoro
Radius
Salamander
Savoir Fare/M
Sonsie
Tremont 647
29 Newbury
21 Federal/N

Jacket Required

Andover Inn
Aujourd'hui
Aura
Bay Tower
Cafe Budapest
Chanticleer/N
Chillingsworth/C
Exchange
Hungry I
Jared Coffin Hse./N
Julien
Locke-Ober Cafe
Ritz-Carlton Din. Rm.
Silks
Summer House/N
Topper's/N

Late Late – After 12:30

(All hours are AM)
Anchovies (2)
Apollo Grill (4)
BARCODE(1)
Boston Beer Works (12:45)
Brasserie Jo (1)
Burren (12:45)
Cafe Pamplona (1)
Caffe Paradiso (2)
Caprice (1)
Chau Chow City (2:45)
Clarke's (2)
Coolidge Corner Clubhse. (1:15)
Cornwall's (2)
Dockside (1)
Dynasty (4)
East Ocean City (3)

Franklin Cafe (1:30)
Fugakyu (1:30)
Ginza (2)
Golden Temple (1)
Good Life (1)
Grafton St. Pub (1)
Grand Chau Chow (3)
Gyuhama (2)
Harry's (1)
Imperial Seafood (3)
Jumbo Seafood (1)
Kaya (1,1:30)
Kowloon (1:30)
Last Hurrah (12:45)
Middle East (1)
Moon Villa (4)
Ocean Wealth (4)
Parker's (1)
Parrish Cafe (1:30)
Peach Farm (3)
Pho République (1)
Rattlesnake B&G (2)
Suishaya (2)
Sunset Grill (1)
Tiger Lily (2)
Top of Hub (1)
Wonder Bar (2)

Meet for a Drink

(Most top hotels and the
following standouts)
Ambrosia on Huntington
Anchovies
Appetito
Armani Cafe
Baja Mexican
Biba
Black Rose
Blue Cat Cafe
Boarding House/N
Border Cafe
Boston Sail Loft
Cactus Club
Casablanca
Chez Henri
Cityside B&G
Clery's
Club Cafe
Cottonwood Cafe
Dali
David Ryan's/M
Delux Cafe
Doyle's Cafe
Florentine Cafe
Franklin Cafe

Geoffrey's
Good Life
Grafton St. Pub
Grill 23
Harvard Gardens
Harvest
Hill Tavern
Iguana Cantina
Il Bacio
Joe's American
John Harvard's
Le Languedoc/N
Les Zygomates
Locke-Ober Cafe
Maison Robert
Matt Murphy's Pub
Milano's Italian Kit.
No. 9 Park
North East Brewing
Papa Razzi
Radius
Rattlesnake B&G
Ropewalk/N
Salamander
Salty Dog
75 Chestnut
Sonsie
Stephanie's
Temple Bar
Top of Hub
29 Newbury
21 Federal/N
Warren Tavern
West Side Lounge
West St. Grille

Neighborhood Rest.
New Bridge Cafe
New Yorker Diner
No Name
On The Park
Penang
Pho République
Pit Stop BBQ
Prose
Rauxa
Redbones BBQ
Red Raven's Love
Rhythm & Spice
Rosebud Diner
R. Wesley's
Santarpio's Pizza
Shilla
6 Burner Urban Diner
Tim's Tavern
224 Boston St.
Uncle Pete's Hickory Ribs
Viet Hong
Village Smokehse.
Vinny's at Night

Offbeat

Anchovies
Atlas B&G
Barking Crab
B.B. Wolf
Billy Tse
Blue Ribbon BBQ
Bob the Chef
Centre St. Café
Dixie Kitchen
eat
Fire & Ice
Frank's Steak
Galleria Umberto
Helmand
Jake's Boss BBQ
Johnny D's Uptown
Magnolia's Southern
Matt Murphy's Pub

Outdoor Dining

(G=garden; P=patio;
S=sidewalk; T=terrace;
W=waterside; best of many)
Adrian's/C (T)
Aesop's Tables/C (P)
American Seasons/N (P)
Andover Inn (P,S)
Angelo's (G,P,S)
Armani Cafe (P,S)
Aspasia (S)
Atlantic Fish Co. (P)
Atlantic 101 (P,S,W)
Back Eddy (W)
Bangkok Blue (S)
BARCODE(P)
Barker Tavern (W)
Barking Crab (W)
Black Dog Tavern/M (W)
Black Goose (P)
Blue Room (P)
Boarding House/N (P,S)
Boston Sail Loft (W)
Brant Point Grill/N (T)
Brown Sugar Cafe (P)
Bubala's by the Bay/C (P,S,W)
Cactus Club (P)
Cafe Edwige/C (T)
Café Louis (T)
Cafe of India (S)

Caffe Paradiso (P,S)
Casa Romero (P)
Chanticleer/N (G)
Chart House (P,W)
Chillingsworth/C (P,T)
Christian's/C (P)
Ciao Bella (P,S)
Claremont Café (P,S)
Colonial Inn (P)
Cottonwood Cafe (P,S)
Cranebrook (G,T,W)
Daddy-O's (G)
Dalya's (T)
Davio's/Cambridge (P)
Dish (S)
El Pelon Taqueria (P,S)
Fire & Ice (P)
Fire King (P,W)
Garden of Eden (P)
Gardner Museum Cafe (P)
Giannino's (P)
Grapevine (G)
Grillfish (T)
Hamersley's Bistro (P,S)
Harvest (P)
Henrietta's Table (P)
Hi-Rise Bread (G,P)
Homeport/M (P)
Hungry I (P)
Il Bacio (S)
India Quality (P)
Intrigue Café (S,T,W)
Ironside Grill (P,S)
Iruna (T)
Jared Coffin Hse./N (P)
Jimmy's Harborside (P,W)
Joe's American (P,W)
John Harvard's (P)
La Campania (T)
La Cucina/M (G,P)
Landing (P,W)
Legal Sea Foods (P,W)
Le Languedoc/N (P)
L'Etoile/M (G,P,T)
Linwood Grill & BBQ (P)
Maggiano's Little Italy (S)
Maison Robert (G)
Mamma Maria (T)
Martin House/C (G,M,W)
Milk St. Café (S)
Mr. & Mrs. Bartley's (P,S)
Offshore Brewing/M (P)
Olé, Mexican Grille (S)
Orleans Inn/C (W)

Other Side Cosmic (S)
Pearl/N (P)
P. F. Chang's (P,S)
Playhouse Bistro/C (G)
Plaza III (P)
Ritz-Carlton Din. Rm. (T)
Ropewalk/N (P,W)
Rowes Wharf (W)
Saffron (P,S)
Sal's Place/C (P,W)
Salty Dog (S)
Sam's (P)
Sandrine's (P)
Sherborn Inn (P)
Sidney's Grille (S)
Silks (T)
Siros (P,W)
Skipjack's (P,S)
Sol Azteca (S)
Sonsie (S)
Stellina (G)
Stephanie's (P,S)
Straight Wharf/N (P,T,W)
Stripers/M (P,T,W)
Summer House/N (P)
Sweet Life Café/M (G,P)
Taberna de Haro (P,S)
Tapeo (P,S)
Tavern on Water (T,W)
Temple Bar (P,S)
Ten Center St. (P)
1369 Coffee Hse. (S)
Tom Shea's (P,W)
Topper's/N (P)
Tratt. Pulcinella (P)
29 Newbury (P,S)
21 Federal/N (P)
Up Stairs at the Pudding (G,T)
Water Club (T)
West Creek Cafe/N (P)
White Rainbow (G)
White Star Tav. (P,S)
Woodman's (G,W)
Wrap (S)
Yerardi's (G,P)

Outstanding View
Amelia's
Anthony's Pier 4
Aujourd'hui
Back Eddy
Barking Crab
Bay Tower
Beach Plum Inn/M
Biba

Black Dog Tavern/M
Boathouse Grille
Chart House
Davio's
High Brewster Inn/C
Homeport/M
Jimmy's Harborside
Landing
Martin House/C
Ritz-Carlton Din. Rm.
Ropewalk/N
Rowes Wharf
Siros
Spinnaker Italia
Straight Wharf/N
Tavern on Water
Top of Hub
Water Club

Parking/Valet

(L=parking lot;
V=valet parking;
*=validated parking)
Abbicci/C (L)
Adrian's/C (L)
Aesop's Tables/C (L)
Akbar India (L)
Al Dente (V)
Amarin of Thailand (L)
Ambrosia on Huntington (V)
Amrheins (L)
Anago*
Andover Inn (L)
Angelo & Son's Seafood (L)
Angelo's (L,V)
Anthony's Pier 4 (L)
Antico Forno*
Appetito (V)
Armani Cafe (V)
Armida's*
Artu*
Atlantic 101 (V)
Aura*
Back Eddy (L)
BARCODE(V)
Barker Tavern (V)
Barking Crab (L)
Barley Neck Inn/C (L)
Bar 10 (V)
Bay Tower (L)
B.B. Wolf*
Beach Plum Inn/M (L)
Bella's (L)
Bernard's (L)
Bertucci's (L)

Biba (V)
Billy Tse (V)*
Black Dog Tavern/M (L)
Black Rose*
Blue Cat Cafe (V)
Blue Ginger (L)
Blue Room (L)
Bombay Club*
Bomboa (V)
Boodle's*
Border Cafe (L)
Brasserie Jo (L)
Brew Moon (L)
Bubala's by the Bay/C (L)
Bugaboo Creek Steak (L)
Cafe Brazil (L)
Café Louis*
Cafe Suisse*
Caffe Luna (L)
Caffe Paradiso*
Cambridge Common (L)
Cantina Italiana*
Cape Sea Grille/C (L)
Carambola (L)
Casablanca*
Casa Mexico*
Centre St. Café (L)
Charley's Saloon (L)
Chart House (L)
Chau Chow City*
Cheesecake Factory (L)
Chillingsworth/C (L)
Christian's/C (L)
Ciao Bella (V)
Claremont Café (V)
Clery's*
Clio (V)
Colonial Inn (L)
Contrast/C (L)
Cottonwood Cafe (L)*
Cranebrook (L)
Dalya's (L)
Demo's (L)
Desmond O'Malley's (L)
Dick's Last Resort*
Dino's Sea Grille (L)
Dockside (L)
Dodge St. B&G (L)
Donatello Rist. (L)
Doyle's Cafe (L)
eat (L)
Elephant Walk (L,V)
Exchange*
Fajitas & 'Ritas (L)

Fava (L)
Federalist (V)
57 Rest.*
Figs (L)
Filippo Rist. (V)
Finale*
Fire & Ice (L)
Fire King (L)
Five Seasons (L)
Florentina (L)
Flume/C (L)
Forest Cafe (L)
Frank's Steak (L)
Fugakyu (V)
Gallerani's/C (L)
Galleria Italiana (V)
Giacomo's (V)
Ginza (L)
Glenn's (L)
Goemon*
Golden Palace*
Golden Temple (V)
Grand Chau Chow*
Grapevine (L)
Green Dragon*
Green Papaya (L)
Green St. Grill (L)
Greg's (L)
Grill 23 (V)
Hamersley's Bistro (V)
Hard Rock Cafe (L)
Harry's (L)
Harry's Too (L)
Hartwell House (L)
Harvest (V)
Henrietta's Table (L)
High Brewster Inn/C (L)
Hilltop Steak (L)
Homeport/M (L)
House of Blues*
House of Siam (V)
Icarus (V)
Iguana Cantina (L)
Il Bacio*
Il Capriccio (L)
Il Giardino (L)
Inaho/C (L)
Intrigue Café (L)
Jacob Wirth*
Jae's Cafe (L,V)*
Jared Coffin Hse./N (L)
Jasmine Bistro (L)
Jimbo's Fish Shanty (V)
Jimmy's Harborside (L)
Jimmy's Steer Hse. (L)

Joe's American (L,V)
Joe Tecce's*
John Harvard's (L)*
Jose's (L)
JP Seafood (L)
Julien (V)
Jumbalaya (L)
Ken's Steak (L)
Kowloon (L)
La Campania (L)
La Groceria (L)
Lala Rokh (L)
Landing (V)
La Paloma (L)
Laurel (V)
Le Bocage (L)
Legal Sea Foods (L,V)*
Le Lyonnais (L)
L'Espalier*
Les Zygomates (V)
Library Grill*
Linwood Grill & BBQ (L)
Locke-Ober Cafe (V)
Lola's/M (L)
Lotus Blossom (L)
Lumière (L)
Lyceum B&G (L)
Maggiano's Little Italy (V)
Ma Glockner's (L)
Maison Robert (V)
Mamma Maria (V)
Manhattan Sammy's Deli (L)
Marino Rist. (L)
Marrakesh (V)
Masa (V)
Ma Soba*
Maurizio's*
Metropolis Cafe (V)
Mistral*
Mother Anna's*
Naked Fish (L)
Nicole Rist.*
No. 9 Park (V)
North East Brewing (V)
Not Your Average Joe's (L)
Oak Room*
Offshore Brewing/M (L)
Olives (V)
Orleans Inn/C (L)
Oskar's (V)
Paddock/C (L)
Painter's/C (L)
Palm (V)
Pandorga's (L)
Papa Razzi*

Passage to India (L)
Peach Farm*
Pellino's (L)
P. F. Chang's (V)
Piccola Venezia*
Pignoli (V)
Pillar House (L)
Pit Stop BBQ (L)
Pizzeria Regina (L)
Playhouse Bistro/C (L)
Plaza III (V)
Polcari's (L)
Ponte Vecchio (L)
Pravda 116 (V)
Radius (V)
Rauxa (L)
Redbones BBQ (L)
Red Clay*
Red Pheasant/C (V)
Rialto*
Rist. Toscano (V)
Rita's Place (L)
Ritz-Carlton Cafe (V)
Ritz-Carlton Din. Rm. (V)
Rowes Wharf*
Rubin's (L)
Ruggieri's (L)
Sablone's (L)
Sage*
Salamander*
Sandrine's (L)
S&S Rest. (L)
Saporito's (L)
Seasons (L)
Sel de la Terre*
75 Chestnut*
Shalimar of India (L)
Shalom Hunan (L)
Sherborn Inn (L)
Sidney's Grille*
Silks*
Siros (L)
Skipjack's*
Sonsie (V)
Sophia's (L)
Spinnaker Italia*
Sports Depot (L)
Stellina (L)
Stephanie's (L)
Stockyard (L)
Stripers/M (L)
Tandoor House (L)
Tapeo (V)
Tasca (V)
Tatsukichi*

Ten Center St. (L)
Thai Basil*
1369 Coffee Hse. (L)
Tom Shea's (L)
Top of Hub*
Topper's/N (L)
Tosca (L)
Tratt. A Scalinatella (V)
Tratt. Il Panino (L,V)*
Tremont 647 (V)
Truc (V)
Turner Fisheries*
29 Newbury (V)
Union Oyster Hse.*
Up Stairs at the Pudding (L)
Vault Bistro/Wine Bar (V)
Verona (L)
Vicki Lee Boyajian (L)
Victoria (L)
Vidalia's Truck Stop (L)
Vin & Eddie's (L)
Vinny's at Night (L)
Vinny Testa's (L)
Walden Grille (L)
Watch City (L)
Wayside Inn (L)
West Creek Cafe/N (L)
West St. Grille (L)
Woodman's (L)
Yama (L)
Yerardi's (L)
Zuma Tex-Mex*

Parties & Private Rooms

(Any nightclub or restaurant
charges less at off-times;
* indicates private rooms
available; best of many)
Abbicci/C
Adrian's/C*
Aesop's Tables/C
Ambrosia on Huntington*
Amelia's
Amrheins*
Anago*
Andover Inn
Angelo & Son's Seafood*
Anthony's Pier 4
Antico Forno*
Appetito*
Armani Cafe*
Artu*
Aspasia
Assaggio*
Atara Bistro/Wine Bar*

Atlantic 101
Aujourd'hui
Back Eddy
Barker Tavern*
Barley Neck Inn/C*
Bawarchi*
Bay Tower*
B.B. Wolf*
Beach Plum Inn/M*
Bella's*
Bernard's*
Bertucci's*
Billy Tse*
Black Rose*
Blue Diner*
Blue Room*
Bob the Chef*
Bombay Club*
Bomboa
Border Cafe*
Boston Beer Garden*
Boston Beer Works*
Boston Sail Loft*
Brasserie Jo*
Bugaboo Creek Steak*
Bull & Finch Pub*
Butterfish American
Cafe Budapest*
Cafe Edwige/C*
Cafe of India*
Cafe St. Petersburg*
Cafe Suisse
Caffe Paradiso
Cambridge Brewing*
Cape Sea Grille/C*
Caprice*
Carla's
Carlo's Cucina*
Casa Mexico*
Casa Romero*
Chanticleer/N
Chart House*
Chau Chow City*
Chef Chow's*
Chillingsworth/C*
China Pearl*
Christian's/C*
Ciao Bella
Cityside B&G*
Claremont Café*
Clery's*
Clio
Club Cafe*
Club Car/N*

Colonial Inn*
Commonwealth Fish*
Company of Cauldron/N*
Cottonwood Cafe*
Cranebrook
Daily Catch*
Dali*
Dalya's*
Desmond O'Malley's*
Dick's Last Resort*
Dino's Sea Grille*
Dish
Dockside*
Donatello Rist.*
Doyle's Cafe*
Ducky Wok*
East Coast Grill*
eat*
Elephant Walk*
Exchange*
Fajitas & 'Ritas*
57 Rest.*
Figs*
Filippo Rist.*
Finale*
Fire & Ice*
Five North Sq.*
Florentina
Florentine Cafe*
Forest Cafe*
Frank's Steak*
Fugakyu*
Glenn's*
Golden Temple*
Good Life*
Grand Canal*
Grapevine
Green Dragon*
Green St. Grill*
Grille at Hobbs Brook*
Grillfish*
Grill 23
Gyuhama*
Hamersley's Bistro
Hard Rock Cafe*
Hartwell House*
Harvest
Helmand
High Brewster Inn/C*
Hill Tavern*
Hilltop Steak
House of Blues*
House of Siam*
Hungry I

Il Bacio*
Il Capriccio
Il Moro*
Inaho/C*
India House*
Indian Club*
India Quality*
India Samraat*
Intrigue Café*
Ironside Grill*
Jacob Wirth*
Jake's Boss BBQ*
Jared Coffin Hse./N*
Jimbo's Fish Shanty*
Jimmy's Harborside*
Joe's American*
Joe Tecce's*
John Harvard's*
Johnny D's Uptown*
Jose's*
Julien
Jumbalaya
Karoun*
Kaya*
Ken's Steak*
King & I*
Kowloon*
La Groceria*
Lala Rokh*
Last Hurrah*
Laurel*
Le Bocage*
Legal Sea Foods*
Le Gamin*
Le Languedoc/N
Le Lyonnais*
L'Espalier
Library Grill*
Locke-Ober Cafe*
Lyceum B&G*
Maggiano's Little Italy*
Ma Glockner's*
Maison Robert*
Mamma Maria*
Manhattan Sammy's Deli*
Marcuccio's*
Marrakesh
Martin House/C*
Ma Soba*
Matteo's
Middle East*
Midwest Grill*
Mistral*
Montien*
Moon Villa*

Mother Anna's
Nicole Rist.*
North East Brewing*
Not Your Average Joe's*
Oak Room
Ocean Wealth
Olé, Mexican Grille*
Olives
On The Park*
Oran Mor/N*
Original Sports Saloon*
Oskar's*
Paddock/C*
Pagliuca's*
Palenque*
Palm*
Papa Razzi*
Pat's Pushcart*
Pellino's*
Penang*
Penguins/C*
Phoenicia*
Pho Pasteur*
Pho République*
Piccola Venezia*
Piccolo Nido*
Pignoli*
Pillar House
Pizzeria Uno*
Playhouse Bistro/C*
Plaza III
Polcari's*
Porters Bar & Grill
Pravda 116*
Prose*
Radius
Rauxa*
Redbones BBQ
Red Clay
Red Pheasant/C*
Red Raven's Love*
Rest. Bricco
Rhythm & Spice*
Rialto*
Rist. Toscano
Rita's Place*
Ropewalk/N*
Rowes Wharf*
Royal East*
Rubin's*
Ruggieri's*
Sablone's*
Sabra*
Saigon*
Salamander*

Sal's Place/C*
Sam's*
Samuel Adams Brewhse.
Sandrine's*
S&S Rest.*
Sawasdee*
Seasons*
Sel de la Terre*
Sherborn Inn*
Siam Cuisine*
Siam Garden
Sichuan Garden*
Sidney's Grille*
Silks*
Siros*
6 Burner Urban Diner*
Skipjack's*
Sonsie*
Sophia's*
Spinnaker Italia*
Stellina*
Stephanie's
Stockyard*
Straight Wharf/N*
Stripers/M*
Sultan's Kitchen*
Summer House/N*
Tapeo
Tasca*
Tatsukichi*
Ten Center St.*
Thai Basil
Thai's*
Tiernan's*
Tiger Lily*
Tom Shea's*
Top Kat Lounge
Top of Hub*
Tosca*
Tratt. Il Panino*
Tremont 647*
Truc
Turner Fisheries*
Uncle Pete's Hickory Ribs*
Union Oyster Hse.*
Up Stairs at the Pudding*
Vault Bistro/Wine Bar*
Verona*
Vicki Lee Boyajian*
Vidalia's Truck Stop*
Village Smokehse.*
Vin & Eddie's
Vinny's at Night*
Vinny Testa's*
Walden Grille*

Warren Tavern*
Watch City*
West St. Grille*
White Star Tav.*
Woodman's*
Yama*
Yangtze River*
Yerardi's*

People-Watching
Ambrosia on Huntington
Aquitaine
Armani Cafe
Bay Tower
Biba
Blue Room
Ciao Bella
Clio
Franklin Cafe
Grill 23
Il Bacio
L'Espalier
Maison Robert
Mistral
No. 9 Park
Olives
Radius
Rialto
Sonsie
Stephanie's
29 Newbury
21 Federal/N

Power Scene
Ambrosia on Huntington
Anago
Aujourd'hui
Bristol Lounge
Green St. Grill
Grill 23
Hamersley's Bistro
Harvest
Julien
L'Espalier
Locke-Ober Cafe
Maison Robert
Mistral
Radius
Ritz-Carlton Cafe
Salamander
Seasons
21 Federal/N
Vault Bistro/Wine Bar

Pre-Theater Dining

(Call to check prices,
days and times)
Bomboa
Boodle's
Brew Moon
Bristol Lounge
Commonwealth Fish
Cottonwood Cafe
57 Rest.
Finale
Galleria Italiana
Grillfish
Jacob Wirth
Jae's Cafe
Landing
Maggiano's Little Italy
Montien
Oak Room
P. F. Chang's
Playhouse Bistro/C
Pravda 116
Skipjack's
Sorella's

Post-Theater Dining

(Call to check prices,
days and times)
Blue Diner
Bluestone Bistro
Brasserie Jo
Brew Moon
Casablanca
Chez Henri
Ciao Bella
Clery's
Cottonwood Cafe
Dockside
Finale
Franklin Cafe
Golden Temple
Good Life
Grendel's Bar
Julien
Jumbo Seafood
Le Gamin
Mistral
Montien
New Yorker Diner
No. 9 Park
Pho République
S&S Rest.
Sonsie
Stephanie's
Suishaya

Top of Hub
Tremont 647
Watch City
White Star Tav.

Prix Fixe Menu

(Call to check prices,
days and times)
Akbar India
Anago
Andover Inn
Aspasia
Aura
Barley Neck Inn/C
Bar 10
Bawarchi
Blue Room
Bomboa
Cafe Budapest
Cafe St. Petersburg
Chanticleer/N
Chez Henri
Company of Cauldron/N
Demo's
Dick's Last Resort
Dockside
Finale
Fire & Ice
Gardner Museum Cafe
Harvest
High Brewster Inn/C
Hungry I
Intrigue Café
Julien
Le Bocage
L'Espalier
Les Zygomates
L'Etoile/M
Maison Robert
No. 9 Park
Oak Room
Palm
Passage to India
Playhouse Bistro/C
Rowes Wharf
Sandrine's
Silks
Skipjack's
Spinnaker Italia
Sultan's Kitchen
Topper's/N
Up Stairs at the Pudding

Pub/Bar/Microbrewery

Amrheins
Anchovies

Black Rose
Blue Cat Cafe
Boston Beer Garden
Boston Beer Works
Brew Moon
Bull & Finch Pub
Burren
Cactus Club
Cambridge Brewing
Cambridge Common
Casablanca
Charley's Saloon
Clarke's
Clery's
Clio
Commonwealth Fish
Coolidge Corner Clubhse.
Cornwall's
Delux Cafe
Desmond O'Malley's
Doyle's Cafe
Franklin Cafe
Grafton St. Pub
Grand Canal
Green Dragon
Grill 23
Jacob Wirth
Joe's American
John Harvard's
Le Languedoc/N
Matt Murphy's Pub
No. 9 Park
North East Brewing
Original Sports Saloon
Rattlesnake B&G
Samuel Adams Brewhse.
Sports Depot
Sunset Grill
Temple Bar
Tim's Tavern
29 Newbury
Union Street
Warren Tavern
Watch City
Whiskey's
Wonder Bar

Quiet Conversation
Aujourd'hui
Bay Tower
Beach Plum Inn/M
Cafe Budapest
Casa Romero
Chanterelle
Claremont Café

Clio
Davide Rist.
Hamersley's Bistro
Hungry I
Il Capriccio
Jasmine Bistro
Le Languedoc/N
L'Espalier
Locke-Ober Cafe
Maison Robert
R Place
Salamander
Sandrine's
Seasons
Straight Wharf/N
Takeshima
Tatsukichi
Top of Hub
Tratt. Il Panino
Truc
Veronique

Raw Bar
Anthony's Pier 4
Atlantic 101
Back Eddy
Barking Crab
Black Dog Tavern/M
Brant Point Grill/N
Brasserie Jo
Christian's/C
Daily Catch
Dancing Lobster/C
David Ryan's/M
Dino's Sea Grille
Dockside
East Coast Grill
Glenn's
Good Life
Grill 23
Jae's Cafe
Jimbo's Fish Shanty
Jimmy's Harborside
Legal Sea Foods
Le Languedoc/N
Lola's/M
Pearl/N
Roggie's
Ropewalk/N
Skipjack's
Turner Fisheries
Union Oyster Hse.
Vault Bistro/Wine Bar
Woodman's

Reservations Essential

Abbondanza Ristorante
Ambrosia on Huntington
American Seasons/N
Aquitaine
Aujourd'hui
Barley Neck Inn/C
Beach Plum Inn/M
Betty's Wok & Noodle Diner
Boarding House/N
Brown Sugar Cafe
Cafe Budapest
Cafe Edwige/C
Café Moxie/M
Cafe St. Petersburg
Cassis
Chanticleer/N
Chillingsworth/C
Clio
Club Car/N
Company of Cauldron/N
Contrast/C
Cranebrook
Donatello Rist.
Federalist
Filippo Rist.
Grapevine
Hamersley's Bistro
High Brewster Inn/C
Hungry I
Inaho/C
Jared Coffin Hse./N
Karoun
Le Languedoc/N
L'Espalier
L'Etoile/M
Library Grill
Locke-Ober Cafe
Lumière
Mamma Maria
Martin House/C
Masa
Medieval Manor
Mistral
No. 9 Park
Oak Room
Oran Mor/N
Prose
Radius
Red Pheasant/C
Rita's Place
Ritz-Carlton Din. Rm.
R Place
Sage

Silks
Spinnaker Italia
Straight Wharf/N
Summer House/N
Topper's/N
Tratt. Il Panino
Tratt. Pulcinella
21 Federal/N
White Rainbow

Romantic

American Seasons/N
Bay Tower
Beach Plum Inn/M
Cafe Budapest
Casa Mexico
Casa Romero
Chanterelle
Chillingsworth/C
Clio
Cranebrook
Dali
Davide Rist.
Euno
Five North Sq.
Grapevine
Hungry I
Icarus
Il Bacio
Iruna
Julien
La Cucina/M
Le Languedoc/N
L'Espalier
Locke-Ober Cafe
Maison Robert
Marcuccio's
Oak Room
Salamander
Sandrine's
Seasons
75 Chestnut
Siam Cuisine
Sol Azteca
Straight Wharf/N
Tapeo
Tasca
Top of Hub
Torch
Tosca
Tratt. A Scalinatella
Tratt. Il Panino
Tratt. Pulcinella
Truc
Veronique

Senior Appeal

Abbicci/C
Andover Inn
Captain's Wharf
Cheesecake Factory
Colonial Inn
Copley's
Dolphin
Gardner Museum Cafe
Grille at Hobbs Brook
Hartwell House
Henrietta's Table
Jimmy's Steer Hse.
Ken's Steak
La Famiglia Giorgio
Legal Sea Foods
Ma Glockner's
Maison Robert
Parker's
Pillar House
Sherborn Inn
Stockyard
Top of Hub
Veronique
Vinny Testa's
Wayside Inn

Singles Scene

Armani Cafe
Atlas B&G
Black Rose
Blue Cat Cafe
Bluestone Bistro
Border Cafe
Boston Beer Garden
Boston Beer Works
Brew Moon
Bull & Finch Pub
Cactus Club
Cambridge Common
Charley's Saloon
Clarke's
Clery's
Dodge St. B&G
Fire & Ice
Good Life
Gyuhama
Halfway Cafe
Joe's American
John Harvard's
Kokopelli Chili
Miracle of Science
New Bridge Cafe
Rattlesnake B&G
Sonsie

Sunset Grill
Temple Bar
29 Newbury
West St. Grille
Wonder Bar

Sleepers

(Good to excellent food,
but little known)
Ajanta
Antonio's
Armida's
Bukhara
Café Moxie/M
Cafe Suisse
Cafe 300
Cape Sea Grille/C
Centre St. Bistro/N
Contrast/C
Court Hse. Seafood
Cranebrook
Dong Khanh
El Pelon Taqueria
Glenn's
Harry's
Hi-Rise Bread
Inaho/C
Intrigue Café
Jasmine Bistro
Jumbo Seafood
Kendrick's/N
La Summa
Le Grenier/M
Le Lyonnais
Library Grill
Nantucket Tapas/N
Nara
Narita
Nicole Rist.
Oran Mor/N
Painter's/C
Pellino's
Piccolo Nido
Pit Stop BBQ
Red Clay
Red Raven's Love
Rita's Place
Sorella's
Suishaya
Taqueria la Mexicana
Viet Hong
Vinny's at Night
V. Majestic
West Creek Cafe/N

White Rainbow
Woo Chun
Yokohama
Zapotec/M

Smoking Prohibited
(May be permissible at
bar or outdoors)
Abbicci/C
Addis Red Sea
Aesop's Tables/C
Amarin of Thailand
American Seasons/N
Andover Inn
Anna's Taqueria
Antonio's
Appetito
Ardeo/C
Aura
Baja Betty's
Baker's Best
B & D Deli
Bangkok Basil
Bangkok Blue
Bangkok Cuisine
Barker Tavern
Barley Neck Inn/C
Bay Tower
Beach Plum Inn/M
Bertucci's
Betty's Wok & Noodle Diner
Bistro 5
Black Dog Tavern/M
Black Eyed Susan's/N
Blue Ginger
Blue Ribbon BBQ
Blue Room
Bluestone Bistro
Bob the Chef
Boca Grande
Bombay Bistro
Bombay Cafe
Brown Sugar Cafe
Bubala's by the Bay/C
Buteco
Butterfish American
Cafe Edwige/C
Cafe Jaffa
Café Louis
Café Moxie/M
Cafe of India
Cafe St. Petersburg
Cafe Suisse
Caffe Luna
California Pizza Kit.

Cantina Italiana
Cape Sea Grille/C
Carambola
Carlo's Cucina
Casa Mexico
Casa Romero
Cassis
Centre St. Café
Chanterelle
Charley's Saloon
Charlie's Sandwich
Chart House
Chef Chow's
China Pearl
Christian's/C
Ciao Bella
Cityside B&G
Claremont Café
Company of Cauldron/N
Contrast/C
Court Hse. Seafood
Daddy-O's
Daily Catch
Dalya's
Demo's
Dish
Donatello Rist.
Duckworth Lane
Ducky Wok
El Cafetal
El Pelon Taqueria
Fajitas & 'Ritas
Fava
Figs
Finale
Fire King
Five North Sq.
Five Seasons
Flora
Front Street/C
Gala Rist.
Gallerani's/C
Galleria Italiana
Ginza
Goemon
Golden Temple
Grand Chau Chow
Green Papaya
Grille at Hobbs Brook
Grillfish
Hamersley's Bistro
Harry's
Harry's Too
Hartwell House
Helmand

Henrietta's Table	Peach Farm
High Brewster Inn/C	Peking Cuisine
Hi-Rise Bread	Penang
Homeport/M	Penguins/C
House of Siam	Pho Pasteur
Hungry I	Piccola Venezia
Icarus	Pillar House
Il Capriccio	Pizzeria Regina
Inaho/C	Prose
Indian Cafe	Purple Cactus
Indian Club	Rangoli
India Quality	Red Clay
India Samraat	Red Pheasant/C
Intrigue Café	Ritz-Carlton Cafe
Iruna	Ritz-Carlton Din. Rm.
Jae's Cafe	Rowes Wharf
Jasmine Bistro	R Place
Jimmy's Harborside	Rubin's
JP Seafood	Saigon
King & I	Salamander
Kokopelli Chili	Sal's Place/C
La Campania	Sandrine's
La Groceria	Saporito's
Lala Rokh	Shalimar of India
Le Bocage	Shalom Hunan
Legal Sea Foods	Shilla
Le Gamin	Siam Cuisine
Le Lyonnais	Sichuan Garden
L'Espalier	Sidney's Grille
Library Grill	Skewers
Lola's/M	Skipjack's
L Street Diner	Sol Azteca
Lumière	Sorella's
Mamma Maria	Sound Bites
Marrakesh	Spinnaker Italia
Martin House/C	Stellina
Ma Soba	Straight Wharf/N
Matteo's	Suishaya
Matt Murphy's Pub	Sultan's Kitchen
Maurizio's	Sweet Basil
Metropolis Cafe	Sweet Life Café/M
Mike's City Diner	Tanjore
Milk St. Café	Taqueria la Mexicana
Mother Anna's	Tatsukichi
Naked Fish	Thai's
New Mother India	1369 Coffee Hse.
Nicole Rist.	Topper's/N
No. 9 Park	Tratt. Pulcinella
Offshore Brewing/M	Turner Fisheries
Olé, Mexican Grille	21 Federal/N
Oran Mor/N	Uncle Pete's Hickory Ribs
Orleans Inn/C	Up Stairs at the Pudding
Palenque	Vicki Lee Boyajian
Pandorga's	Vidalia's Truck Stop
Passage to India	Viet Hong

Village Smokehse.
Vinny's at Night
Vinny Testa's
Warren Tavern
Wayside Inn
West Creek Cafe/N
Wrap
Yama
Yangtze River
Zaatar's Oven
Zaftigs Deli

Tasting Menu

Anago
Aujourd'hui
Barley Neck Inn/C
Bistro 5
Bomboa
Butterfish American
Clio
Club Car/N
Donatello Rist.
Hamersley's Bistro
Karoun
La Campania
L'Espalier
Library Grill
Marcuccio's
Olives
Pravda 116
Radius
Rest. Bricco
Rialto
Rita's Place
Salamander
Sandrine's
75 Chestnut
Silks
Top of Hub
Topper's/N
Tremont 647

Tea

(See also *Hotel Dining*; the
following are highly touted)
Caffe Paradiso
Cranebrook
Grand Canal
Skewers

Teenagers & Other Youthful Spirits

Bertucci's
Bishop's
California Pizza Kit.
Cheesecake Factory

Figs
Fire & Ice
Galleria Umberto
Hard Rock Cafe
Jimbo's Fish Shanty
Johnny's Luncheonette
Kokopelli Chili
Pizzeria Uno
Vinny Testa's

Teflons

(Get lots of business, despite
so-so food, i.e. they have
other attractions that prevent
criticism from sticking)
Amrheins
Anthony's Pier 4
Baja Mexican
Black Rose
Blue Diner
Bugaboo Creek Steak
Bull & Finch Pub
Burren
California Pizza Kit.
Cambridge Brewing
Cambridge Common
Charley's Saloon
Cheesecake Factory
Cityside B&G
Commonwealth Fish
Coolidge Corner Clubhse.
Doyle's Cafe
Duckworth Lane
Grendel's Bar
Hard Rock Cafe
Jacob Wirth
Joe's American
Kokopelli Chili
Milano's Italian Kit.
Pizzeria Uno
Rattlesnake B&G
Sports Depot
Vidalia's Truck Stop
Vinny Testa's
Watch City
Whiskey's

Theme Restaurant

Bishop's
Bisuteki
Border Cafe
Bugaboo Creek Steak
Bull & Finch Pub
Cactus Club
Cafe Budapest
Casa Mexico

Casa Romero
Coolidge Corner Clubhse.
Hard Rock Cafe
Iguana Cantina
Joe Tecce's
Kowloon
Matt Murphy's Pub
Original Sports Saloon
Tapeo
Tatsukichi
Union Oyster Hse.

Wine/Beer Only

Abbondanza Ristorante
Addis Red Sea
Al Dente
Alloro
Amarin of Thailand
Angelo's
Antico Forno
Antonio's
Armida's
Artu
Aspasia
Atara Bistro/Wine Bar
Baker's Best
Bangkok Basil
Bangkok Bistro
Bangkok Blue
Bangkok Cuisine
Bangkok House
Bernard's
Bertucci's
Bluestone Bistro
Bob the Chef
Bombay Bistro
Bombay Cafe
Boston Beer Works
Brown Sugar Cafe
Buteco
Butterfish American
Cafe Brazil
Cafe Jaffa
Café Louis
Cafe of India
Cafe Sushi
California Pizza Kit.
Cambridge Brewing
Carlo's Cucina
Cassis
Centre St. Café
Chanterelle
Chef Chow's
Claremont Café
Commonwealth Fish
Company of Cauldron/N
Contrast/C
Daddy-O's

Daily Catch
Dali
Demo's
Duckworth Lane
Finale
Five North Sq.
Flora
Full Moon
Gala Rist.
Galleria Italiana
Gardner Museum Cafe
Geoffrey's
Giacomo's
Ginza
Grand Chau Chow
Green Papaya
Harry's
High Brewster Inn/C
House of Siam
Il Giardino
Il Moro
Imperial Seafood
India Pavilion
India Quality
India Samraat
Iruna
Isabella
Jasmine Bistro
John Harvard's
Johnny's Luncheonette
JP Seafood
Kaya
Kebab-N-Kurry
King & I
Lala Rokh
Le Gamin
L Street Diner
Lumière
Marcuccio's
Marrakesh
Ma Soba
Maurizio's
Metropolis Cafe
Midwest Grill
Mike's City Diner
Moon Villa
Nicole Rist.
Offshore Brewing/M
On The Park
Passage to India
Pat's Pushcart
Peach Farm
Phoenicia
Pho Pasteur
Piccola Venezia
Piccolo Nido
Pizzeria Regina
Ponte Vecchio

Poppa & Goose
Prose
Rangoli
Rasol
Roggie's
Roka
Royal East
R Place
Rubin's
Sage
Sal's Place/C
Salts
Sam's
Sandrine's
Sawasdee
Shilla
Siam Cuisine
Sorella's
Suishaya
Sultan's Kitchen
Sweet Life Café/M
Taberna de Haro
Tacos El Charro
Tandoor House
Tasca
Thai Basil
Tratt. Il Panino
Tratt. Pulcinella
Truc
Uncle Pete's Hickory Ribs
Verona
Vidalia's Truck Stop
Watch City
Zaatar's Oven
Zaftigs Deli

Winning Wine List

Anthony's Pier 4
Boarding House/N
Caffe Bella
Federalist
Grapevine
Green St. Grill
Hamersley's Bistro
Il Bacio
Il Capriccio
L'Espalier
Les Zygomates
Lumière
Maison Robert
Mamma Maria
Radius
Salamander
Silks
Taberna de Haro
Tremont 647
Vault Bistro/Wine Bar
Veronique

Worth a Trip

Andover
  Cassis
Bedford
  Dalya's
Cape Cod
  Chillingsworth/C
  High Brewster Inn/C
  Regatta of Cotuit/C
  Regatta of Falmouth/C
Concord
  Colonial Inn
Hingham
  Tosca
Hull
  Saporito's
Lawrence
  Bishop's
Martha's Vineyard
  La Cucina/M
  L'Etoile/M
  Savoir Fare/M
Nantucket
  Summer House/N
  Topper's/N
  21 Federal/N
Needham
  Fava
Newburyport
  Glenn's
Randolph
  Caffe Bella
Salem
  Grapevine
Scituate
  Barker Tavern
Tyngsboro
  Silks
Wellesley
  Blue Ginger
Westport
  Back Eddy

Young Children

(Besides the normal fast-food
places; * indicates children's
menu available)
Adrian's/C*
Aesop's Tables/C*
Amrheins*
Anthony's Pier 4*
Appetito*
Atlantic 101*
Aujourd'hui*
Aura*
Baja Betty's*
B & D Deli*
Barking Crab

B.B. Wolf*
Bertucci's*
Bishop's
Black Dog Tavern/M*
Black Rose*
Blue Ginger*
Bluestone Bistro*
Boodle's*
Border Cafe*
Boston Sail Loft*
Brasserie Jo*
Brew Moon*
Bristol Lounge*
Bugaboo Creek Steak*
Bull & Finch Pub*
California Pizza Kit.*
Charley's Saloon*
Chart House*
Chau Chow City
Cheesecake Factory
Clery's*
Colonial Inn*
Commonwealth Fish*
Cottonwood Cafe*
Daddy-O's*
Desmond O'Malley's*
Dish*
Dockside*
Fajitas & 'Ritas
57 Rest.*
Fire & Ice
Fish Landing B&G/C*
Frank's Steak*
Full Moon
Gala Rist.*
Galleria Umberto
Grand Canal*
Green Dragon*
Grille at Hobbs Brook*
Halfway Cafe*
Hard Rock Cafe
Harry's*
Henrietta's Table
Hilltop Steak*
Hi-Rise Bread*
House of Blues*
Iguana Cantina*
Intrigue Café*
Ironside Grill*
Jacob Wirth*
Jared Coffin Hse./N*
Jimbo's Fish Shanty
Jimmy's Harborside*
Joe's American*
John Harvard's*
Johnny's Luncheonette
Jose's*

Jumbalaya*
Kokopelli Chili
Kowloon*
La Groceria*
Landing*
La Paloma*
Legal Sea Foods*
Library Grill*
Maddie's Sail*
Ma Soba*
Mr. & Mrs. Bartley's*
Naked Fish*
Not Your Average Joe's*
Oak Room*
Olé, Mexican Grille*
Orleans Inn/C*
Paddock/C*
Papa Razzi*
Parker's*
Pat's Pushcart*
Penguins/C*
Pizzeria Uno*
Polcari's*
Red Clay*
Ritz-Carlton Cafe*
Ropewalk/N*
Rowes Wharf*
Rubin's*
Rudy's Cafe*
Ruggieri's*
Sal's Place/C*
Sam's*
Sel de la Terre*
Sherborn Inn*
Sidney's Grille*
Siros*
Skewers*
Skipjack's*
Sorella's*
Stars
Stripers/M*
Ten Center St.*
Tom Shea's*
Tratt. Il Panino*
Turner Fisheries*
Union Oyster Hse.*
Vidalia's Truck Stop*
Village Smokehse.*
Vinny Testa's
Walden Grille*
Warren Tavern*
Woodman's*
Wrap*
Zaatar's Oven*
Zaftigs Deli*
Zuma Tex-Mex*

Wine Vintage Chart 1985-1998

This chart is designed to help you select wine to go with your meal. It is based on the same 0 to 30 scale used throughout this *Survey*. The ratings (prepared by our friend **Howard Stravitz**, a law professor at the University of South Carolina) reflect both the quality of the vintage and the wine's readiness for present consumption. Thus, if a wine is not fully mature or is over the hill, its rating has been reduced. We do not include 1987, 1991 or 1993 vintages because, with the exception of cabernets, '91 Northern Rhônes and '93 red Burgundies and Southern Rhônes, those vintages are not especially recommended.

	'85	'86	'88	'89	'90	'92	'94	'95	'96	'97	'98
WHITES											
French:											
Alsace	25	20	23	28	28	24	28	26	24	25	24
Burgundy	24	25	19	27	22	23	22	27	28	25	24
Loire Valley	–	–	–	26	25	18	22	24	26	23	22
Champagne	28	25	24	26	28	–	–	24	26	24	–
Sauternes	22	28	29	25	26	–	18	22	23	24	–
California:											
Chardonnay	–	–	–	–	–	24	22	26	22	26	26
REDS											
French:											
Bordeaux	26	27	25	28	29	18	24	25	24	23	23
Burgundy	24	–	23	27	29	23	23	25	26	24	24
Rhône	26	20	26	28	27	15	23	24	22	24	26
Beaujolais	–	–	–	–	–	–	21	24	22	24	23
California:											
Cab./Merlot	26	26	–	21	28	26	27	25	24	25	26
Zinfandel	–	–	–	–	–	21	23	21	22	24	25
Italian:											
Tuscany	27	–	24	–	26	–	–	25	19	28	25
Piedmont	25	–	25	27	27	–	–	23	25	28	25

Bargain sippers take note: Some wines are reliable year in, year out, and are reasonably priced as well. They include: Alsatian Pinot Blancs, Côtes du Rhône, Muscadet, Bardolino, Valpolicella and inexpensive Spanish Rioja and California Zinfandel and are best bought in the most recent vintages.